The Jazz Tradition

The Jazz Tradition

MARTIN WILLIAMS

New York
OXFORD UNIVERSITY PRESS
1970

For Martha

ACKNOWLEDGMENTS

My first debts are to Donald Allen and Barney Rosset who started this when Allen asked me to write about Thelonious Monk in *Evergreen Review* No. 7. From that beginning, *The Jazz Tradition* and some of its theories evolved. My second debt is to Sheldon Meyer who saw what sort of book this could be and encouraged me to revise the material and make it that sort of book.

It may be that I am indebted to every writer on jazz I have ever read and to every musician I have ever heard and spoken with. Specifically, I am indebted to those writers whose names are included herein. The theoretical aspect of my work owes a debt to André Hodeir, particularly to his exposition of the role of Louis Armstrong in jazz history.

Many of the chapters in this book have appeared previously in different form. As included here, they have all been somewhat revised. Some have been thoroughly rewritten and expanded. Also, I have sometimes deleted repetition of basic ideas from one piece to the next except when the repetition seemed to me to serve the purpose of emphasis. I have previously had something to say between hard-covers on Jelly Roll Morton, Billie Holiday, and Horace Silver. I hope anyone acquainted with those earlier comments will agree that I have things to add here.

The essays on Louis Armstrong, Bix Beiderbecke, Billie Holiday, Count Basie and Lester Young, John Lewis and the Modern Jazz Quartet, Sonny Rollins, Horace Silver, Charlie Mingus, Coleman Hawkins, and Ornette Coleman originally appeared, in different form, in the *Evergreen Review*. The section on Jelly Roll Morton includes several paragraphs from an essay in the *Evergreen Review* but its major portions, here somewhat revised, come from a study written for *Jazz*, edited by Nat Hentoff and Albert J. McCarthy and published by Rinehart in the United States and Cassell in Great Britain.

The chapters on Duke Ellington, Thelonious Monk, and Miles Davis combine material which has appeared in the *Evergreen Review* and in the *Saturday Review* in editor Irving Kolodin's "Recordings" section.

The chapter on Charlie Parker combines material which appeared in the *Evergreen Review* and in *Down Beat*. My comments on John Coltrane first appeared in slightly shorter form in *Down Beat*.

M. W.

September 1969

CONTENTS

1. INTRODUCTION: A Contemporary Art, 3

2. JELLY ROLL MORTON: Three-Minute Form, 16

3. LOUIS ARMSTRONG: Style Beyond Style, 47

4. BIX BEIDERBECKE: The White Man's Burden, 60

5. COLEMAN HAWKINS: Some Comments on a Phoenix, 70

6. BILLIE HOLIDAY: Actress Without an Act, 78

7. DUKE ELLINGTON: Form Beyond Form, 87

8. COUNT BASIE AND LESTER YOUNG: Style Beyond Swing, 107

9. CHARLIE PARKER: The Burden of Innovation, 120

10. THELONIOUS MONK: Modern Jazz in Search of Maturity, 138

11. JOHN LEWIS AND THE MODERN JAZZ QUARTET:
     Modern Conservative, 156

12. SONNY ROLLINS: Spontaneous Orchestration, 167

13. HORACE SILVER: The Meaning of Craftsmanship, 178

14. MILES DAVIS: A Man Walking, 186

15. JOHN COLTRANE: A Man in the Middle, 197

16. ORNETTE COLEMAN: The Meaning of Innovation, 207

     Discographical Notes, 221

The Jazz Tradition

1

INTRODUCTION

A Question of Meaning

One observer has suggested that jazz music—or all jazz music but the most recent—represents a kind of cultural lag in which the devices of nineteenth-century European music have been domesticated and popularized in the United States, adding that at the same time these devices were inevitably influenced by an African-derived rhythmic idiom.

I am sure that proposition is untrue. It assumes that European ideas of harmony and melody are fundamental to jazz, and are used in jazz in the same way that they were in Europe, whereas the truth may be that in jazz, rhythm is fundamental.

Jazz did not exist until the twentieth century. It has elements which were not present either in Europe or in Africa before this century. And at any of its stages it represents, unarguably it seems to me, a relationship among rhythm, harmony, and melody that did not exist before. Whatever did not exist before the twentieth century is likely to express that century.

If we undertake a definition of jazz, we would begin with the fact that it is an Afro-American musical idiom, and we would already be in trouble, for almost all our music is in an Afro-American or Afro-influenced idiom.

And so, to digress for a moment, is much of our culture Afro-influenced. Most of our slang comes from the gallion (as the black ghetto was once called), although numbers of our population continue to believe it is the invention of the teenagers in the corridors of our largely white high schools. So does most of our dancing. And how many Americans realize the origins of the strutting and baton twirling of our drum majorettes—and how would they react if they did know? More than one foreigner has observed that Americans do not walk like their European and Asian relatives, and one observer has gone far enough to declare that they walk more like Africans. Modes of comedy in America have been deeply influenced by our minstrelsy, which, however much it was distorted by white blackface, was still black in origin and, more important in device, in attitude, and in outlook.

To return to our music, it might surprise the patrons at the Nashville Grand Old Opry to learn how deeply their so-called "Country and Western" idiom has been influenced by an Afro-American one, but their reaction would not change the facts. And it should be widely acknowledged that no one in any musical idiom any longer writes for (let us say) the trumpet as he once did because of what jazzmen have shown that instrument can do. Most of our musicians also know that American symphonic brassmen generally have an unorthodox vibrato because of the pervasiveness of the jazzman's vibrato.

It should be acknowledged, that today jazz is not *the* popular idiom of American black men. And jazz shares such contributions as its "blues scale" and its unique musical form, the twelve-bar blues, with other popular idioms. But jazz is the most respected Afro-American idiom, the most highly developed one, and the idiom to which improvisation is crucially important.

I hope that from the chapters that follow, two ideas will emerge of how jazz has evolved. One has to do with the position of certain major figures and what they have contributed to jazz. The other has to do with rhythm.

I should say at this point that I did not begin with these ideas as preassumptions. They emerged in my own mind and related themselves to the theories of other commentators only as I undertook to write the chapters themselves. They offer, I hope, a more comprehensive and perhaps more musical view of the way jazz has developed than has previously been available.

If we take the most generally agreed-upon aesthetic judgments about jazz music, the first would undoubtedly be the dominant position and influence of Louis Armstrong—and that influence is not only agreed upon, it is easily demonstrable from recordings.

If we take a second generally agreed-upon opinion, it would concern the importance of Duke Ellington, and most particularly Ellington in the maturity of 1939–42.

And a third opinion? Surely the importance of the arrival of Charlie Parker. And after Parker, what made jazz history was the rediscovery of Thelonious Monk. And after that, the emergence of Ornette Coleman—or so it would be if one were looking for evidence of originality after Parker and Monk.

The pattern that emerges from those judgments would be a kind of Hegelian pendulum swing from the contributions of an innovative, intuitive improviser (Armstrong, Parker), who reassessed the music's past, gave it a new vocabulary, or at least repronounced its old one, and of an opposite swing to the contributions of a composer (Ellington, Monk), who gave the music a synthesis and larger form—larger, but not longer.

And before Armstrong? As I hope my essay demonstrates, Jelly Roll Morton's music represented a synthesis and summary of what jazz, and Afro-American music in general, had accomplished up to the moment of his arrival.

There remain the matter of the direct influence of the great figures on some of their immediate followers, and the matter of the few players whom one might call dissenters.

Following Armstrong I have written of Bix Beiderbecke, whose ends were comparable with Armstrong's but whose means and origins were somewhat different. I have spoken of the direct but very different effect of Armstrong on Coleman Hawkins and on Billie Holiday, and of the somewhat less direct effect of his work on the Count Basie orchestra. Similarly, I have tried to discuss Charlie Parker's effect on Miles Davis and on Horace Silver, and to discuss their own contributions. I have endeavored to point out the things that Monk, John Lewis, and Sonny Rollins have in common, along with the things they do not.

The question of where a study like this stops becomes fairly arbitrary at some point. One's final word on where it stops must be that it had to stop somewhere, and it stopped where I stopped it. Were I to continue, my next choices for individual chapters would probably be King Oliver, Sidney Bechet, Earl Hines, Roy Eldridge, Art Tatum, Charlie Mingus, Albert Ayler . . . But, as I say, my book stops where it stops.

If we examine the innovations of Armstrong and Parker, I think we see that each of them sprang from a rhythmic impetus. Similarly, if we look at pre-New Orleans music— cakewalk tunes, then ragtime—we can again identify a definite and almost logical rhythmic change. Similarly, looking beyond Parker to more recent developments we see important changes in rhythm.

Dizzy Gillespie has said that when he is improvising he thinks of a rhythmic figure or pattern and then of the notes to go with it, and I am sure that any important jazz musician from any style or period would give us a similar statement. Indeed, the musicians and fans give us the key to the changes in the music in the style-names themselves: cakewalk, ragtime, jazz, swing, be-bop. Casual as they are, regrettable as they sometimes may seem, these words do not indicate melodies or harmonies. They indicate rhythms.

In all the stylistic developments of jazz a capacity for rhythmic growth has been fundamental. And in saying that, I believe we are saying more than we may seem to be saying. There is nothing in the outer environment of the music, nor in the "cultural influences" upon its players, to guarantee such growth. Quite the contrary. One might say that during the past hundred years of jazz and the African-American music that preceded it, American black men have relearned a rhythmic complexity (in different form) which was commonplace to their African ancestors.

And here we find ourselves up against the "liberal" bugaboo of "natural rhythm" and whether Negroes have it or not—up against the position which holds that Negroes do not and could not have something called "natural rhythm," and that it is insulting and even racist to say that they do.

Negroes certainly could not have *un*natural rhythm. The music ultimately comes from people, not alone from their environment or their cultural influences. Certainly blacks must have a rhythm natural to their own music and their own dances (which does not of course mean that "all" Negroes have such a thing, nor that others may not acquire it). Nor is the rhythm simply personal to certain musicians, otherwise there would not be such a wide response to it on the part of others—other musicians, dancers, listeners.

My sense of human justice is not, I hope, dependent on the assumption that black men *could* not have a natural rhythm. Differences among peoples do not make for moral inequality or unworthiness, and a particular sense of rhythm may be as natural as a particular color of skin and texture of hair. No, it does no damage to my sense of good will toward men or my belief in the equality of men, I trust, to conclude that Negroes as a race have a rhythmic genius that is not like that of other races, and to concede that this genius has found a unique expression in the United States.

It is worth pointing out that the rhythmic capacities of a jazz musician are not directly dependent on other aspects of technique in the traditional sense. Players either *think* rhythmically in a particular style, or they do not. Oscar Peterson has prodigious facility as a pianist but rhythmically he does not think in the manner of "modern" jazz, and when he undertakes a Parker-esque run we may hear an incongruous fumbling in the fingers. Similarly, Buddy Rich, an astonishingly accomplished drummer technically, still plays swing-era drums rhythmically.

I think that a rhythmic view of jazz history provides the most valuable insight into its evolution. But I do not mean to set up absolute standards in pointing it out, and there are contradictions when one comes down to individual players, particularly white players. Thus, such harmonic and linear modernists as Stan Getz, Gerry Mulligan, and even Art Pepper think in an older rhythmic idiom of alternate strong and weak accents or heavy and light beats, within a 4/4 time context. Still, pianist Al Haig, for example, who is white, grasped quite early the rhythmic idiom of Gillespie and Parker. Coleman Hawkins, on the other hand, once he had absorbed early Armstrong and begun to develop his own style, became almost European in his emphasis of the "weak" and "strong" beats. (I expect, by the way, that this is because Hawkins is not a blues man.)

Jazz is a music evolved by black men and in general best played by black men, which white men can play and sometimes play excellently. But at the same time it is a music which obviously has deep meaning for extraordinary numbers of men of all races the world over.

From this point on, my book will have little to say on the meaning or "content" of jazz music. And particularly for that reason, I should like to undertake to say something on that subject now.

The question of meaning in music is one of the most difficult and tenuous that one can undertake. And particularly so in jazz which, although it obviously has a direct emotional appeal to a relatively broad audience, also has standards of its own to which traditional aesthetic categories in music (such as they are) should be applied only with the greatest care.

Traditionally, there have been two approaches to the question of the content of jazz; we might call them "impressionist" and Marxist. In the first, a commentator offers his emotional response to the work at hand, describes the feeling he gets from Miles Davis or Billie Holiday, or whoever. Often he is convinced that what he is describing is in Billie Holiday's singing. But inevitably, he must be describing what the response in himself is to her singing.

Such comments can be enlightening and valuable. We may feel they give us insight into our own responses to the music, responses which would otherwise remain vague, unformed, unconscious, unexpressed. But such descriptions tend to be self-limiting and tend to set up self-contained categories labeled "Billie Holiday" or "Miles Davis." Like the descriptions in impressionist criticism of all kinds, they tend to become substitutes for the experience of the music itself.

Marxist critics have of course taken an apparently broader view, and they find in jazz a confirmation (not to say an affirmation) of their views of society and man. To the more fundamental Marxists, jazz is musical "social protest." (When one tries to tie down such a concept, he will find precious little confirmation in the lyrics to traditional blues, incidentally, which deal far more often with the problems of courtship, personal morality, and natural forces—storms, floods—than with society.) I find Marxist interpretations unsatisfactory for it seems to me that they see the complexities of man and his art as merely the transient tools of "social forces." It seems to me that even most perceptive and receptive Marxists—certainly the narrow and doctrinaire ones—turn art into a reductive "nothing but" proposition, robbed of its complexities and its humanity.

Perhaps, then, we might try a somewhat different approach, one which hopefully is based more directly on the "knowable" aspects of music, and on those ways in which jazz differs from other musics—or at any rate other Western musics.

First, jazz knows of no absolutes: there is no one "best" way of performing a piece. Each day, each moment has its way, and hence its own meaning. Tomorrow's way is not today's; today's is not yesterday's.

That does not mean that there are no standards. Yesterday's way may have been better than today's, or not as good. Tomorrow's may be better still, or less good. And I may be perfectly clear and specific about where the inferiority or superiority lies. But I accept such differences as inevitable and natural, and I take each day's way of performing for its own meaning. At the same time, my standards themselves change with my own growth and change. And I accept these changes too.

Thus, in several respects, the dimension of time is acknowledged in the nature of the music. And, again, there are no absolutes.

Philosophically, then, jazz is a twentieth-century music. Through *doing*, jazz musicians have arrived at, and have lived, a fundamental insight of contemporary philosophy.[1]

1. Thus phonograph records are in a sense a contradiction of the meaning of the music. That is, they tend to make permanent and absolute music that is created for the moment, to express the meaning of the moment. On the other hand, records attest that what is made up for the moment *can* survive that moment aesthetically.

Jazz is philosophically contemporary in another sense. The Greeks, as José Ortega y Gasset has pointed out, made the mistake of assuming that since man is the unique thinking animal (or so they concluded him to be), his thinking function is his superior function. Man is at his best when he thinks. And traditionally, Western man has accepted this view of himself. But to a jazz musician, thought and feeling, reflection and emotion, come together uniquely, and resolve in the act of doing.

No music depends so much on the individual as jazz. Indeed, jazz requires not only an individual interpretation of melody, it demands spontaneous individual invention of new melody, individual articulation of emotion, and individual interpretation of musical sound.

No jazz player is supposed to sound like any other player. A musician's instrumental voice should be as uniquely personal as is his speaking voice, but obviously its quality must be more a matter of deliberate, conscious development than that of his speaking voice. One could probably tell the history of jazz in terms of the way in which this concept of individual sound has been developed, modified, and enlarged over the years.

But at the same time that jazz depends on the individual, it also depends on group co-operation. In all its styles, jazz involves some degree of collective ensemble improvisation, and in this it differs from Western music even at those times in its history when inprovisation was required. The high degree of individuality, together with the mutual respect and co-operation required in a jazz ensemble carry with them philosophical implications that are so exciting and far-reaching that one almost hesitates to contemplate them. It is as if jazz were saying to us that not only is far greater individuality possible to man than he has so far allowed himself, but that such individuality, far from being a threat to a co-operative social structure, can actually enhance society.

Art does not reflect society and environment and consciousness so much as it tells us what environment and society and consciousness do not know. It compensates for conscious attitudes; it reveals to us that there are other, perhaps opposite, but still tenable ways of looking at things or of feeling about things. Art tells us what we do not know or do not realize. And it prepares the way for change. If it is superior art, it may also resolve at a deeper level the conscious and unconscious attitudes through paradox.

In the 1930s, in the midst of the Great Depression, when no people were harder hit than American black men, the Count Basie orchestra played with a surging, joyous momentum and a new rhythmic flexibility. Such qualities not only characterized the Basie orchestra itself, they fundamentally and permanently affected the most basic jazz idiom—the twelve-bar blues. Such musical-aesthetic facts (and one might cite many more of them) involve, it seems to me, a strong criticism of narrowly Marxist or "social" interpretations of the art.

Now it is true that many listeners hear only the "happy" side of Basie's music—or Fats Waller's or Louis Armstrong's music—and they interpret jazz only in such terms. They miss the paradoxical melancholy and pain in Basie's music. They hear the joy in King Oliver but miss his anguish— or at least their consciousness misses it. And this is particularly true of white listeners.

The joy in the music is of course not a simple, facile effort to cheer oneself up in the face of hard times—a sort of "have a drink and forget about it" attitude toward something which cannot be forgotten and needs to be faced. At the same time, the paradoxical pain and melancholy in the music are never self-indulgent, and they go deeper than the outer circumstances of poverty and denigration.

Indeed, jazz is a music of the most profound paradox, capable of finding joy in pain, capable of being at once banal, or even grotesque, and grandiose (the essence of Louis Armstrong's art). It can be collective, even "primitive" if you will, and yet personal and individual quite beyond standards so far acknowledged by Western man.[2]

In general, as I say, white Americans recognize the "happy" side of jazz. Historically we have scorned the music, pushed it into the most despised and unrecognized areas of our lives. In righteous, high-minded, middle-class America jazz has taken its place in the barroom, in the whorehouse, in burlesque houses, in tawdry night clubs, and on the soundtracks of crime films—areas with an inevitable and still persistent association with big-time crime.

It would surely take a lot of research, thought, and exposition to dig deeply into the social meanings of the musics of the black American, but if one were going to undertake such a task, I think he might start with the hypothesis that, for whites at least, the music represents important aspects of our lives, but aspects that are associated with all our unresolved problems, with our unrecognized lack of self-knowledge, with all the truths about ourselves which we refuse to admit to or face up to—things, some of which James Baldwin described so perceptively in *Notes of a Native Son*. Those things, however, are positive as well as negative in that they involve a fundamental redemption if we could acknowledge them.

Jazz, then, has to do with vital and crucial things about Americans that are not a part of the comfortably benign, self-righteous, innocent picture of ourselves we like to pre-

2. Paradox is a part of the inherently contrapuntal nature of the music, to be sure. It is obvious in the New Orleans style, in the simultaneous improvising of the horns. But even for a soloist with rhythm accompaniment there is at least a counterrhythmic juxtaposition. However, I here refer to the dual emotional nature even of a single improvising hornman.

sent both to the world and to ourselves. Those unadmitted
things are sometimes joyful as they are sometimes painful.
They are potentially tragic, which does not mean that they
are defeatist but that they may be ennobling.

I offer here a remarkable statement on the meaning of
the music by one of its earliest artists, Sidney Bechet, in his
autobiography, *Treat It Gentle*:

> After emancipation . . . all those people who had been
> slaves, they needed the music more than ever now; it was
> like they were trying to find out in this music what they
> were supposed to do with this freedom: playing the music
> and listening to it—waiting for it to express what they
> needed to learn once they had learned it wasn't just white
> people the music had to reach to, nor even to their own
> people, but straight out to life, and to what a man does
> with his life when it finally *is* his.

Now, if I may be allowed to interpret him a bit, it seems
to me that Bechet acknowledges here that the music reaches
beyond its immediate circumstances, even beyond its ethnic
origins, and tells all men something about themselves which
they do not know and have never heard before.

We are living in a time of the rebirth of the gods, as a
contemporary psychologist has put it, that is, a rebirth of
the fundamental principles and symbols by which men live
and by which the spirit of man survives.[3] And there can be
no doubt that much contemporary art has as its purpose the
breakdown of the old principles and the old symbols. But
at the same time as it destroys, some contemporary art perhaps also rebuilds, and perhaps jazz rebuilds in ways that
are unique.

Jazz not only exalts the individual finding his own way,

3. See C. G. Jung, *The Undiscovered Self* (Mentor Books).

it also places him in a fundamental, dynamic, and necessary co-operation with his fellows. It handles paradox—the paradox of emotion but also the paradox of thinking and doing —in ways that perhaps no other music has. It does not deal in absolutes, and it does not deny the relative function of time.

Why is it the music of so many people? It was made by American blacks, and they have provided its leadership, still do, and I have no doubt will continue to. But as I say, all sorts and conditions of men the world over respond to it deeply. It is easy enough to say that the conflicts with the outer world experienced by Negroes gave the music its birth and have kept it alive. But I believe that if those social conflicts were somehow resolved, the conflicts that are fundamental within each human being would then keep jazz alive and developing, for jazz has been deeply in touch with those fundamental conflicts all along. And it is from these inner conflicts that comes the true impetus of art.

Jazz is the music of a people who have been told by their circumstances that they are unworthy. And in jazz, these people discover their own worthiness. They discover it in terms that mankind has not experienced before. I have deliberately borrowed a theological term in saying "unworthy." I think it is an apt one because the experience of feeling unworthy is fundamental to the twentieth-century man who, whether he admits it or not, is in danger of losing his old gods or has lost them already. But the music involves discovery of one's worthiness from within. And it is thus an experience that men of many races and many circumstances have responded to.

Perhaps in jazz, then, the gods, in some small way, prepare for their metamorphosis.

2

JELLY ROLL MORTON

Three-Minute Form

One thing that leads us to believe that we should call jazz an art, and not just acknowledge it as a remarkable expressive folk culture, is the fact that its best works survive the moment. In doing that they defy all, for not only are they intended for the moment (as is most folk culture), but they are often improvised on the spur of the moment.

Much jazz does survive but, to hear that it does, we must be willing to forget what is merely stylish and what is merely nostalgic. Probably no man in jazz was ever more the victim of both stylishness and nostalgia than Ferdinand "Jelly Roll" Morton. Because of the innovations of Louis Armstrong, he was already going out of style before his major work had been recorded. The colorful character of Jelly Roll Morton seems to be one of the abiding clichés of jazz history. The attitude may come from writers' efforts to get people interested in Morton by hooking them on the "character," and it is certainly encouraged by one kind of look at a life that was full of wandering, pimping, bragging, and wild ostentation in dress and possessions. And the braggart, the blowhard, the exaggerator, the liar (often just the audacious kind of liar who does not really expect to be believed)—they were Morton too, and these images encourage one to make a cozy, implicitly patronizing account of him. But in his life and his wanderings, amid all the delusions and painful paranoid railings, was a kind of larger integrity: the music in him always seemed to triumph and led him on.

Morton was an exasperatingly complex and even contradictory man, and he had a large and fragile ego that hardly encourages one to try to understand the man and, what is more important, his music. From his life one grasps what seems enlightening. One wonders at much and one can only repeat a great deal. But the ultimate point is the music. Our knowledge of his life and his world is important only insofar as it enlightens us about his music. And, hearing his music, we know that it expresses more of the man and his deeper feelings than his public masks, his pride, his snobbery, his pontifications, and his prejudices can show us.

One of Morton's best recordings is of a piece he called *Dead Man Blues*. Like W. C. Handy's blues, and like ragtime pieces before them, *Dead Man* is built on several themes—specifically three. The themes obviously need to work well together. And they need to be put into an order that gives the piece as a whole a sense of musical and emotional development.

In planning a performance, one concern of a jazz composer-arranger is to decide who plays what, who improvises when and how much: how to bring out the best in each player without letting him overpower the total performance. The whole, in an ideal performance of a great jazz composition, has to be greater than the sum of its parts.

Musically, Morton's recording of *Dead Man* begins with an echo of a funeral procession, an introductory strain from the familiar Chopin *Funeral March*, the lead played on trombone with a hint of humor. From this point on, *Dead Man* attempts the difficult task of being sober without being stodgy.

The first theme in *Dead Man* is stated in a dancing po-

lyphony[1] by the trumpet's lead, with the clarinet in a
quietly simple second part behind it, and a trombone in a
rhythmic-melodic bass line. There is a buoyancy of melody
and rhythm in this chorus; it is quite unlike the heavy,
plodding, and strident Dixieland of earlier and later years,
and such masterful ensemble playing in this style is perhaps
a lost art.

The second section of *Dead Man* is a series of variations,
overlapping two of its themes. The first is a chorus by Omer
Simeon's clarinet, a variation on the first theme. The second
is a two-chorus solo by cornetist George Mitchell, compris-
ing the second theme plus one variation on it. Mitchell
shapes lovely, logically developed, simple melodies. They
hang together but his second chorus develops his first, and
it further prepares for the entrance of the third *Dead Man*
theme. It is rare that a solo can have such structural uses
and still be beautiful in itself, but the great jazz composers
can always encourage such playing.

The third part of *Dead Man* begins simply, with a trio of
clarinets playing a lovely, riff-like blues line in harmony.[2]
As they repeat the chorus, Kid Ory's trombone enters behind
them with a deep, moaning countermelody. In the third
chorus, as if encouraged by Ory, Mitchell and Simeon join
the trombonist, the other two clarinets drop out, and the
three horns play a lovely, three-part polyphonic variation

1. I have followed the general practice in jazz commentary of calling the
New Orleans style polyphonic. However, polyphony implies several melodic
lines of equal importance, but in New Orleans jazz the trumpet (cornet)
or trumpets obviously carry a lead melody to which the lines of the clarinet,
trombone, and rhythm are secondary. In some of its later developments—
the interplay of Sidney Bechet and Tommy Ladnier for example—New
Orleans jazz did approach polyphony.
2. This theme was not used in Morton's other versions of *Dead Man*; it
does not appear in the sheet music nor in the piano roll version of the
piece. However, King Oliver had recorded the strain as *Camp Meeting
Blues* in 1923.

based on a return to the opening theme. Thus the closing section balances the polyphonic chorus which opened the record. The three clarinets then tag the performance with a brief echo of the third theme. The overall scheme of *Dead Man Blues* is therefore intro/A/A1 (clarinet solo)/B and B1 (cornet solo) /C/C1/A2/tag.

In some accounts, Morton's music is placed in a neat category called "New Orleans style," and there the explanations stop and the enthusiasm starts.

That category is not so neat. The usual explanation is that New Orleans style is something the Original Dixieland Jazz Band was attempting to play, the style Kid Ory was first to put on records in 1921, the style King Oliver's Creole Jazz Band recorded in 1923, the style certain of Johnny Dodds's groups (The Wanderers, The Boot Blacks, The Black Bottom Stompers) recorded later, and that the early Armstrong Hot Fives reflected. Such an effort to place Morton historically is far too general to be very enlightening. There were many kinds of music played in New Orleans and a number of these, from the propriety of A. J. Piron to the crudeness of Sam Morgan, we would be willing to call jazz, pre-New Orleans jazz, near-jazz. They were not all alike. Furthermore, despite the similarities, it should be obvious that there are certain very basic differences in conception between Morton's orchestral music and Oliver's. Oliver's music was, one might say, improvisational blues played by a group of musically integrated instrumentalists, whose greatest virtue came from the individuals involved and the way they blew together. Morton's is an individually, compositionally conceived music with orchestrational variety and form. Rhythmically, Morton's music represents an earlier stage in jazz than Oliver's. But for the moment he does represent, Morton was a modernist, as far as we can tell. He was also perhaps something of an innovator, but his music showed more sophistication, consciousness, and formal musical knowledge than Oliver's, and he had definite theories about what he was doing. At the same time, Morton never abandoned the expressive and earthy realities of jazz and the blues.

As far as we can tell—as far as written documents, published scores, and recordings enable us to tell—Morton was the first great master of form in jazz. In this respect, he belongs with Duke Ellington, John Lewis, and Thelonious Monk. By the late 1930s, Ellington had absorbed into his music the innovations which Louis Armstrong, as an improviser, had announced. Lewis (partly by assimilating and transforming form from Europe) and Monk (by working more directly with the implicit resources of jazz itself) found form within the innovations represented by Parker, Gillespie, and Monk himself.

With what resources at hand did Morton work? Buddy Bolden's? If we accept Bunk Johnson's re-creations of Bolden's style, Bolden's sense of form as an improviser was a strong one and strikingly like Morton's as an orchestrator (and, incidentally, like Monk's). We can say that despite his exemplary handling of single-theme compositions, Morton's conception represents an extension of the form established by the great ragtime composers, but it also incorporates rhythmic, harmonic, and variational elements of the jazz movement and the blues. Morton's conception was later than Scott Joplin's or perhaps Bolden's, earlier but more sophisticated than Oliver's. In effect, Morton's music represents a summary of all that jazz had achieved before Armstrong's innovations reinterpreted its basic language.

There are some curious likenesses among these leaders of form: Morton, Ellington, Lewis, Monk. All are pianists (or at least they all play piano) and all have been called poor pianists which in some, usually irrelevant, senses, several are. All are major composers, of course, perhaps *the* major composers in jazz. All may show, at least part of the time, an orchestral (rather than horn-like) conception of the piano, which can make them all sometimes unorthodox but extremely effective accompanists. All have taken strikingly similar approaches to the problem of improvisation vs. form, freedom vs. discipline, individuality vs. total effect. And for Morton and Ellington at least, as their messages of form began to take effect, revolutionary improvisers arrived. The maturing of Ellington's sense of form was followed by Parker's innovations, but Ellington had a lot to do with planting the seeds. There were signs of another revolution as Monk's sense of form began to be recognized, and Monk planted the seeds. Morton was the unluckiest of the four, for he had hardly begun recording and regular publication before Armstrong's revolution had already taken effect. He began almost as an anachronism, a leader of a style already becoming unstylish. But perhaps hints of Armstrong's innovations are to be heard in his music. And obviously it is not against Armstrong that Morton should be judged artistically.

One other thing that all these men (Morton, Ellington, Lewis, and Monk) share is a crucially important movement —ragtime. Ellington was steeped in its Eastern, later "stride" branch. Monk got it indirectly from Ellington and somewhat more directly from James P. Johnson and Fats Waller. Lewis got it indirectly and largely from Ellington, but he has professed an admiration for James P. Morton's relationship to ragtime was direct, and it was to the Midwestern-Sedalia-St. Louis version.

In itself, ragtime proved to be a kind of blind alley, but its contribution to jazz, and to form in jazz, is probably immeasurable. From one viewpoint, it was the most formal, most "European," even most "highbrow" movement associated with jazz. It is incredible that in so short a time its folk themes, ring shouts, church themes, European dances, and military strains could be so transformed and formalized as to create a unique, identifiable body of pianistic music. Within a decade after the emergence of ragtime (beginning in about 1899) exploitation, excess, popularization, decadence, and its own implicit limitations had largely destroyed it. Meanwhile, for the greater jazz movement, its work had been done and would abide for fifty years.

Although Morton respected the best ragtime men and said so, he apparently saw what was happening and what was missing. The music had become, in the hands of pseudo-ragmen, a kind of showman's piano for vapid displays of fingering; and in the hands of publishing-house hacks, it was a style in which to compose banalities. Joplin's work aside, by about 1905 the style had become rigid, and even some of the more legitimate rag composers simply decorated or reworked ragtime commonplaces. Morton was part of a movement which saved things from decadence. Ragtime was structurally, rhythmically, and emotionally limited, and Morton seems to have known it.

The printed scores of Morton's typical multithematic pieces—*Wolverines, King Porter Stomp, The Pearls, Kansas City Stomps, Grandpa's Spells,* etc.—show three themes, a developing or contrasting melodic and tonal relationship among them (often as ABC or ABAC), plus one or two choruses of variation on the third theme. A very few ragtime scores survive which include written variations. In performance, spontaneous variations, or at least decorative embellishments and fills, were sometimes made, but variation is not essential to this music. Written variation is obviously essential to Morton's music, and we know that in performance, improvised melodic variation is a part of its substance.

There are other differences: in rhythm, harmony, and emotional range.

JELLY ROLL MORTON   23

One could describe Morton's smoothing out of ragtime rhythms as the result of the addition, to the clipped 2/4 and simple syncopations of ragtime, of more complex tango-derived syncopations and of polyphonic bass melodies borrowed and transformed from certain marches and European folk dances. One could also describe his harmonic progress as based on his knowledge of European music and the intuitive freedom with which he could relate tonalities and arrive at simple substitute chords—something which neither King Oliver nor James Scott knew as much about. And his emotional range was perhaps the result of his feeling for the blues. But these categories make very arbitrary separations, they overlap in practice, and they do not give a complete picture even of Morton's "sources."

Many of the ragtime composers were well-schooled, some undoubtedly better schooled than Morton. Most of the resources that Morton used were there in the European music to which he was exposed—ready and waiting to be used, as it were, for a long time. But, as the history of jazz has shown repeatedly, the Promethean task is always a matter of showing that such European-derived techniques will work as jazz, how they will work, and assimilating them into the jazz idiom. Making a musical resource work into jazz is never easy, never the result of only formal musical knowledge nor of will. It takes what we can only describe as an intuitive genius and insight into the nature of jazz.

A crucial point of Morton's theories was that the rhythm in his scores—the bass line and the way in which phrases are placed upon it—gives enough rhythmic and melodic variety to constitute an intermittent but interplaying polyphonic and polyrhythmic part—of anticipated downbeats, delayed accents, syncopated Spanish rhythms, and trombone-like melodies.

In *Mr. Jelly Roll*, Alan Lomax invited us to see Morton's music as an ingenious combination of "Downtown" and

"Uptown" New Orleans elements: the largely European (but "folk" and therefore rhythmic) music of the colored Creoles, plus the earthier music—blues, work songs, spirituals—of the uptown Negroes and ex-slaves, some of whom had migrated from nearby plantations.

Similarly, one might see it as an alliance between ragtime and the blues, with importations from French and Spanish folk musics, Baptist hymns, and martial music—the last at least analogous to rags.

Unfortunately, most discussions of the constant flirting of jazz with "Latin" music soon bog down into a listing of compositions, beginning with Joplin's *Solace* and including Horace Silver's *Señor Blues* or Ornette Coleman's *Una Muy Bonita*. The source of the syncopated 2/4 (which led towards 4/4) of jazz may well be the tango. The source of the behind-the-beat delays and "around-the-beat" accents which are so important to Morton's *New Orleans Blues, New Orleans Joys, The Crave*, or *Mamanita* could also be the tango. The very placement of the melodic phrases in, for example, the third theme of Morton's *Wolverine Blues* corresponds with the placement of the heavy beats in a tango—but *Wolverines* is not a jazz tango. Clearly, "the Spanish tinge" (Morton's name for this Latin influence) goes deeper than certain compositions, than an occasionally brilliant effect which one hears not only in Morton's but in Oliver's rhythm section, and than Morton's own comments might lead one to believe.

And from the blues the music gained further rhythmic character and variety, depth, honest passion, and spontaneous variation and improvisation.

Between the waning of ragtime and the ascendancy of New Orleans jazz music, there was an overlapping popular movement in American music called "the blues craze," which was announced by the song publications of W. C. Handy, pieces like *St. Louis Blues* and *Beale Street Blues*.

In some ways, Handy's approach was more formal even than ragtime's. It was also perhaps a little arty. He took folk blues melodies, made them regular, harmonized them, and evolved a system in which the "bent" tones of the blues "scale"— notes found in every music in the world except Western concert music, by the way—could be imitated by putting the third and seventh notes of the scale in minor. He built several of these melodies into often splendidly organized multithematic compositions on the model of rags. Even in Handy's somewhat fussy approach, rhythmic variety, "breaks" (suspensions of a stated pulse), and passion were captured.

As is evident from Morton's re-creations on his Library of Congress recordings of the kinds of blues that were played in the lowest dives in New Orleans, there was a lot of structural and, more important for the moment, rhythmic diversity in this music. There were blues in the clipped 2/4 of ragtime, in the smoother and syncopated 2/4 of Creole jazz, in a 4/4 swing suggesting the rhythm of Armstrong, and even in the eight-to-the-bar of boogie woogie (which, by the way, suggests the rhythmic patterns of modern jazz). Handy's records of his own blues used a mechanical version of rag rhythm and a rather arty dance band approach. When others played Handy's blues, a rhythm almost like New Orleans Creole jazz often emerged.

Even in the most formally compositional blues, there can be emotion unknown to ragtime. There would be no jazz without the blues or, to put it a bit differently, without the blues jazz would be a sterile music. But without ragtime, what a melodically limited kind of rhythm-making jazz might be. The European tradition of form, discipline, and order probably affects jazz more *directly* today than before, but these ideals crucially affected it indirectly through ragtime long ago.

The blues had rhythmic variety, passion and, chiefly be-

cause of Handy's work, a certain public respectability. Like
most folk music, the blues were performed with improvisation. Combining the melodic-compositional emphasis of rags
and the improvisational-variational emphasis of blues, we
have the basis for Morton's principle of thematic variation.
Inevitable or not, simple or not, it was an almost brilliant
stroke, for it combined and developed the virtues of both
forms but the dangers of neither. It made variation meaningful, but channeled and controlled it. It kept the music
fresh and alive, but gave it order and purpose. It also opened
up many possibilities for future developments. Later conceptions might have allowed more freedom, but at this stage,
and with polyphonic structures, it was precisely this discipline of Morton's that helped immeasurably to transform
emotional impulse and musical craft into art.

Morton's "theory of jazz" which he gave to Alan Lomax
is not so much a theory as it is a specific response to the
definition of jazz which used to be in certain American dic-
tionaries (something about loud, fast, blatant, cacophonous
noises) and similar "Aunt Sallies." But it does give certain
principles that were important to him and, perhaps more to
the point, does affirm that his mind was the kind which
thought about practice and arrived at principles. The fact
that he acknowledges that he worked out his style at medium
tempos (which permitted him to work on note-doublings,
embellishment, and accentual displacements) not only indicates a fundamentally rhythmic approach to jazz but coincidentally indicates the basis on which most subsequent
innovations were also worked out. Hear the recordings made
at Minton's in the early 1940s; hear the Armstrong of the
late 1920s and early 1930s. Much has been made of Morton's
remark, "Always keep the melody going some way." It does
acknowledge that thematic variation is Morton's way, but
it is actually an afterthought to his insistence on proper and
interesting harmonization.

Much has been made of Morton's insistence that riffs
(simple, rhythmically pronounced melodic phrases repeated
over and over) are for background, not for themes. No one
could doubt that the great effectiveness of riff melodies is
often bought cheap, but Morton himself wrote some riff
melodies, and the very riff he used to demonstrate his point
was the final theme of his rewriting of Santo Pecora's *She's
Crying for Me* into *Georgia Swing*. Many of his other
themes, like many rag themes, are simple and brief enough
in their basic ideas to amount to riffs. At any rate, one could
hardly doubt the effectiveness of riffs behind soloists. Nor
could one question that his principle that a jazz pianist
should imitate an orchestra has the confirmation of time;
from Morton through Bud Powell, Earl Hines through
Erroll Garner, pianists follow either band or horn styles.

As Morton put it, using "breaks"—brief two-bar, suspensions of a stated rhythmic pulse—is "one of the most effective things you can do in jazz." In a sense they are a culmina-
tion of the rhythmic resources of the music (unless "stop
time," two-bar breaks in series carries things a step further)
but Morton is probably the only man, musician or critic,
who made them a principle. They continue to be used today
(often at the beginning of choruses instead of as a climactic
device), and the subtle sense of time and suspense they
require is the bane of many a "revivalist" dixielander and
an excellent test of a musician's swing.

Morton's assertion that jazz can be played soft, sweet,
slow, with plenty of rhythm (or, as André Hodeir later put
the same principle, "swing is not the same as getting hot")
is, of course, crucial. The problem of swing at slow tempos
plagues jazzmen periodically.

Morton was, as I say, something of a modernist. That is
why he so frequently ridiculed "ragtime men." He was part
of a movement which saved Afro-American music from de-
generation at the hands of pseudo and second-rate ragtimers

and continued its development. He obviously respected the *best* ragtime and its composers, however. And that is also why he frequently scorned blues instrumentalists ("one tune piano players"). His work was more sophisticated, formal, knowledgeable, resourceful, and varied than theirs. It was a product of intelligence and theory as well as emotion and intuition.

Morton's real reputation depends on a brilliant series of orchestral recordings he made for the Victor company between September 15, 1926 and June 11, 1928—a short enough period, but greater reputations in jazz have been made on less finished work.

These recordings are the real successors to the striking series of piano solos he made for Gennett, Paramount, Rialto, and Vocalion between 1924 and 1926. He had made other orchestral records before the Victors, none of them really worthy of him as a pianist nor anticipating the orchestrator and leader he was to become. But in those early band records he did try out some of the devices and effects he was later to perfect.

The exception among the early band recordings, and a real success, are the simplest in scoring, the pair of titles on Paramount, *Big Fat Ham* and *Muddy Water*—polyphony plus solos. Jasper Taylor's excellent (if overrecorded) woodblock drumming falls into just the right rhythmic role for Morton's music. There is fine group swing, the right balance between discipline and expressiveness in the playing, with the Keppard-Oliver-like trumpet and the clarinet understanding and displaying this relationship excellently. But Morton's attempt to use a saxophone as an extra polyphonic voice is a failure; it was something he would try again and something he seldom made much of, partly because few of these saxophonists ever got any swing.

Otherwise, an inept clarinetist, an amateurish trumpeter, or a rhythmically awkward ensemble usually spoils these early recordings. The Morton-directed version of *London Blues* by the New Orleans Rhythm Kings ably alternates passages in harmony, counterpoint, and solo, and breaks, along the lines he later perfected. The later Okeh *London Blues*, reorchestrated in polyphony and spoiled only by bad clarinet, shows for the first time on records the effective variety and thoughtfulness of Morton as an accompanist. Among the remaining records, the Gennett version of *Mr. Jelly Lord* (1926) features a three-man reed section which plays, and swings, in harmony.

As I have said, Morton's achievement, before the Victor orchestral recordings were made, was his piano, and we should take a closer look at that style.

In 1944 William Russell wrote an analytical review of Morton's rediscovered *Frog-i-More Rag* solo for the magazine *The Needle*, which, I think, offers a definitive statement of Morton's style:

> Jelly Roll's piano style and musical greatness are nowhere better demonstrated. . . . All the most typical features . . . are abundantly evident: his wealth of melodic invention and skill in variation; the tremendous swing . . . his feeling for formal design and attention to detail; his effective use of pianistic resources; the contrasts of subtle elegance with hard hitting drive; the variety of harmony, and yet freedom from complication and superficial display. . . .
>
> Jelly Roll had a more formal musical training and background than many New Orleans musicians. . . . At times the close-knit design is marked by an economy of means that amounts to understatement. *Frog-i-More* follows the usual form of Morton's stomps—introduction, a short three-part song form, and a trio section. A definite musical idea

is used for each new part. Since the opening idea for the
first strain, an ascending succession of 7th chords, does not
immediately establish the tonality, a curious effect of an
extension of the introduction is created. The contrasting
second strain is unusually forceful, employing a repeated-
note motive and powerful left hand bass figures in Jelly's
full *two-handed* style. After a modified return of the first
strain a characteristic Morton trill bridges over to the
trio. . . .

Jelly took great pride in his "improvisations" (on theme)
. . . listen to the trio section to discover Jelly's phenomenal
skill in variation. And if one were to study the four different versions of *The Pearls* or the half-dozen recordings
of *Mr. Jelly Lord*, and perhaps also take time to compare
some of these variations with the published versions, he
would begin to get an idea of Jelly's unlimited imagination
and mastery of motival variation. . . . The beautiful
chorale-like melody of the *Frog-i-More* trio is first played
very simply, in a style reminiscent of the sustained trio of
Wolverine Blues. . . . On paper the tune, with its constantly repeated motive, presents a singularly four-square
appearance, but Jelly's performance is a revelation of
rhythmic variety by means of such devices as shifted accents,
slight delays, and anticipations. . . . As raggy as Jelly's
performance of this chorale is, it nevertheless is in perfect
time; the regular pulse can be felt throughout with no loss
at all in momentum. . . . The melodic invention of this
finale is as notable as its immense rhythmic vitality. . . .
Jelly's rhythmic impetus and melodic embellishment give
the effect of a fantastic and frenzied variation. Actually,
each bar is directly related to its counterpart in the first
simple statement and all of Jelly's characteristic and fanci-
ful "figurations" are fused with the basic idea as though
they belonged there originally . . . with Jelly Roll, no
matter how exuberant rhythmically or varied melodically
the final choruses become, there is never any doubt of their

musical logic and that each note grows out of the original motive. Nor is the typical flavor of the unique Morton style ever . . . lost.

When Morton recorded his music, reminiscences, and fabrications for the Library of Congress, beginning May 21, 1938, he gave us documents that are revealing, exasperating, and delightful. His piano invention is extended, unhampered by such things as the time limits of recording for a ten-inch 78 r.p.m. There are unique revelations of his resources and fine inventiveness on the extended versions of *Wolverines, The Pearls, Creepy Feeling.* But this man, aging, sick, inwardly discouraged behind the pride and bravado, sometimes faltered in fingering and time.

One of his most revealing performances is of Joplin's *Maple Leaf Rag,* first in St. Louis-ragtime style, then in his own. The performance speaks for itself of his innovations in rhythm, tempo, polyphonic effect, improvised variation. Guy Waterman has said of Morton's reorganization of Joplin's *Original Rags*:

> The most obvious indications of Jelly's jazz approach stem, in the right hand, from the improvisation and, in the left hand, from the anticipated downbeats and the octave runs of four sixteenth-notes, Jelly's trademark. Actually, however, these devices do not explain the full transformation which Jelly brings about. There is a gulf which separates ragtime, as the early rag composers understood it, from jazz as Jelly epitomized it. This gulf has more to do with the type of beat which the two develop and the nature of the momentum which builds up. The difference is reflected in the entire organization of the performance.[3]

Two other performances on the Library of Congress series are worth examining for what they show us about Morton's

3. *The Jazz Review,* December 1958.

ideas of structure. The first is an extended version of *Kansas City Stomps*. As published, *Kansas City Stomps* consists of an introduction (a "tune-up" motif) and three themes: A (*e* flat), A (an exact repeat), B (*e* flat), B (an exact repeat), C (*a* flat), C' (a melodic variation). Both A and B are sixteen-bar themes (out of ragtime, polkas, and marches) and C is an unusual twelve-bar melody with a double break at bar one and at bar seven, making two six-bar units.

In this performance Morton plays: introduction, A, A' (a variation), B, B' (a variation), A" (another variation), C, C' (a variation), introduction (a modulational interlude), A''' (a third variation). Thus an implicit rondo is completed, with each return to each theme a variation on that theme.

Then there is the challenge of a single theme. *Hyena Stomp* is a simple sixteen-bar melody of pronounced rhythmic character—an extended two-bar riff, if you will, on one of Morton's favorite chord structures. As a comparison of the shortened printed score and the orchestral version he did for Victor records will show, the basic outlines of the way Morton handled variations on it were compositionally preset—but that is true of much jazz. As is also true in jazz, the way the outlines are *used* in performance can be another matter.

The basic motive of the theme is stated in the first two measures, then moved through a chorus of sixteen bars which serves as an introduction. There follows a second sixteen-bar chorus in which the melody is again stated in bare form. In these first two statements the harmony is deliberately rung clear so that an almost lyric mood is set with that riff, but there are hints of the kind of rhythmic variation to come. There follows a series of six variations. Each is based on a musical idea which Morton works out; each is related to what immediately precedes and follows it, either as contrast or complement; each is also part of the total pattern of the performance; and each is orchestrally or instrumentally conceived.

Chorus three is primarily rhythmic, an appropriate contrast to the careful harmonic-lyric emphasis of the first two. Morton simplified the melody and harmony drastically in a kind of "barrelhouse" destruction of the piece, in which the swinging momentum and a partly polyphonic bass line are first introduced. From this simplification, Morton rebuilds *Hyena Stomp* in various ways. The fourth chorus is an elaborate lyric transformation—melodically the most complex—of the theme, dancing lightly after the heavier motion of what has preceded it. From this point on, as we gradually return to and build on the pronounced rhythmic momentum introduced in the third chorus, we hear a melodic simplification from this peak, and dynamic building. The fifth chorus is an excellent stroke. It still refers to the melody but it also transforms (by simplification) the fourth, forming a kind of two-chorus unit with it. The sixth chorus is a contrast, but one which had been subtly prepared for. It is a variation in the bass (a rather complicated one for the time) under a simple treble statement, and in the preceding chorus there has been much activity in his left hand, readying our ears for this one. In the seventh chorus we are reminded of trumpet figures, and these gradually build into an ensemble variation in the eighth. Morton leads into and makes his climax. The dynamic-rhythmic ideas continue to build excitement and the rhythm swings freely and simply.

Assigning the styles of the variations to instruments, we would have:

Chorus 1   ensemble in harmony
Chorus 2   ensemble, hints of polyphony
Chorus 3   polyphony

Chorus 4   clarinet solo, lower register
Chorus 5   clarinet, upper register, trombone in polyphony
Chorus 6   trombone solo, broken polyrhythms behind
Chorus 7   trumpet into riffs, hints of polyphony
Chorus 8   unison brass-like riffs, still on theme

On the basis of the various ways that Morton handles his simple theme, we have heard some remarkable things, but there is even more in some of the details.

As we have seen, our chorus unit is sixteen measures. But Morton used variations which joined two groups of choruses (four and five, seven and eight). At the same time, each chorus, by the nature of the theme, may fall into two eight-bar units. These, in turn, may fall into units of four bars. Then there is the fact we began with: the basic melodic motif can be stated in two bars. To some, such a thing is evidence of melodic crudeness. Morton, apparently aware of these limitations, took interesting advantage of them and made them principles of his structures. The final chorus, for example, consists of an unbroken eight-bar line followed by two four-bar units, held together emotionally. Also, the first melodic fragment in chorus one is not exact; an improvised shift of meter is then corrected in bars three and four. And in the two clarinet choruses Morton handles bar lines with further ingenuity: the first is based on a parallel repetition of two-bar units; the second begins with contrasting two-bar units. Thus Morton builds variations in continuity within choruses, combines some of these into double choruses and, within this, works out small structures of two, four, and eight bars, all of which contribute by contrast, parallel, and echo to a total development and unity.

Any such an attempt at scrutiny as the foregoing is bound to make a music that is warm, passionate, and spontaneous seem a contrived and pat set of devices. The point of it, of course, is to illustrate general and subtle principles of style. In any given performance, the application of Morton's ideas will be different. But once one grasps the nature of these ideas and their relationships, the excitement, beauty, and uniqueness of Morton's work will, I think, possess him even more strongly and lastingly.

Behind the success of the Victor recordings are a maturity in Morton's conception, the availability of a group of musicians equipped both to play well and to follow Morton's exacting instructions and leadership, careful rehearsal, and a series of exceptional orchestrations.

Like the question of how many of his compositions Morton stole or otherwise obtained from others (a question hardly confined to him—it might be raised about many major jazzmen), the question of how much musical knowledge he actually had and how much help he had with scoring is perpetually unresolved. One can get testimony, often from excellent jazzmen, that Morton knew little about music and played badly. One can get just as much reputable testimony that he was an excellent musician, ahead of his time in several respects, and could play extremely well. The only answer, of course, is his playing—*with* its faults and with its evident evolution and refinement. The answer to the complaint that Morton did not make his own orchestrations is the obvious fact that a single musical intelligence and taste is behind them. Doc Cook, Tiny Parham, Mel Stitzel, and others have been mentioned as helpers with scoring. The answer undoubtedly is that, even if Morton needed help, the conception was nevertheless his.

The ensembles for the Victor recordings were sometimes written—always at least sketched—in advance. Obviously those with harmonized parts were written or at least carefully rehearsed, but so were some of the polyphonic ensembles. They are the disciplined perfection of integrated, inter-

woven, early New Orleans polyphonic improvising, surpassing all others we have on records. The release of alternate
"takes" of the recordings confirms that in ensemble nearly
everyone except Morton played ad lib upon a presketched
outline of his part.

The solos, more often than not, were improvised. There
are exceptions: Johnny Dodds obviously plays (or plays
from) two written choruses on *Hyena Stomp*, and Omer
Simeon obviously allows himself little freedom on *Shreve-
port Stomp*. On the other hand, the release of a very different and superior take of the excellent trio recording of
Wolverine Blues confirms that, for that performance, Johnny
Dodds improvised entirely, using the chord structure alone,
while Morton varied the trio theme behind him. And, as
several of Omer Simeon's and George Mitchell's solos on the
alternate takes demonstrate, Morton would often work out
with the instrumentalist a sketch or plan which the latter,
in turn, was free to fill in or ad lib. Surely the similarities
between Morton's way of working with his musicians and
that of both Ellington and the Modern Jazz Quartet confirm
that there has been only one really successful, variously
arrived at solution to the problem of improvisation and
total form, of spontaneity and group discipline, in jazz.

One thing that immediately strikes one about the Victor
recordings is the extraordinary way in which the players in
the various groups work together. Such unity (and it is beautifully recorded) would be rare even for a group that had
been playing together for many months, regardless of the
stylistic sympathy of its members with one another. For
pick-up groups, even ones so carefully selected and rehearsed as these were, it is almost unthinkable. And one
should remember that such discipline as Morton exacted
may easily produce negative results in the playing of jazzmen of any school.

Smokehouse Blues, from the first recording date, is exceptional if only for the polyphony of its last chorus and because it is so movingly and passionately played. One must wait almost until Morton's last years for so moving a blues.[4] The orchestration is largely soloistic, however, and the soloists were equipped for it. They were equipped not only to play expressively but also to let emotional subjectivity contribute to the performance as a whole rather than detract from its development—a task few jazzmen have been able to fulfill unless they were willing to submit their talents to the direction of a Morton or an Ellington. One brief break in the clarinet chorus has Simeon double-timing while Morton's piano and Johnny St. Cyr's banjo quadruple-time beneath him! Yet the effect of this sudden contrast is to enhance the mood of the piece, not to interrupt it. Morton's own unaccompanied solo does not seem to fit rhythmically with the rest of the recording, but before one decides that his sense of rhythm was failing him (as it sometimes did), one should be aware of the deliberate rhythmic variety that is a part of so many of these recordings, and be aware that the successful use of it is a crucial part of Morton's achievement. *Black Bottom Stomp,* an excellent case in point, was also made at this first Victor date.

Black Bottom, one of Morton's best compositions, is built on two themes:[5] one of sixteen measures, and a second of twenty. The version by the Red Hot Peppers is easily one of Morton's best recordings.

The ensemble included cornet, George Mitchell; trombone, Kid Ory; clarinet, Omer Simeon; piano, Morton; banjo, Johnny St. Cyr; bass, John Lindsay; and drums, An-

---

4. Charles Luke's *Smokehouse* is not a twelve-bar blues, of course, but a sixteen-bar piece in the slow blues mood. However, Morton's *Wolverine Blues* is not a blues but is in post-ragtime "stomp" style.
5. I am grateful to Gunther Schuller for correcting me in several points in my previous comments on this remarkable piece.

drew Hilaire. In the brief performance, these men interpret
the themes of *Black Bottom* and make solo variations on
them. Some of their variations are thematic and some are
fresh inventions on their chord patterns. They offer passages
in harmony, polyphony, and patterns broken four bars at a
time between soloist and group. Morton's piano solo is unaccompanied, but the other soloists play with the rhythm
section, sometimes with banjo, sometimes without, and one
clarinet solo is accompanied only by the banjo. Sometimes
the beat is a pronounced heavy/light/heavy/light; at other
times it is an even 4 and there is one climactic chorus with a
pronounced back beat. There is the "black bottom" variant
of the Charleston rhythm: there are two-bar breaks, sometimes by one instrument, but once split between two of them.
There is a wide variety of combinations of instruments and
textures. Morton had the audacity to try something which
is still highly unusual: his strongest climaxes are made, not
simply by increasing dynamics or by accumulating masses
of instruments, but by holding back Lindsay's string bass
and Hilaire's tom-tom and bass drum until key moments.

My brief description makes the performance sound absurdly cluttered and pretentious. But it is neither. *Black
Bottom Stomp* flows with such apparent simplicity and
almost fated logic that one barely notices its astonishing
variety. One thing that holds it together is its patterns of
echo as various effects appear and reappear: this polyphonic
passage is balanced by that one later on; this rhythmic pattern is echoed in a later one; the clarinet lead here is balanced by the clarinet solo there—the very variety is given
in an orderly manner.

To be a bit more detailed, *Black Bottom* begins with an
eight-bar, written introduction for the ensemble given as
four bars plus an exact repeat. The first chorus of the first A
theme is offered in written harmony, but at a couple of
points the clarinet and the trombone momentarily break

away into a kind of polyphony. In A1, we are given four
bars ad lib by cornet in solo, followed by four bars written
for ensemble, four more for cornet, four more for ensemble.
Mitchell's second four bars are a sprightly variant of his first.
In A2, the third appearance of the first theme, the clarinet
plays a paraphrase over a lightly sketched "black bottom"
rhythm by the banjo alone.

A four-bar interlude introduces the stomping B theme
which we hear in improvised polyphony, and in this opening
chorus a two-bar break is shared by cornet and trombone.
Also evident in this chorus is the important role that bassist
John Lindsay plays, and is to play, in the arrangement. B1,
the second appearance of the second theme, is a nonthematic
clarinet invention of eighteen bars, and an ensemble figure
of two bars. B2 is an unaccompanied piano solo by Morton,
also nonthematic and followed by the same two-bar ensemble figure that ended the previous chorus. B3 is a cornet solo,
a thematic paraphrase over a stop-time variant of the black
bottom rhythm. B4 is a nonthematic banjo solo, under
which Lindsay varies his pattern ingeniously between 2/4
and 4/4. Some of the banjo's figures may be familiar, but
the playing is wonderfully spirited. B5, due to be an all-out
ensemble climax, has the cornet, clarinet, and trombone
delicately interweaving in polyphony over a very lightly
played, understated rhythm, with a superbly placed break
by Hilaire's cymbal. B6, the final ensemble, is the true
"stomp" chorus, with Lindsay and Hilaire in strong, the
latter with emphatic bass drum plus the aforementioned
tom-tom back-beat, with an unexpected trombone break.

Morton's music reflects a deep understanding of the value
and purpose behind a device or an effect, and all parts of
Black Bottom Stomp are intrinsic to a knowingly paced
whole. Could anyone else in jazz history—even Ellington—
put so much into a brief performance with such success?
The Red Nichols-Miff Mole version of *Black Bottom*, made

a few months after this one and apparently using the same orchestration as its point of departure, is a rhythmically unsure, superficial, ineptly played sequence of lumbering effects.

The strongest contrast to the complexity of stomps like *Black Bottom* is a recording like *Jungle Blues*. It is a deliberately archaic piece, whose basic ingredients are a primitive blues bass line and a simple riff. Before he has finished, Morton has in effect formed the riff into three themes (and they are good ones), handled the heavy "four" of the bass with some variation, occasionally relieved it briefly and, as he usually could, spun the performance to the brink of monotony, ending it at exactly the moment-too-soon.

Between the complexity of *Black Bottom Stomp* or *Grandpa's Spells* and the comparative simplicity of *Jungle Blues* or *Hyena Stomp* lies the range of an artist.

Dead Man Blues is probably the masterpiece of the Victor series for its superior themes, its orchestration, and its performance.[6] There are wonderful details in *Dead Man Blues*: the easy swing of Mitchell's never-obvious lead, the strength of Omer Simeon in both his ensemble and solo melodies, the beautiful outward simplicity of the two trio choruses. The opening and closing ensembles seem the fruition of the years of New Orleans ensemble playing, of its simultaneous improvisation. They are choruses which in themselves might make reputations for an orchestrator and his players and which, as part of a whole performance, are among the most effective understatements in jazz recording.

Dead Man redeems *Sidewalk Blues* wherein Morton was

---

6. I have not mentioned the verbal exchanges between Morton and Johnny St. Cyr, the lame jokes, that begin the record. Such things are apt to seem either pointless or annoying to us in Morton's records even when they are used sparsely and intended humorously. Perhaps more important, they indicate an approach to one's audience that is more real than arty.

perhaps a bit too preoccupied with the excellence of his ensemble's swing and a bit careless with the quality of his melodies in the introduction and trio, and with some of his trombone lines. Some kinds of failure are necessary to an artist, particularly if they show him by contrast just what he does best. To have followed *Dead Man* by the excessively corny and banal added parts for two violins on *Someday Sweetheart* is perhaps a bit like John Lewis's having followed *Sait-on Jamais* with *European Windows*; because if Morton's intentions were more "dance band" and Lewis's more "concert hall," both tended, perhaps equally, toward "acceptability." Morton's other "experiment" in the Chicago recordings—that of again adding the extra voice of an alto saxophone—cannot be called a failure. Stomp Evans swings more than the saxophonists on Morton's earlier records and, for all the modified slap-tonguing in his solos, his part interferes far less in the polyphonic sections. Indeed, particularly on the trio of *The Pearls* he seems to contribute to an interesting texture and ensemble swing.

If *Black Bottom Stomp* has a serious rival among the fast stomps, it is *Grandpa's Spells*. *Grandpa's Spells* is perhaps better written. Its orchestration is exceptional, lacking only the touches of brilliance one hears in *Black Bottom*, and it is very well played. Its plan is ingenious but, again, an outline is only an introduction. There is the same variety among polyphony, harmony and solo, rhythmic emphasis, breaks, etc. There is also an ingenious use of rhythm instruments, this time an apparently innovative conversation of breaks among string bass, trombone, and ensemble. Is there anything comparable in jazz recording until Ellington's *Jack the Bear*?

Grandpa's Spells illustrates a further point about Morton's instrumental music. New Orleans jazz, like all jazz, retains highly "vocal" elements, but in it we hear a relatively developed instrumental style, not simply a vocal style transferred to instrument. Morton was a pianist, and his piano imitated a jazz orchestra, but he knew that some of his ideas were too directly pianistic to be simply transferred to the horns and rhythm. When working with the Peppers he did not simply rescore his conception back to its orchestral source; sometimes he needed to recompose and he knew it. *Grandpa's Spells* in the Hot Peppers version opens with a recomposed first theme played on St. Cyr's banjo.

The more one hears Chicago-made Hot Peppers recordings, the more one is impressed with Morton's remarkable ability in choosing and rehearsing his musicians, particularly George Mitchell and Omer Simeon. Both men understood Morton rhythmically. Simeon's strength was his ability to improvise from a sketch or outline, and particularly to make responsive countermelodies in ensemble passages. Mitchell's elusive rhythmic sense was perfectly suited to Morton's, lying between the staccato 2/4 accents of an earlier day and the even 4/4 accents to come. Most important, Mitchell's cornet melodies were probably as complex as they could be and still remain an integrated lead voice in the polyphonic ensembles. A little more of the virtuoso cornet soloist and the ensemble begins to collapse, as Louis Armstrong's work of this period made increasingly evident.

To single out moments from these recordings is obviously unfair since I am claiming such unity of conception for the best of them. But, with that in mind, there are some moments that should be mentioned: the chorus on the trio of *Cannonball Blues* when the banjo carries the theme against the double-time piano comments of the leader; the conversation in "twos" on *Wild Man* between clarinet and piano, then clarinet and alto, in which one will intermittently egg the other into double-time; the announcement which *Steamboat Stomp* makes that Morton's orchestral style has dealt with the problem of faster tempos; and the entirely infectious movement and swing of *Doctor Jazz*, a jazz composer's version of a single-theme pop tune. On June 11, 1928, Morton held his first Hot Peppers recording session in New York. I think that the location probably accounts for the final fulfillment of Morton's rhythmic conception which we hear on *Georgia Swing, Kansas City Stomps, Shoe Shiner's Drag,* and *Boogaboo.* Many Northeastern players were using, and continued to use, an older rhythm that was rather closer to ragtime, and Morton could take direct advantage of that fact. It was easier to get these players to swing *his* way than it would be for Red Allen or J. C. Higginbotham on later records. *Shoe Shiner's Drag (London Blues)* was apparently impressive enough to be remembered and recorded by Lionel Hampton and it is a blues on a sophisticated, substitute chord structure. But the best work from this recording date is *Kansas City Stomps.* At a medium tempo, it features excellent polyphonic writing and playing on several themes, and it sustains throughout the swing of some of the Chicago recordings which have slower tempos, with their same easy understatements in climaxes. *Georgia Swing* is almost as good. Ward Pinkett is a fine trumpeter for Morton to have chosen: his sense of time and accent is almost equal to George Mitchell's, and Morton knew how to use the variety of effects he could produce with mutes.

The last of the great Victors—in 1928—is a quartet based on Oliver's *Chimes Blues,* which Morton called *Mournful Serenade.* None of his subsequent recordings is supposed to be as good as the earlier ones. But the point is that he had too much taste and insight merely to repeat and decorate, to reiterate and complicate what he had already done.

Twenty-five sides had displayed his music, as complete and close to perfection as an artist can ask. It was time to try other things, and among those other things are some real successes.

The first date announced the things he would work on. *Red Hot Pepper* successfully modifies the earlier manner towards big-band scoring. The blues, *Deep Creek*, is a string of solos on more than one theme with opening and closing ensembles. Certainly many of Morton's big-band arrangements suffer by comparison with what Don Redman, Fletcher Henderson and Ellington did, but Morton's best were done in 1928 and 1929, and their best a bit later. *New Orleans Bump* is a successful example of the same kind of thing his successors were to do, and it is another excellent example of pushing simplicity to the brink of monotony, then saving it by a hint of variety and by knowing exactly when to stop.

In others of these later records there are fine moments: the clean swing and passion of the last chorus of *Pontchartrain*; the well-paced and varied textures of *Burning the Iceberg* (the familiar integration of section harmony, polyphony, and solo now being used in the new conception for a larger group) despite its rather anachronistic basic rhythm; and the handling of the first theme in its various appearances on *Pretty Lil* (by an immediate reduction in the second chorus, later by solo variation, etc.). If the scoring or the handling of elements on a later record is not quite on that level, there may well be other things: the superb interplay of piano and guitar on *Little Lawrence* or the very effective piano breaks and solo on *Tank Town Bump*. When one of these records fails, it does not fail because the music on it is pedestrian or banal. Even when the arrangements are based on familiar chord structures or melodic patterns, Morton may handle them with a freshness that will discover in them something alive and unhackneyed, if not always artistically satisfying.

Finally, a performance like *Blue Blood Blues* shows that Morton knew exactly what the theme/string-of-solos/theme approach might achieve, and that recording is still one of the best of its genre—possibly *the* best before some of the small-group recordings of the late 1930s.

A decidedly minor artist (or minor craftsman) may be a major influence—even on a major artist. But it is also quite possible for a major artist to have little influence on his immediate successors. The kind of after-the-fact argument which elevates a man on the basis of influence often avoids a crucial evaluation.

I would like to present Morton on his own terms. If one cannot quite see his achievement on those terms, if one needs comparisons with the work of those around him to help, there is the evidence of: the inept, unswinging, monotonous recordings of his own pieces made by Red Nichols and Miff Mole, The Original Memphis Five, or the California Ramblers; King Oliver's pedestrian *Dead Man Blues*; the Fletcher Henderson version of *The Chant*; or the more recent versions of the Morton repertory made by Turk Murphy and Pee Wee Erwin. One can also learn much by comparing the hesitant versions which some of the Southwestern bands made of his things in the 1920s—the Bennie Moten version of *Midnight Mama*, for example.

But it is the Southwest that one can gather the most verbal evidence of Morton's influence. Interviews bring testimony that Morton, his compositions, his musical training, or his scores were an inspiration. Andy Kirk, Jimmy Rushing, Don Redman, and Ben Smith have all attested to it.

In *King Porter*, we can see one specific and clearly identifiable influence of Morton's work on jazz. In the variations on the trio, we hear figures which are typical of Morton, which Henderson's arrangement used and passed on to Benny Goodman—a kind of scoring for brass (and Morton clearly had brass in mind in such sections) which set a pattern used by almost everyone during the swing period, even Ellington. Hear *Bojangles* for the clearest instance. One can hear it still in everyone who writes big-band jazz scores.

But the real challenge of Morton's work is not a simple result of Morton the composer, the orchestrator, the theorist, the master of form; it is the more complex challenge that in him jazz, by the mid-1920s, had produced an artist.

One can find a lot of reasons for finding this man with the clown's nickname still important in the jazzman's heritage. In him jazz did produce one of its best composers, best leaders, and one of its first theorists. More important, he first demonstrated the only way jazz has ever found to free its larger structures and groups from the tyranny and subjectivity of the moment.

3

LOUIS ARMSTRONG

Style Beyond Style

The history of jazz conventionally begins with music from the western Congo and evolves as a style in New Orleans around the turn of the twentieth century. The contrast between the percussive music of Africa and New Orleans jazz is startling, not so much in that these musics seem similar as that, in some very basic ways, they do not seem similar. To be sure, jazz is played on European melody instruments and has borrowed from European melody and harmony. But the gross dissimilarity is in rhythm. Congolese music is so sure and so complex rhythmically as to make early jazz seem child's play, and for some of the players, rather awkward child's play.

There is a point of view which holds that Louis Armstrong brought rhythmic and melodic order to jazz out of crudeness or chaos. It may seem so, and because of his remarkable freshness it may even have seemed so in the 'twenties. But actually an honorable and often aesthetically successful tradition had preceded him and prepared his way.

It is only in quite recent developments that jazz has begun to approach the rhythmic complexity of African music. The history of jazz represents a gradual coming together of ideas of melody and ideas of rhythm. The sizable task that every major innovation has performed—in cakewalk music, in ragtime, in New Orleans jazz, in swing, in be-bop—is basically rhythmic and shows itself in phrasing, in melodic rhythm, as well as in percussion. It is as if the music had to have a constantly renewed rhythmic vitality as it changed in melody and harmony. Each step finds jazz expanding its rhythmic and harmonic language while retaining its immediacy and its emotional concurrency with contemporary life.

A major step in this evolution was taken in New Orleans in the first two decades of this century. It was taken gradually and it happens that we have it documented on records in almost all its stages, from the rather clipped cornet phrasing of Freddie Keppard and Mutt Carey to the easier more legato melodies of Tommy Ladnier's trumpet and Sidney Becht's soprano sax. It culminated in the durable genius of Louis Armstrong.

There are difficulties inherent in discussing Armstrong. For one thing, he has been called a genius. Call a man a genius often enough, no matter how justly, and his work gets to be beyond comment. On the other hand, Louis Armstrong has been treated by some as a sort of embarrassment. He has functioned as a vaudevillian and, partly because he uses the stage manner that many black *and* white performers employed during the 'twenties and 'thirties, he has been dismissed as an Uncle Tom. Also, with the constant demands placed on him in almost nightly performances, he has learned, as many jazzmen of all schools inevitably have learned, to coast and shuck his way genially through many nights. One cannot be truly creative and truly concerted emotionally six nights a week on demand, and one finds substitutes. Finally, jazz has taken at least one major step since his first contribution was made, and is taking still another; to some jazz listeners Armstrong seems only a piece of history.

New Orleans contributed a durable ensemble style, of course, popularized as Dixieland. I think that it was also the New Orleans players who established improvisation as basic to jazz. Most popular or folk musics involve some kind of improvisation, but before New Orleans it had not been so important in any American style. Earlier players employed embellishment and casual spontaneous change in performance, but many of the New Orleans players really worked on improvisation and many of them thought of it as a cardinal part of their equipment. New Orleans musicians made a basically emotional contribution. Even before Armstrong's appearance, players from all over the country knew that New Orleans musicians had impressively preserved the depth and the immediacy of the folk idiom, both sacred and secular, in a comparatively sophisticated instrumental style.

It has been said that the New Orleans style evolved as the musical sophistication of the downtown colored Creole players came together with the earthier passion and rhythmic vitality of the uptown black performers: to put it briefly, European melody and harmony plus blues feeling. The various traditions which came together in New Orleans were more complex than that but the equation may stand for what happened. Once that music had been established at home, it was assimilated by others and began to spread. But in New Orleans it continued to develop. I think what Armstrong did was to reintroduce at a later stage an even larger measure of the blues emotionally, rhythmically, and melodically.

Certainly Armstrong's first elaboration of the elements of his style was even more than a brilliant sum of its parts, and it went quite beyond anything that had happened before him. He also opened up even greater possibilities both for himself and for all jazzmen for twenty years and longer.

Despite the importance of such near contemporaries as

Sidney Bechet, Armstrong's achievement was also more re-
sponsible than anything else for the fact that jazz irrevocably
became not so much a collective ensemble style as a soloist's
art. Armstrong's impact was startling and almost immediate.
Through the crudeness of the recording techniques and the
complexity of the collective improvising, his part in the
1923 King Oliver Creole Jazz Band recordings is clear
largely because of his phrasing. He has acknowledged Oliver
as his stylistic mentor, and the Oliver whose phrasing is
closest to Armstrong's is probably the most familiar: Oliver,
the poised and flowing soloist of *Dippermouth Blues*. Conversely, Armstrong is closest to Oliver on the Clarence Williams Blue Five recording *Everybody Loves My Baby* and
in accompaniment to Ma Rainey's *Courtin' the Blues*. However, some older players remembered the ideas Armstrong
uses in his *Chimes Blues* solo as having come from Bunk
Johnson, and they remembered Johnson as an inspiration
for Armstrong's generation of New Orleans trumpeters.
Johnson's first records were made in 1942, but if they reflect
Johnson's earlier style, then he was a more legato and rhythmically relaxed player than his predecessors, and his work
might well have been the basis for the later New Orleans
trumpet style.

During 1924 with the Fletcher Henderson orchestra in
New York, Armstrong made his message even more clear,
and his solos with that group still shine through beautifully
on the records.

On these earlier recordings by contrast some of Armstrong's fellow players seem to flounder rhythmically. His
ideas of rhythm and phrasing were not established among
other instrumentalists, even among many New Orleans instrumentalists. Some men used an earlier rhythmic tradition.
Some tried to emulate him and wobbled between two traditions. Some few did grasp his message, and I suspect the

grasp was easier for those who knew and felt the blues idiom and could play it well.

Armstrong's early work remains fascinating, but in the light of what he did later even early Armstrong seems a prelude. Perhaps to establish his idiom for himself as well as others, he used a great many note doublings and triplings and other embellishments which have a primarily rhythmic function. This often makes it appear as if his early playing has an excess of notes in comparison with his later solos. It is not that these notes do not fit melodically, but that the early solos do not have the sublime melodic ease of his later work. Many players who learned from his early work continued to use the predominantly rhythmic embellishments, notes whose primary function was to make accents. Muggsy Spanier was one who did, and there are comparable "rhythm notes" in the phrasing of men like Coleman Hawkins, Don Byas, even Roy Eldridge—indeed players in every style of jazz use ornamentation with a primarily rhythmic function.

An instructive Armstrong record is *Twelfth Street Rag* (1927, but unissued until 1940). As written, *Twelfth Street* is a fair rag-style piece, but its manner was already dated by the 'twenties and it is still used today as a vehicle for a deliberately corny quasi-jazz. Armstrong's performance, a brilliant revelation, opens up the jazz tradition. To recompose the tune so drastically, he slowed it down and removed its jerkiness. In effect, he rephrased it into a passionate blues, and there is hardly a note that is not directly consumed with melody. In its way, *Twelfth Street* is more interesting, or at least more indicative, than such justly celebrated Armstrong performances as the brilliant stop-time choruses of *Potato Head Blues*, the series of sublime descents on *Gully Low (S.O.L.) Blues*, the recomposition of Morton's *Wild Man Blues*, the sustained exuberance of *Hotter Than That,* or the lovely and sober form of *Big Butter and Egg Man*. With *Twelfth Street Rag*, we are prepared for the beautifully free phrasing on the 1928 recordings with Earl Hines, *West End Blues* and *Muggles*. We are prepared for the later passionate melodies that swing freely without rhythmic reminders and for the double-time episodes that unfold with poise. We are prepared for a fuller revelation of Armstrong's genius.

By the late 'twenties, Armstrong in effect had reinterpreted the jazz tradition although he used all the familiar forms, all the melodic and harmonic patterns. Some of the records with Hines (*Skip the Gutter, Knee Drops, Two Deuces*, and the like) reinterpret episodes from his own earlier recordings with the Hot Five and Hot Seven, and the brilliant duet, *Weather Bird*, even reaches back to the Oliver repertory. It soon became obvious that so compelling a player was to become a popular musical figure with a large audience.

In *Early Jazz* Gunther Schuller remarks of Armstrong's subsequent work that, "Records like *West End Blues, Weather Bird, Potato Head Blues*, and *Beau Koo Jack* showed Louis Armstrong at the full extent of his mature powers. It would have been beyond even his genius to develop past this point, even if the temptations of commercial success had not been as strong as they now were." I cannot agree. I think that not only some of his best improvising, but also some of his most far-reaching work, were still ahead of him.

It was not simply for reasons of popular expediency that Armstrong undertook new materials, popular songs, and more sentimental Tin Pan Alley ballads. What other material was there for him to try? And he had to in another sense. To a player of Armstrong's abilities such pieces, although they might not be as good in one's final judgment as Fats Waller's *Squeeze Me* or King Oliver's *West End Blues*, were written with greater sophistication and offered harmonic and structural challenges which did not exist in the jazz tradition as Armstrong found it. One result of course was that he created a new tradition: piece after piece that Armstrong undertook after 1928 has remained in the repertory.

I expect that if Louis Armstrong had one jot of taste concerning the kinds of materials he has used, if he had the kind of taste that would reject some of the trite, silly, and sentimental ditties he has played, and about the shallow, soggy, and affected musical accompaniments with which he has sometimes played them, then he would have been able to do nothing at all. For a moment's critical reflection, were he inclined to it, would have cut him off from all material and all performance. And his genius is such that he can apparently take any piece, add a note here, leave out a note there, condense or displace this melodic phrase a bit, rush this cadence, delay that one, alter another one slightly, and transform it into sublime melody, into pure gold. He can turn something merely pretty into something truly beautiful and something deeply delightful. Conscious taste has little to do with such transformations; they are products of an intuitive genius, and of the kind choice where reason cannot intrude.

There are times when Armstrong has totally, or almost totally, departed from melody into a free invention within an harmonic framework, as with the celebrated 1938 version of *I Can't Give You Anything But Love, I Double Dare You* from the same year, the 1932 *When It's Sleepy Time Down South, Swing You Cats* from 1933, and a few others.

However, Armstrong's most innovative work can be heard in a select group of recordings which begins with *West End Blues* and includes, chiefly, *Sweethearts on Parade* (1930), *Between the Devil and the Deep Blue Sea* (particularly the faster, third take, 1931), and his second version of *Basin Street Blues* (1933). It is a commonplace that great figures outline and suggest many more possibilities than they are able to develop in their own work. But for any development, or even acknowledgment, of the brilliant ideas of phrasing and melodic rhythm in these Armstrong recordings we must wait for Lester Young in the late 'thirties and, even more decisively, for Charlie Parker and the jazz of the mid-'forties.

Armstrong's contributions to *West End Blues* represent a beautiful balance of brilliant virtuosity and eloquent simplicity. His arresting opening cadenza leads him to his opening theme statement, which begins simply and then rebuilds to the complexity of rising triplet arpeggios of its final measures. It ends on a high *b* flat. A passionate *b* flat held for almost four measures marks the simple beginning of Armstrong's reentry for his final chorus on *West End Blues*. Then follow the bursting, descending virtuoso phrases that lead him to his conclusion.

In the beginning and conclusion of this performance in Armstrong's fresh and unexpected accents and rhythmic patterns, it seems to me we are very far from the simple, double-time effects of *I'm Not Rough* and *Muggles*, and have entered into a quite different kind of rhythmic thinking.

Armstrong begins his opening chorus on *Sweethearts on Parade* so obliquely off the melody that one gets the effect of an introduction and opening statement all in one. Indeed, he seems almost to be tossing random asymmetrical phrases in the air until a particular phrase comes along that somehow ties the previous phrases together. And when he does allow us to glimpse the melody, he quickly veers away from it again into inventions of his own, usually complex ones that dance around the beat and offer hints of what is to come. After the vocal, a repeated, blues-inspired paraphrase

of the song's opening idea leads to a deliberately earth-
bound, drum-like phrase,[1] thence to his flying interpolation
of the motive of the *High Society* obbligato (here is where
Charlie Parker must have gotten that favorite lick). From
this point to the end of the chorus, we are once again into a
kind of rhythmic thinking that was innovative even for
Armstrong.

Sweethearts on Parade, then, is built up in brief, intriguing but ultimately logical fragments. *Between the Devil
and the Deep Blue Sea* takes a different approach. Armstrong's first contribution to the performance in both versions is a vocal chorus, a free invention that barely glances
at the melody as written (did any other singer take up this
idea until Sarah Vaughan?). On the faster, third take of the
piece, Armstrong plays his first chorus (minus the bridge)
with a straight mute—a rare event for him. Again, his thinking is quite bold rhythmically, but melodically his phrases
link and flow together uniquely: his first covers only two
bars, but his second is an unbroken six bars, and his third
(granted a quick breath in the middle) consumes eight. The
only flaw in this singular performance comes after Armstrong
removes his straight mute during the song's final eight bars
and for the reprise of eight more that finishes the record. On
open horn he rather abruptly introduces an episode of Armstrong grandiloquence which, this time, he had not properly
prepared for.

The 1933 *Basin Street Blues* is an improvement over the
earlier, 1928 version, and a good arrangement of which the
leader takes superb advantage. The first trumpet chorus
ends on a hint of the virtuosity to come. The vocal chorus,
"scat" sung without words, is an invention and it is virtually
as bold rhythmically as the astonishing trumpet solo that

1. The *Nagasaki* lick, one might call it, later to become the *Salt Peanuts*
octive jump and drum lick in a be-bop jazz dialect.

follows, in which the episodes of simple grandiloquence are prepared for by the soaring grandiloquence of the more complex phrases.

At the same time, along with such bold, improvised invention and rhythmic innovations, the years 1931–33 saw some of Armstrong's most brilliant melodic paraphrases and transmutations.

The recordings Armstrong made for Victor during that period I think reflect such playing at its peak. There is that eloquently recomposed *I Gotta Right to Sing the Blues*, with Armstrong's melody suspended almost above the piece, certainly floating majestically over his accompaniment, yet in perfect time and perfect swing. One has to wait almost until the jazz of the 'sixties for such freedom of musical phrase. In an almost opposite approach, he juggles and rejuggles the phrases *I've Got the World on a String*.[2] There is also the justly praised *That's My Home* from 1932, where Armstrong's lovely paraphrasing and compelling passion transform a silly and mawkish ditty into stark experience. And there is the version of *St. James Infirmary* that makes beautiful melody more beautiful.

Thus, it was in the years 1928 through 1933 that Armstrong found the highest expression of his genius.

Certainly there are failures from the great years, and a number of them are all of a piece. Armstrong's greatest work came at slow and medium tempos; the fast things—the *Shine, Ding Dong Daddy,* and *Tiger Rag* showpieces—sound oddly unfinished and rather like amiably raucous build-ups for events that never take place. It seems to me that a major contribution of both Roy Eldridge and Dizzy Gillespie was

---

2. In view of the excellence this recording of *I Got a Right to Sing the Blues* and of *Between the Devil and the Deep Blue Sea*, it might be pointed out that the author of these pieces, Harold Arlen, was one of the first of our popular songwriters whose work shows the effect of Armstrong's ideas.

that they did something sustained and musical within such fast tempos, as Armstrong often did not.

I have said nothing so far about Armstrong's singing, and that is partly because I am of two minds about it. It is usually said that his vocal style is like his trumpet style. On his 1932 version of *When It's Sleepy Time Down South*, for example, the vocal and instrumental choruses are very similar in ideas and phrasing, particularly in the release. Yet the emotional import of Armstrong's voice seems to me different from that of his horn. Armstrong's trumpet has a melodic sweep and a sometimes staggering emotional comprehension and depth; his voice often seems to carry only a part of the power of the majesty of his horn. There is much of the stage manner, of the "genial Satchmo," in his voice, and his stage humor has sometimes seemed to me forced and embarrassingly unfunny. In contrast I find Fats Waller's spontaneous humor and presence still a delight on many of his recordings and in the few films he made. Armstrong's manner has a likeably engaging surface, to be sure, but I think it sometimes solicits our feelings in order to buttress a certain frank amateurishness. His horn instructs us; his comments and jokes might even invite our willing indulgence if he were not so honestly being himself and so likeable a man. But so likeable a man, if he is as complex as Louis Armstrong, must have an opposite side to his nature. Both sides and all of his complexity show in his horn.

Louis Armstrong functions as a musical entertainer, as a vaudevillian, but to see this only in its narrowest terms is to miss his essence. When we see a celebrated American vaudevillian like Al Jolson or Judy Garland, I think we see the appealing dramatization of an ego and the dramatic projection of a kind of emotional self-indulgence which off-stage and in reality might be repulsive. At any rate, the musical "act," the vaudevillian, the torch or cabaret singer,

is not necessarily musically interesting and is more often
emotionally narrow. By contrast Louis Armstrong is nearly
always musically interesting.

If we do not hear anything truly new from Armstrong
after 1933, we often hear an ability to sustain the eloquence
of his earlier discoveries from the 'thirties. I will cite *Jubilee,
The Skeleton in the Closet, Ev'n Tide,* and *Lyin' to Myself.*
There was inevitably a kind of solidification and simplification in much of his work. And I suppose it was this simplification which prepared the way for a greater popularity.
But actually the popularity which has made him a kind of
international figure did not begin for him until after 1947,
when he reverted to a small quasi-Dixieland format. It is
surely a confirmation of all theories about cultural lag that
Louis Armstrong gained his largest audience only after his
ideas had been imitated and popularized—sometimes gro-
tesquely so—by scores of trumpeters and arrangers, and
after his own playing had suffered from inevitable simplifications and the inevitable nights of emotional lassitude. At
the same time, when the popularity did come, Armstrong
rediscovered something of the sweep and the bravura which
had often been subdued during the mid-'thirties.

It is a commonplace that Armstrong's groups have always
been inferior to Armstrong. Inevitably so, but many of them
have been grossly inferior to him as well as to the other jazz
groups around him, even when their personnels might lead
one to expect much more than one got. When he used Earl
Hines in the late 'twenties, he also had Jimmy Strong, who
despite his technical abilities could give no emotional com-
petition to Armstrong's earlier clarinetist, Johnny Dodds.
But in the 'forties, in the group which reunited him with
Hines and which included Jack Teagarden and Sidney Cat-
lett, he had an exceptional jazz assemblage, individually if
not collectively. His art continued in the 'fifties; he recorded

new versions of *Struttin' With Some Barbecue, Basin Street Blues, Lazy River,* and *Georgia On My Mind* which are a credit to a major jazzman. And he redid *King of the Zulus* in a version as emotionally powerful as any of his recorded performances. Well into his sixties, Armstrong would play on some evenings in an astonishing way—astonishing not so much because of what he played as that he played it with such power, sureness, firmness, authority, such commanding presence as to be beyond category, almost (as they say of Beethoven's late quartets) to be beyond music. When he played this way, matters of style, other jazzmen, and most other musicians simply drop away as we hear his eloquence. The show biz personality act, the coasting, the forced jokes and sometimes forced geniality, the emotional tenor of much of Armstrong's music past and present (that of a marvelously exuberant but complex child)—all these drop away and we hear a surpassing artist create for us, each of us, a surpassing art.

4

BIX BEIDERBECKE

The White Man's Burden

One commentator has called cornetist Bix Beiderbecke the baby-faced darling of the 1920s. If he was that, it was only in retrospect, and the Shelleyan, Keatsian, Billy-the-Kid-like jazz myth about him is decidedly a product of the 'thirties. Notes to a reissue LP reveal that he was mentioned in the public prints only twice during his life[1] (there were no jazz journalists then) but he was a kind of demigod to musicians. Louis Armstrong has even said that he and Bix were working on the same thing, presumably on making jazz improvising primarily a soloist art.

I doubt if one should discuss Beiderbecke without offering at least some preliminary and general remarks about white jazzmen, at least the white jazzmen of the 'twenties and early 'thirties. Perhaps the best approach is by means of some remarks about players other than Beiderbecke. For example, a discussion of jazz drumming might be incomplete without a mention of Dave Tough's name. Jack Teagarden was an exceptional and dedicated jazzman. And Pee Wee Russell seems to me one of the most interesting clarinetists in jazz history.

For one thing, Russell was a dedicated improviser; in his

1. By Charles Edward Smith in *Symposium* and Abbe Niles in *Bookman*.

own modest and shy way he dared, explored, and took chances. He may sometimes have failed, but he seldom played without a real effort at musical adventure and a genuine belief in improvisation. Perhaps too much so, for one even gets the feeling that he had to summon up the proper way to handle his horn each time he used it. His style was a thoroughly personal expression; if he had a major inspiration, it was Bix Beiderbecke.

I think that Beiderbecke's work has affected the whole of jazz. Such a thing has been said of Jimmy Dorsey, but Dorsey, whatever one's final evaluation of him as a jazzman, was a challenge, I expect, only because he was such a good saxophonist. Older recordings by, say, Rex Stewart, Benny Carter, "Hot Lips" Page, Jimmy Noone, and more recent recordings by Johnny Hodges and Roy Eldridge have made direct interpolations from Beiderbecke or obvious use of his ideas. In a sense the same might be said of phrases from Greig or from a dozen second-rate "light classics." Eldridge has said that his youthful models included Red Nichols and Beiderbecke, and I am sure that the experience directly affected the way he later used the trumpet, although his style became much transformed. However, a comparable tribute might be paid to cornetist B. A. Rolfe whose playing inspired Louis Armstrong to use the full range of his instrument. On such a basis one could argue that everyone from John Phillip Sousa to David Raksin has affected jazz, but I am arguing for an important contribution within the idiom that eventually affected not just a few obvious followers but nearly all jazz players.

One problem in any discussion of jazz and race involves a holdover liberal cliché from the 'thirties. Having heard so many racial generalizations that are destructive, demeaning, or absurd, we have become afraid of any kind of generalization. It might help clarify matters to return to the well-worn

phrase, to the dictum that I have mentioned above, that
"Negroes have natural rhythm," which has become hor-
rendous. But what if blacks did have "natural rhythm"?
Would it be a sign of inferiority to have "natural rhythm"?
Is it insulting to say that they have dark skin? Why is it
really enlightened or unprejudiced to assume that Negroes
could *not* have something called "natural rhythm"?

Does it imply an inability to treat Orientals as individuals
to say that they have black hair or brown eyes? We may
know the subtle touchiness of the subject but, after all, is it
not the truth, rather than a counterstatement, that shall
make us free?

Our liberal clichés long ago put us in the position of
assuming that differences imply an innate moral or intellec-
tual superiority on the one hand and inferiority on the
other. We cannot allow for differences or allow them to be
differences. And we assume thereby, surely without realizing
it, that all men are equal only if they are the same. (Or is
it that all men are equal only if they are willing to accept
American middle-class standards?)

I realize that I have discussed these questions before in the
first chapter of this book, but perhaps they bear repetition
and perhaps there are some things to add.

It would be perfectly easy to show that not all blacks have
"natural" rhythm nor very good acquired rhythm necessarily. And one can think of black jazz musicians who have
had rhythmic problems and have overcome them, and of
some who have had them and have them still. There are
Negro players who swing but keep poor time and there are
some who keep time well but don't swing. There are Negroes
who can't really improvise, and for whom jazz is merely a
style with a set of devices that is not too difficult to acquire.
Still, it seems to me perfectly valid to say (whether the basis
is racial, ethnic, environmental, or whatever) that black

jazzmen in general have had fewer rhythmic problems than white jazzmen.

On the other hand, one apparently cannot hold that white jazzmen, even the most derivative white jazzmen generally do not sound like Negroes without somehow being insulting to someone (but insulting to whom?). Of course, one response to this proposition is that "those white men are not playing real jazz." If one chooses to call what white musician A is playing "not jazz" one invites a fruitless, semantic argument on the meaning of the word *jazz*. By an objective or technical definition, musician A plays jazz. By aesthetic judgment he may play good jazz and good music.

My proposition is that the white players of the 'twenties and early 'thirties brought a particular lyric sensibility to jazz and this sensibility has had an effect on its subsequent development. Bix Beiderbecke was the most gifted and important of those players, important not only because his work was the most influential, but also because he was intrinsically an exceptional, original soloist. Certainly Beiderbecke's effect was not as grandiose, not as pervasive, and nothing like as important as Louis Armstrong's. But it is there. And jazz would not be the same if it had not been there.

Bix Beiderbecke is the first white jazzman whose work one can take seriously, and that is at least partly because he took jazz seriously. The original Dixieland Jazz Band of 1917 seems to me to have caught little more than the surface irreverence of the music. The New Orleans Rhythm Kings caught more, but they were sincerely and admittedly trying to sound like the Negro players. Beiderbecke heard something more than the spirited irreverence. In his best work he is not merely imitating the Negro idiom but, inspired by it, he is working out his own idiom. Beiderbecke took jazz seriously enough to be personal, and he was gifted enough to be more than simply personal. Certainly he did not sound like a Negro; it is to his everlasting credit that he did not and that he did not try to. It was his tribute to the music that he perceived that to do so would be to go against its deeper purport and meaning.

Bix Beiderbecke knew records by Nick La Rocca and the Original Dixieland Jazz Band (ODJB), and those were almost the only jazz records that were made between 1917 and 1923.

It is remarkable how many white players worked out comparable styles, apparently independently, by knowing La Rocca and following through on what they heard. Next to Bix, Red Nichols is the best known. Whatever one may think of the music and intentions of the ODJB, they gave Beiderbecke an important impetus. (There is talk of the influence of a cornetist named Emmet Hardy, but he is only a name to us now.) Bix later heard others, of course, and was affected by them. A recently rediscovered solo of his in *I Didn't Know* might almost be the young Louis Armstrong, and several years earlier he had flashed through *Big Boy* in much the way Armstrong burst through the records by Erskine Tate's Chicago pit band.

In some ways Beiderbecke's earliest records outline his career. They were made with a midwestern group called the Wolverines. Their intentions were serious, but the Wolverines didn't make much more creditable jazz than the less dedicated big dance bands, or the almost equally dedicated small groups, that Bix later recorded with.

The Beiderbecke we hear with the Wolverines is both ahead of his times and behind them. His commitment and integrity show on *Tiger Rag*. It was a pretty corny showpiece as the ODJB played it, and it has led many a player to banality since. Beiderbecke avoids the corn and the banality, and he does not attempt to have it both ways with the

kind of bravura that Armstrong later developed. He simply
works on fairly legato, improvised melodies within the frame
of the piece.

Beiderbecke had rhythmic problems. He was basically
working with La Rocca's rhythmic ideas and smoothing
them out, if you will, but a lot had happened in jazz rhythm
meanwhile. We can take it that La Rocca was playing a
rather stiff version of the early rhythmic ideas of New Orleans jazz, the clipped accents we hear on Freddie Keppard's
few records and that Mutt Carey retained throughout his
life.

I do not believe that it is entirely useful to declare that
Louis Armstrong first arrived at that magic, illusive, but
empirical rhythmic phenomenon that came to be called
"swing." I believe that in an earlier rhythmic style Keppard
and Carey both "swing." [2] However, in his brief *Royal Garden Blues* solo with the Wolverines Beiderbecke is playing
a kind of parade horn that does not even seem intended to
swing, whatever the rhythmic style.

Beiderbecke could swing within the outlines of his style.
And he could also fall between two stools when he reached
for something like Armstrong's delayed, behind-the-beat, or
even his anticipatory phrasing. The dilemma sometimes

2. The term "swing," although it remains undefined and continues to be
carelessly used, is a part of the technical vocabulary of jazz music. It came
into general use with Louis Armstrong, indeed may even have been introduced by him, and was at first a musicians' term to describe Armstrong's
early rhythmic contribution to the music. Subsequently, the word was used
as the name of the style, largely built on his contribution and that of the
early "big band" arrangers, the kind of jazz that was popular during the
'thirties. But the term has been retained in the jazz vocabulary and applied
to subsequent styles and players. Similarly, it has been applied to earlier,
pre-Armstrong styles, and fruitfully so, I think. That is to say, it is possible
to play pre-Armstrong jazz, and even ragtime, with or without the appropriate rhythmic character and momentum, i.e. "swing," and swing is
empirically present or not present in a performance.

made his time seem shaky, but the same sort of thing was happening to many jazz players during the late 'twenties— on occasion even to so authoritative a man as King Oliver. However, in his best solos, Beiderbecke handles his ideas of rhythm with ease and they answer to his basic conception, answer to his ideas of melody and his exceptional harmonic ear.

Some of Bix's Wolverine solos—*Sensation, Riverboat Shuffle*—may almost seem patchworks of the jazzy mannerisms and clichés of the 'twenties. His problem, we realize, was to make something out of the musical materials available to him and he did not really have a background of folk sources on which to draw. But even in the *do-wacka-do* and *voe-dee-o-doe* figures one can hear a rare sense of melodic order trying to assert itself, and an emotional dedication to improvisation. Comparing this *Riverboat* to the one he made three years later, we hear an enormous improvement: he has discovered lyric melodies of his own. His ear and sense of melody are central. He was self-taught but could make even a fairly mechanical follow-through on the cornet valves an expressive part of a solo. Even with the Wolverines, his unique approach to improvising can already be heard in his memorably fluent and original solo and last chorus lead in *Jazz Me Blues*.

There soon began the association with C-melody and alto saxophonist Frankie Trumbauer which was to carry both of them through the big dance orchestras of Jean Goldkette and Paul Whiteman, and into recording studios with groups under their own names. Beiderbecke's small groups attempted jazz even if the men weren't up to it; Trumbauer's groups sometimes attempted it but at other times sounded like little brothers to the Whiteman band.

Trumbauer too was an influential man. Johnny Hodges has indicated that almost the only guides he had as a young saxophonist were Sidney Bechet and Trumbauer. Trum-

bauer worked in many of the same musical areas as Bix (and
I expect he got most of his ideas directly from him) but,
although there is a kind of melodic purity in him at his best,
he never had any swing, and his playing projects far less
emotional expressiveness and conviction that Beiderbecke's.
Trumbauer's solo in *Way Down Yonder in New Orleans*,
for example, has good ideas, an interesting and provocative
handling of saxophone sound and phrasing, and steady time
(more dependably steady than Bix's?), but no swing. It is
almost a merely historical phenomenon. (One might also
note the shocking deterioration in Trumbauer's playing
after Beiderbecke's death.)

Beiderbecke on the same piece does not show the same
effort at invention but leans more heavily on a paraphrase
of the melody. And the paraphrase is not Bix at his best,
being less interesting than, say, the way he handled the
bridge of *Sweet Sue* with Whiteman. Still there is an urgent
emotional cohesion and melodic logic in Bix's *Way Down
Yonder* solo that makes Trumbauer's seem almost an
abstraction.

I don't think you could say that paraphrase or melodic
embellishment[3] was the rule for these men. More often they
seemed to be reaching for original variations made on chord

3. The distinction which Gunther Schuller makes in *Early Jazz* between
embellishment and improvisation does not seem entirely satisfactory to me
as applied to jazz, however well it fits eighteenth-century European practice. One may not wish to celebrate the improvisational aspects of certain
simple and obvious embellishments in jazz. However, by the early 'thirties
jazz had produced so dazzling an embellishment and ornamental style as
that of Art Tatum, and one would surely want to celebrate the improvisational prowess with which Tatum used such resources. It *is* useful, it seems
to me, to make a distinction between an improvisation that is thematic and
one that is nonthematic, i.e., an "invention" or "harmonic variation."
Furthermore, André Hodeir's borrowing of the grammarian's term "para-
phase" seems to me most useful in describing the particular kind of
thematic variation at which Louis Armstrong was so superb, one that moves
away from embellishment and is part thematic transformation and part
invention.

structures. Frequently they succeeded, and this was before such inventions were really the rule in anything but blues playing or in a blues approach adapted to a few, simple chord progressions in music other than blues. *For No Reason at All in C*, improvised in the chords of *I'll Climb the Highest Mountain*, is an obvious example. There are also Bix and Tram's solos on the justly celebrated *Singin' the Blues*, and several of the solos with Goldkette and Whiteman, like Bix's fine episode in *Lonely Melody*. There are also things like Bix's *Dardanella* solo which use the opening melody phrase almost as a recurring motif around which to build an original line.

Despite the inferior surroundings, the integrity and beauty of Beiderbecke's best work survives. In its own time, Bix's work came at the right moment. When jazz was irrevocably becoming a soloist's art, he made crucial steps away from simple embellishments and arpeggios toward melodic invention. He gave jazz harmonic and linear enrichments and showed how lyric it might become. He also affirmed from his own perspective, something that many jazz melodies affirm: that melodic completeness need not obey traditional ideas of form, that a melody can be a continuous linear invention, without the rather mechanical melodic repeats of popular songs, and still be a satisfying aesthetic entity. Bix's personal melodic intervals, his warm tone, his handling of sound, his plaintive bent notes, and his easy phrasing are a part of his contribution too. But they are all only manifestations of the real import of his playing, which was emotional. It suggested that there was a largely neglected kind of lyric feeling which might also find expression in jazz.

Many jazzmen got these things directly from Beiderbecke. Many more got them when his message was caught, absorbed, and elaborated so brilliantly by Lester Young, and through him they have affected almost the whole of jazz since

the mid-'thirties. Young himself gave most of the credit to
Trumbauer, which would mean it was a saxophonist's debt
and at second hand, but I doubt if a man who carried *Singin'
the Blues* around in his tenor case was unaffected by Bix's
part in it.

There is more than coincidence in the echo of Beiderbecke that people hear in Miles Davis, for Davis owes a debt
to Lester Young. Perhaps there is the same kind of link in
the pairing of Davis with Lee Konitz; Young was a major
influence on Konitz too. And for me *For No Reason at All
in C* seems at least the indirect ancestor of the best of the
Lennie Tristano–Lee Konitz–Warne Marsh recordings.

If Beiderbecke's short life was a tragedy, it was the tragedy
of an artist for whom there was little or no tradition that
was meaningful, and few guides available. It has been said
that he was misguided about jazz, looked in the wrong places
for his inspiration, was too preoccupied with impressionistic
concert music, etc. I expect he looked wherever he could for
whatever would help him. Growing up an American of
German descent in Davenport, Iowa, he heard all the jazz
he could hear. Ragtime was widespread but it had already
been sifted of its meaning for jazz by the early 'twenties.
Like many young men of his generation he virtually stood
in awe of Bessie Smith and King Oliver, yet I doubt if the
blues could have been essential to him as a guide for his
own sensibilities. He could not rely on that rich interpolation of folk and blues phrases and devices that so many
players were employing in improvising—even white players
by this time—not because he did not know, did not love,
or could not absorb these things, but because for him they
did not really carry the unique story he had to tell and the
lyric contribution he was to make. Beyond a point, the jazz
tradition that existed then, remarkable as it was, could not
help him. He had to work much of it out for himself.

5

COLEMAN HAWKINS

Some Comments on a Phoenix

Periodically jazz musicians and listeners rediscover tenor saxophonist Coleman Hawkins. Even during the time of major changes in the mid-'forties, the avid be-bop partisan accepted Hawkins as a part of the jazz scene, as he accepted no others of Hawkins's contemporaries of the 'twenties and few of his companions of the 'thirties. One might call Hawkins a thorough professional, but he was also a major performer and he belonged to a generation in which these two things might go together as a matter of course.

Periodically Hawkins also seemed to rediscover himself. He listened to everyone, but however much his own playing reflected what he heard around him, Hawkins remained Hawkins.

Probably everyone who knows Hawkins's work has a favorite, relatively late recording on which he feels the saxophonist played particularly well. My own is the Shelly Manne–Hawkins LP called "2 3 4." Not only did Hawkins remain an exceptional player for decades he also recorded prolifically. An exhaustive survey of his records would be a lengthy and perhaps pointless task. But it might be useful to suggest the nature of his early style, indicate the course of his development, and point out what seems to me some of his more durable performances.

Coleman Hawkins's contribution has been so comprehensive that it is impossible for any tenor saxophonist to avoid some reflection of his influence unless that player were to do a fairly direct imitation of Lester Young or perhaps Bud Freeman. Yet, when one listens to Hawkins on his very earliest records, one hears no promise of his stature as a player. One hears a young man performing with calculated and rather superficial raucousness, a slap-tongue tenor player with little more than shallow irreverence to recommend him.

However, one can note that this clowning soloist obviously knows his instrument, knows his chords, and has a sure sense of time and tempo. Thus the Coleman Hawkins heard on his 1923–24 solos with the Fletcher Henderson orchestra. However, the Coleman Hawkins heard on Henderson's *T.N.T.*, recorded in October 1925, is a very different player. The basis of the difference is quite apparent: rhythmically and melodically, Hawkins's brief solo is early Armstrong. *The Stampede*, made a few months after Armstrong's departure from the orchestra, is even more revealing. Cornetists Rex Stewart and Joe Smith burst forth with brass hyperboles, reaching for Armstrong's excitement. Coleman Hawkins follows Armstrong's lead too, but he treats his style not as a series of effects but rather as a series of definite musical ideas in a cohesive structure.

A year or so later, on *Goose Pimples*, the young Hawkins has become more himself, cutting through with the hard staccato phrases that characterize his playing of this period. However, on the 1928 version of *King Porter Stomp* we hear Hawkins still echoing the young Armstrong fairly directly.

The disappointing Hawkins of this period is the Hawkins of the twelve-bar blues. He is not a blues man, and he seems to have known it. But unlike some of the early stride pianists, he was not content merely to play the blues form without the feeling. And unlike, say, Earl Hines or Benny

Carter, he was not prone to work out a personal and introspective style within the idiom. Hawkins set out to learn to
play the blues with blues feeling. He did learn and he has
played some very good blues, but to the end of his life he
sounded as if the slow blues were, for him, something
acquired.

Blazin', from early 1929, seems to me one of the best early
revelations of a developing Coleman Hawkins style, and in
it we hear the increasing reliance on the vertical, on
Hawkins's exact and growing knowledge of chords, and on
spreads of arpeggios. From a sound, youthful grounding in
music, especially in piano instruction, Hawkins knew the
notes in chords and learned to form passing chords between
assigned ones. He also had the clear example of jazz reed
players like Jimmy Noone and Buster Bailey who played
arpeggio styles. But it is interesting to learn that an encounter with the harmonic and embellishmental sophistication of pianist Art Tatum was a turning point in Hawkins's
development.

His solos on the Mound City Blue Blowers' *Hello Lola*
from 1929, and Henderson's *Chinatown* from the following
year, show some of the dangers of his new approach. It is
as if in making all the chords, Hawkins also became determined to make all the beats, and he made them in a more
or less regular, heavy/light/heavy/light pattern. At faster
tempos, once he was past his entrance, Hawkins's phrasing
settled into a rhythmic regularity, and an almost brilliant
articulation of proper notes sometimes trails off into a kind
of rhythmic mutter. The risks involved became increasingly
obvious in later performances: his knowledge of harmony,
his regularity of rhythm, and his hardness of tone could
lead him to mechanically formed solos delivered with a
forced emotion.

On *New King Porter Stomp, Underneath the Harlem*

Moon, Honeysuckle Rose, and other pieces from 1932, Hawkins found a temporary rhythm solution. He would assume a momentary rhapsodic stance: triplets and more complex phrases flutter and curve away from the beat, apparently without intending to swing. Although the ideas in these solos are fine, the rhapsodic phrases are delivered with an earnestness that is almost affected and sentimental—a showy use of techniques approaching the manner of the quasi-romantic "hotel tenor" player. He was using the same approach as late as 1937 on the justly celebrated recordings of *Honeysuckle Rose* and *Crazy Rhythm* done with Benny Carter in Paris.

Hawkins's early celebrated ballads, *One Hour* with the Blue Blowers (1929) and *Talk of the Town* with Henderson (1933), are both exceptional and both indicative of the mood that would yield his later masterpieces. But both are imperfect in revealing ways. *Talk of the Town* is a good improvisation weakened by lush effusiveness. *One Hour* is a better solo, a combination of lyric ideas and traditional jazz phrases; it makes all the chord changes properly and it is showy without being untidy. But Hawkins's tone is still especially hard and brittle, as if his only protection against sentimentality were to take on the mask of toughness.

A blues man might not have had problems with excess of tone and emotion because he might not have had sentimental temptations. Not that the Hawkins of this period had no emotional protections. On *Wherever There's a Will, Baby,* with McKinney's Cotton Pickers, he combines a fine sense of musical fun and hokum with firm musical ideas.

One should also mention *Queer Notions* that Hawkins made with Henderson, on which the increasingly sophisticated Hawkins provided himself with just the sort of challenging medium-tempo vehicle he wanted. As one would expect, the challenge is largely harmonic. But I think that

Hawkins's two choruses on *Hocus Pocus* from 1934 are probably the best of all his solos with Henderson. They are perhaps not typical, being more directly melodic and less arpeggiated, but they combine the robustness of his early work with a sophisticated melodic sense and a touching, almost nostalgic lyricism. The choruses seem also to have been highly influential: they outline the essentials of the style used by Herschel Evans and his associates and successors, Buddy Tate, Illinois Jacquet, and (most recently) Yusef Lateef. Of course it is possible that Hawkins, as a constant listener, may have picked up such phrases as these touring the Southwest with Henderson, but it is also possible that this so-called Southwest tenor style was first expounded by Coleman Hawkins in a New York recording studio.

When Coleman Hawkins returned from Europe in 1939, he entered his great period as a jazz soloist. He had continued to expand his basic harmonic techniques. He had come to terms with his own lush and sentimental temptations, which means that he had learned to sustain a true lyric mood and therefore no longer needed the sometimes forced and usually brittle edge to his tone that he had apparently found necessary before. The sharpness of vibrato heard on *One Hour* cannot be heard on *Body and Soul*.

Rhythmically, however, there sometimes seems to have been no solution, and Hawkins's double chorus on *The Sheik of Araby*, recorded in January 1940, fails almost as it succeeds. It is a *tour de force* of the sort which dazzled and delighted his fellow musicians, yet Hawkins's swift, knowing harmonic disentanglements are nearly lost in a predictably regular accentuation. In such moods Hawkins is in effect attempting to be not only his own soloist, but his own harmonist and his own rhythm section as well. However, he does build these choruses gradually, both emotionally and technically, without resorting to bathos or musical banality. Other solos from the same period show Hawkins's final and best rhythmic solution. His chorus on *Dinah*, recorded with Lionel Hampton a month earlier, is another harmonic delight. Rhythmically it frankly sets up the expectation of more or less regular heavy/light/heavy/light accents and varies them just briefly enough, often enough, and obviously enough to relieve any encroaching monotony.

Body and Soul (1939) is the accepted Hawkins's masterpiece. The record reveals not only Hawkins's knowing use of increasingly sophisticated techniques but his brilliant use of pacing, structure, and rhythmic relief. He saves his showiest arpeggios, opening melodiously and introducing implied double-time along the way. His second recorded improvisation on the *Body and Soul* chords, originally called *Rainbow Mist* (1944), is not quite the equal of the original but his absolute sureness and ease at what he is about, and his ability to let the performance build, are the work of a great musician.

They are also the work of a great improviser. I have heard Hawkins's work deprecated as "just arpeggios," and the complaint has been lodged that in his solos he leans heavily for a sense of order on the fact that the modifying chords in popular songs repeat in relatively short cycles. But arpeggios and cyclical patterns of harmony are Hawkins's means, much as they were J. S. Bach's in certain moods, never his end. Anyone who has heard him replay a standard Hawkins piece, or heard him play the same piece successively, will understand the committed creativity with which Hawkins approaches his means.

I would say that the great period that began in 1939 for Hawkins continued through 1944. That latter year was a prolific one in records for an always prolific player, and it found Hawkins present on several very good sessions and two excellent ones. One of the finer sessions was with players who had also been outstanding in the mid-'thirties, Teddy Wilson and Roy Eldridge, and produced *I'm in the Mood for Love*. The other excellent session produced *Sweet Lorraine, Crazy Rhythm*, and the superb *The Man I Love* by Hawkins and a rhythm section.

Sweet Lorraine, the one slow ballad recorded on the date, shows Hawkins forming his chord-spreads into meaningful melodic phrases. Rhythmically he glides easily from one heavy beat to the next, variously curving around the light ones. His tone is firm but not harsh. Hawkins's decision to play *The Man I Love* at medium tempo, but with the soloists taking it in "long" meter, set up a dramatic basis for exploring Gershwin's chord changes. Hawkins plays with uncompromising involvement and a plentitude of ideas. A variety of traditional-sounding riffs and blues phrases interplay in surprising cohesiveness with showy arpeggios. Brief phrases which break up Hawkins's regular accents are placed with great effectiveness, and the performance is perhaps Hawkins's masterpiece of relieving rhythmic contrast.

The fact that the years 1939–44 found Hawkins at a peak had a more than personal importance, for in these years most young saxophonists were under Lester Young's influence, and Young often overrode harmony in the interests of melody and his original rhythmic ideas. After 1944 Hawkins fell in easily with the young modernists because his knowledge of chords, both theoretical and pragmatic, allowed him to. Rhythmically, he continued to live in the early 'thirties— but, again, with more regular accents than many players of that period. Hawkins also did not seem out of place, I expect, because younger players like Dexter Gordon had arrived at a synthesis of Hawkins and Young.

Hawkins did begin to sound dated harmonically by the mid-'fifties. On a Thelonious Monk date, made in 1957, he was momentarily intimidated by some of the thick complexity Monk gives to his chords. However, Hawkins's quick solution, to go ahead and play what he knows, is the solution of a mature man, and his solos show it. Hawkins continued to listen: later he used simple scalar embellishments in his solos that echoed the more complex ones of John Coltrane.

Among Hawkins's more direct pupils, one thinks most particularly of two men. The most brilliant is Don Byas, but Byas was never as successful as Hawkins in varying his phrasing; even the staggeringly sophisticated techniques of finger and harmony on Byas's *I Got Rhythm* or *Indiana* are phrased and accented with freight-train regularity. Perhaps the greatest pupil of all is Ben Webster, who is almost Byas's opposite. Long an exceptional soloist, Webster became a great one, I think, after he accepted the limitations of his fingers and embouchure and became a simple and eloquent melodist.

One might call Webster a player of great natural musical instincts, and Hawkins a player of great natural musical curiosity making use of the techniques that his innate curiosity led him to acquire and assimilate. Thus Hawkins survived more than four decades, a player whose commitment to improvisation was essential.

6

BILLIE HOLIDAY

Actress Without an Act

"All I ask of popular songs," a journalist once wrote, "is that they be beautiful"—which is to ask everything or nothing. Pretty they may sometimes be, but beautiful they usually are not. And if they were beautiful, an artist like Billie Holiday might have nothing to do. Her repertory abounded in trivial melody, in ugly melody, in merely pretty melody. To be sure, a part of the meaning of jazz comes from its spontaneity—improvisation and variation have meanings of their own. But in another sense there would be no point in Miss Holiday's changing a melody if it were already beautiful. Her particular musical talent was that she could find emotional and melodic beauty in banality.

Her style evolved in the early 'thirties, when she began singing professionally, and although she picked up a couple of mannerisms from later players, she stayed with it all her life. She was respected by jazzmen of all eras. That respect had to do, in part, with her stage manner: she came out, sang, bowed, and left—no vaudeville showmanship. It had to do also with the special emotion of her performances, and with her superb musicianship.

Some of the qualities of her musicianship are dramatized

on an LP done at one of her late public appearances, a 1956 Carnegie Hall concert. She was in good spirits and good voice that evening, and she varied her program in tempo and mood from song to song. She sang *Yesterdays*; in her first version of the piece she had transformed its calculated nostalgia into real pathos, and here again she moved into an up-tempo section without interrupting her continuity or mood. She took *I Cried for You* very fast and with such poised rhythmic sureness that she seemed to be teasing her accompanists about the speed—or paying no attention to them at all—and she did not falter. More musicians gathered on stage for *What a Little Moonlight Can Do*. They were more enthusiastic than discreet or appropriate in accompanying her, but they did not faze Miss Holiday. She sang *Fine and Mellow* (one of the very few true blues in her repertory, by the way) patiently and beautifully, and it is a piece she must have done many hundreds of times. Swing, rhythmic poise, and emotional presence were crucial parts of her equipment, but she was a jazz singer and her real greatness rested on her ability to extemporize. Basically hers was a musicianship not of voice but of rhythm and melody. On occasion she sang a song straight, without much variation; then she might be an interesting and even moving singer, but she was not a great one.

Billie Holiday began recording regularly, first with Teddy Wilsons's studio groups in 1935, then on her own the following year. If we know how these early records were made, we respect them even more. They were primarily intended for an urban Negro audience, and during those depression years they sold largely to jukebox operators. Like Henry "Red" Allen and Fats Waller before them, Teddy Wilson and Billie Holiday were asked to come to the studio with a group of the best musicians available (they would most often be drawn from the Fletcher Henderson, Count Basie,

Duke Ellington, and Benny Goodman bands). There were
no preparations or rehearsals. The performers would be
given "lead sheets" to the latest popular songs, many of
which they had not seen or heard before, with indications
of melody, simple harmony, and words. They did some
"standard" songs too, but the new material seems to have
been selected with little care or taste, and it sometimes
reached ludicrous proportions. The jazzmen proceeded to
transmute the material into their own idiom—they worked
up fairly innocent arrangements and they improvised solo
variations. Certainly not all of what they did was good—
inspiration falters and some songs can't be helped much—
but they apparently felt much at ease in handling material
they had never laid eyes on before. When they succeeded,
they succeeded brilliantly—Miss Holiday perhaps most of
all.

The quality and timbre of Billie Holiday's voice was entirely her own, and it can be rather a shock when one hears
it for the first time. It is not like that of any blues singer one
knows of or any earlier jazz singer. But the more one hears
it the more one realizes how perfect it was to the import of
her singing. Her very earliest records, 1933 ditties with the
titles *Your Mother's Son-in-Law* and *Riffin' the Scotch*, are
obviously the work of a younger Billie Holiday, but she
was still using some of the mannerisms of the "hot" singer
of the late 'twenties (of Ethel Waters, perhaps). By the
1936 *A Fine Romance*, it was entirely clear where her
allegiance lay. As she said herself, she liked Bessie Smith's
feeling and Louis Armstrong's style. And her taste led her to
the greatest Louis Armstrong, the Armstrong of 1928–33.
On *A Fine Romance*, she glides above her accompaniment
with perfect poise and perfect rhythm, and without the
rhythmic filigrees that even the younger Armstrong had
found necessary to his development. This allegiance is con-

firmed by one performance after another, and particularly on pieces that Armstrong himself had done: *I Can't Give You Anything But Love, Georgia on My Mind, Pennies from Heaven.* One comparison is most revealing: her 1939 *I Got a Right to Sing the Blues* directly echoes Armstrong's version. But it is not Armstrong's voice alone that she respected. She also followed his trumpet; she went beyond Armstrong the singer and grasped some of the technical and emotional possibilities of his horn. Certainly her voice did not have the commanding sound of Armstrong's horn or its grandiose import of feeling, but it is perhaps in just that subtle difference of the sound and the emotions it implies that we might find the essence of her art. In her own way, Billie Holiday probably developed the musical language of Louis Armstrong as much as any other performer and carried jazz more directly along the path he implied.

Billie Holiday did absorb Armstrong's phrasing in its best aspects early in her career. More important, she had a comparable talent for altering a few notes, a few accents, a few rhythmic contours to make a popular ditty into real music as in *Time on My Hands* (1940), *All of Me* (1941), *I Cover the Waterfront* (1941), and many another. And, perhaps most important, she took the crucial step of barely echoing or virtually abandoning a melody if it did not suit her and improvising a new one, as in the main strains of *The Man I Love* (1939), *Body and Soul* (1940), *Love Me or Leave Me* (1941). It might be argued that when Billie Holiday raises the opening notes to a song like *Moanin' Low* she is merely making the song more comfortably suited to her own, admittedly small, range. Or it might be said that her alterations in Gershwin's *Let's Call the Whole thing Off* actually avoid a rather tricky chord change. But the effects of these changes are musically and melodically fascinating. One's final judgment is that her point of departure (the song at hand), her natural voice and emotional equipment, her innate melodic taste and perception, have come together to produce a work of *individual* art of a kind which only jazz—in its dependence on both the individual's virtues and shortcomings—can countenance. And further, if we decide that it was her natural sense of drama that enabled her to find substance in such ephemera as *Painting the Town Red* or *You Let Me Down*, we should also acknowledge that she never changed a song merely for a passing dramatic effect, and that, for her, dramatic effect and musical effect are the same thing. (Certainly there are precedents: when Bessie Smith approached a pop song she did so as an authoritative blues singer. For *I Ain't Got Nobody* or *After You've Gone* this meant that she bent its melody into a different shape.)

It must have been a revelation to Billie Holiday to work with members of the Count Basie rhythm section, for they actually played the kind of even, swinging, light accompaniment that Armstrong's lines had implied—the Basie rhythm section not only played them but played them so well that they could begin to take liberties with them. But I cannot agree that the meeting of Lester Young and Billie Holiday was the meeting of like styles. It may have been the meeting of similar approaches to musical sound or of compatible personalities. (But would Lester have been capable of her implied sarcasm and bitterness?) In style, however, it is the meeting of a brilliant and personal extension of Armstrong and a sublime departure from him. In Buck Clayton, she found the stylistic kinship of another jazzman who was indebted to Armstrong's ideas. In Lester Young she found rapport but emotional and stylistic contrast, and two eras of jazz met in a sometimes transporting musical discourse.

The younger Billie Holiday could not bring off everything, to be sure. The near monotone of *The Very Thought of You* (1938) does not inspire her, nor does she overcome

the "pretty" steps in *The Mood That I'm In* (1937) . In her
1936 version of *These Foolish Things,* the written melody
of the piece intimidated her a bit, and she relied heavily on
simple blues devices in an effort to avoid it—almost the way
Bessie Smith might have done. But as André Hodeir has
pointed out, in her 1952 version of the song she became its
master, retaining only its best phrases, providing new melodies for its inferior ones, giving the piece a superior recomposition. Other indications of her growing abilities came
when two versions of a piece done at the same recording
session happen to have been issued. The take of *I'll Never
Be the Same* in *"Billie Holiday: The Golden Years, Vol. I,"*
for example, was much better than a previously issued one,
and was probably done after the performers had the material
down a bit better.

On her January 1938 date, with Teddy Wilson and some
of the Basie sidemen, she is not intimidated by a familiar
piece like *Back in Your Own Backyard,* and she changes it
boldly. But as is remarkably often the case, the bridge comes
off close to the original. Yet on *On the Sentimental Side*
and *When a Woman Loves a Man,* she is suddenly subdued
and almost complacent, which might give pause to those
who believe that her only successful subject was unrequited
love. Similarly, she does *If Dreams Come True* as if she
half-believed its absurdly rosy lyric. Perhaps the great paradoxical summary of this period is *Trav'lin' All Alone* in
which medium tempo and perfect swing are in suspenseful
tension with the bitterness of her emotion. At any rate, this
sort of paradox seems more lastingly effective than the
spiritedly sardonic way she treats *Getting Some Fun Out of
Life* or *Laughin' at Life.*

Her response to the presence of the Basie men was, as I
say, always special: *I'll Get By, You're A Lucky Guy, Mean
to Me, I Must Have that Man,* and *I Can't Believe That*

You're in Love with Me are excellent Holiday, particularly the last two.

Even if one's subject is Billie Holiday, one cannot leave these early recordings without further praise for the musicians involved: for Teddy Wilson's improvisations on *The Way You Look Tonight, Pennies from Heaven, These Foolish Things, Laughin' at Life*. For the contrasting inventiveness both of Miss Holiday and of Teddy Wilson on *More Than You Know*, a brilliant record and possibly their joint masterpiece. For Lester Young's beautiful solo on either take of *When You're Smiling*, and on *The Man I Love* and *All for Me*. For the accompaniments of Wilson and Buck Clayton, especially, on many of the early performances. And for the simultaneous improvising of Holiday and Young on *Me, Myself and I,* particularly, along with *A Sailboat in the Moonlight* and *He's Funny That Way*. They are among the great and revealing pleasures of the recorded jazz of the 'thirties. *Body and Soul* clearly reveals Buck Clayton's position in jazz history in his brief solo; it departs from the melody virtually into an invention, but in a style clearly dependent on Armstrong's.

Some performances with the Count Basie orchestra taken from broadcasts have been issued on records, and they find Billie Holiday singing with rare optimism. The rhythmic rapport between the whole Basie band and her on *Swing! Brother, Swing!* is even more revealing than the studio dates with only men from the rhythm section.

By the 1937 *Without Your Love*, bold melodic departures were the rule for Billie Holiday. But gradually her accompanists used more formal arrangements—the price of a growing fame, perhaps. Soon Miss Holiday was a success with much the same sort of supper club following that earlier heard the jaded, sometimes self-deluding emotions of a Helen Morgan, and that later attended an Edith Piaf. Her

tempos got slower and slower, her material more and more
that of a torch singer. But there could be no better comment
on her art than the emotional directness and depth with
which she transformed the affected and self-conscious decadence of *Gloomy Sunday.*

With a new record company and a new contract in 1944,
her songs were still sometimes not well-selected. The stilted
atmosphere—which often included arrangements for still
larger orchestras, sometimes with strings—did not encourage
quite her former emotional and melodic freedom. But at
this time she did record at least one really beautiful song,
Lover Man.

Probably she needed more emotional rapport, if not with
her fellow musicians, then with an audience. Each time an
"in person" performance has been preserved it has been
special, and there is a concert from April 1946 on records
that is more distinguished than most of her recordings of
the time. She did her *Strange Fruit* (moving propaganda
perhaps, but not poetry and not art), *Body and Soul,* her
beautifully transformed *Trav'lin' Light, He's Funny That
Way, The Man I Love,* and *All of Me,* almost all but the
last of them at slow tempos.

After 1952 her recordings were again less formal, with
fewer musicians accompanying her, and a variety of tempos
restored. Her sense of variation had become even surer, but
her voice had not. We can account for this by saying that
most untrained voices, and some trained ones, are very apt
to deepen and deteriorate with the years. Possibly so with
Billie Holiday. But for me the frayed edge of her sound in
her later years seems to come from a deeply suppressed sob
which, if she ever let go, would bring tears she might never
be able to stop. Perhaps I mean that quite literally; perhaps
I mean that she seemed so determined not to feel a deeper
self-pity that she couldn't see the terrible sadness of her self-

destruction. She may have done a great deal of sympathy-begging, feeling sorry for herself, but that is not the same thing. Her life was truly tragic in that no one could help her and she could not help herself.

Through it all she maintained artistic distance; she was not merely indulging her feelings in public. In a sense, she was an actress, a great natural actress who had learned to draw on her own feelings and convey them with honest directness to a listener. And like a great actress, she did not entirely become what she portrayed, but in some secret way she also stood aside from it, and gave us the double image of character and of an implied criticism.

She was an actress. And she was a great musician. But she never had an act.

7

DUKE ELLINGTON

Form Beyond Form

Main Stem was made in 1942 and therefore comes from
Duke Ellington's greatest period as a jazz composer, orchestrator, and leader of a large ensemble. I am not sure that it
is one of the masterpieces of that period, but it is a very good
recording. On the face of it, it may seem casual enough: a
blues in a relatively fast tempo. It opens with a theme played
by the orchestra, followed by a succession of one-chorus
solos by sidemen, and a final return to the theme. It is a
big band blues, then, apparently like many another casually
conceived and executed big band blues of the time.

The opening chorus of *Main Stem* is its twelve-bar theme.
But the theme involves some interesting accents and phrases;
it is not the usual simple two or four-bar riff, repeated over
and over, moved around to fit blues chords. Then there is
its orchestration: a casual listening might not reveal which
instruments and which combinations of instruments are
playing what. Also, there is an interplay of accents from the
brass: the manipulation of plunger mutes by the trumpets
sets up one kind of rhythm, while a more conventional
accentuation of notes sets up and interplays with a slightly
different rhythmic pattern.

The second chorus is a cornet solo by Rex Stewart, taking

over for the band's recently departed plunger-mute soloist, Cootie Williams. However, the chorus is not exactly a solo; it is a call-and-response episode in which the saxophones deliver simple statements—simple, but taking off from one of the phrases in the opening theme—to which Stewart gives imitative, puzzled, plaintive, or humorous answers. Next is an alto saxophone solo by Johnny Hodges, and Hodges the melodist is left to himself with no background but the rhythm section. Then Stewart returns in his own style. He gets a background, with saxes predominating, obviously in contrast to his own brass instrument. But the background is also an imaginative simplified version of the opening theme. Then trumpeter Ray Nance solos, and behind him the theme returns more strongly, almost exactly. The next soloist is clarinetist Barney Bigard; he juxtaposes a melodic fragment, suggested by the theme, over still another simplification of the theme, this time scored with the brass predominating. Behind Joe Nanton's plunger trombone solo there is another sketch of the main melody, this one with saxes predominating.

Perhaps *Main Stem* approaches monotony—or at least repetitiousness—at this point. What we hear next initiates a contrast. It begins with a brief orchestral transition, almost lyric in its pronounced contrast to the rhythmic character of what has preceded it. Then there is a solo by Ben Webster, the hint of lyricism continuing in his accompaniment. We are into a different chord sequence and chorus length. Webster improvises on a sixteen-bar sequence and we are into a second section to *Main Stem*. Webster's earnestness is followed by a robust trombone solo by Lawrence Brown, again on the sixteen-bar pattern, but with a brass accompaniment that is increasingly rhythmic, preparing for what follows. What follows is a recapitulation of the opening theme, but not an exact one. As if to balance both his twelve and sixteen-bar sections, Ellington extends the twelve-bar theme's ending to make it sixteen bars.

Main Stem, then, with such organization and unity, is a far from casual performance. Yet it is a relatively casual one for Duke Ellington.

I suppose it is the greatest tribute to Duke Ellington's music when one realizes that from *The Duke Steps Out* and *Ring Dem Bells* through *Main Stem* some of his most effective pieces have been basically strings of solos by his sidemen. Yet all these are all fully Ellington performances, and not just because his soloists are men whose styles we associate with Ellington. It is a high achievement to have been able to parade solos by Rex Stewart, Johnny Hodges, Stewart again, Ray Nance, Barney Bigard, Joe Nanton, Ben Webster, and Lawrence Brown in rapid succession on *Main Stem* without haste or overloading, and with no loss of the effect of a single, purposeful piece of music. And when one notes the details of theme-orchestration, background, and transitional scoring that contribute variety and yet help make such unity of effect possible, one also notes that these group effects are essentially simple—and perfect. And how perceptively Ellington could use, for example, the very special qualities and limitations of Nanton's trombone, Stewart's cornet, and Bigard's clarinet.

Duke Ellington's first recordings date from 1924. They may seem to preserve an inauspicious beginning for a major talent; they may make him seem a jazz musician on the wrong track, even in danger of derailment; or they may make him seem no jazz musician at all. They are stiff and jerky rhythmically, and they abound in the sort of superficial jazziness of the period. But I think we can now see that, for him, Ellington was on the right track.

Under the surface, Ellington showed in *Rainy Nights* that he had gone to the right source to learn what was then

known about orchestrated jazz, to Don Redman and specifically to his score for Fletcher Henderson called *Naughty
Man*.[1] He also had several promising instrumentalists, particularly trumpeter Bubber Miley. Ellington has said that
it was Miley, as the dramatic soloist and the introducer of
strong, folk-derived themes, who affirmed for him his calling
as a leader of a jazz orchestra. Although there are some
spurious moments in his playing on the early records, Miley
was obviously an authentic and developed jazz musician.
His inspiration and model was King Oliver, and through
Miley we can hear one route by which New Orleans music
has affected all jazz, that is, how much feeling and expressive depth could be retained in an increasingly sophisticated
and developing instrumental music.

The music on most of the early Ellington records is
basically in the dance band style of the day, a fairly sophisticated version of that style. From just such music, Ellington
first absorbed the technical basis on which to build his own.
He needed ideas of harmony, melody, orchestral color and
form, and, like all jazzmen in all periods, he readily absorbed
many of them from the music he heard around him, then
sifted them, and transmuted them into his own jazz language.

I do not mean to dismiss the earliest Ellington records.
Besides Miley's work on several of them, there is *L'il Farina*,
with its succession of solos, which compares favorably with
the orchestral jazz being recorded in New York at the time.
And by praising Miley, I do not mean to dismiss trombonist
Charlie Irvis, nor saxophonist Otto Hardwick and Prince
Robinson as soloists, nor the young Sonny Greer's drumming. In *Choo Choo* we meet Ellington the composer and,
especially in its chord patterns, meet him interestingly.

1. I am indebted to John S. Lewis for pointing this out. However, one
cannot be positive about it, for apparently the first version of *Naughty Man*
was made at almost the same time as *Rainy Nights* and the influence might
have gone in the other direction.

Then there is the fact that Ellington's piano (what one can hear of it on these early records) reflects his upbringing in the Eastern "stride" school. I believe that the traditions of that school probably go back even earlier than the ragtime style of the 1890s, but its players subsequently learned much from the great rag men. By the middle 1920s stride piano was at a peak in New York. All of the stride men were interested in a technical expansion, busily absorbing everything they could from musical comedy scores and "light classics" (even some heavier ones)—there are times when the stride men seem bent on developing a kind of American Negroes' version of "proper" parlor piano. Admittedly, few of these men could play with real blues feeling, and most of them were rather stiff rhythmically compared to the New Orleans men, but each of them felt required to evolve his own style, settle on his own harmonic devices, and I think such standards tellingly influenced Ellington's ideas of music.

The stride style is largely orchestral; it imitates a band. Thus, in orchestrating, the young Ellington had his band directly imitate his piano. If we compare, say, the 1928 Ellington piano version of *Black Beauty* with his orchestration, we can hear him virtually assigning the piece, finger by finger, off the keyboard to his horns and reeds.

By late 1926 Ellington was making recordings of Miley's pieces—*East St. Louis Toodle-oo* was the first—and was writing jazz pieces of his own. He was also still acquiring outstanding instrumentalists: Nanton was present, as was baritone saxophonist Harry Carney. By late 1929 there was New Orleans bassist Wellman Braud, and if Braud lacked steadiness and harmonic correctness in those days, he knew what jazz was all about. His strong feeling and his spirited rhythm changed the character of Ellington performances.

It was in late 1927 that another crucial event in Ellington's career took place. Curiously, it again involved King

Oliver. Oliver turned down an offer to play at a night club
called the "Cotton Club," and Ellington's orchestra got the
job in his place. It meant work and keeping an orchestra
together, and it turned out to mean national fame through
a radio wire. But most important for the music, it meant
playing "floor shows" and "production" numbers. In providing the music for these shows, Ellington began to discover what kind of jazz he was to make, and he began the
radical expansion of the jazz orchestral language that was
necessary for him to make it.

Ellington became the great composer-orchestrator of jazz
and the great leader of a large ensemble, the master of form
in jazz and the great synthesizer of its elements. He had to
take the idiom that Miley represented, take what he had
learned from Redman and Henderson, take his own innate
urbanity and sophistication, and start all over again, with a
completely new approach to big band jazz.

Ellington made big band jazz by making a show band or
pit band into a jazz band. Others had approached the proposition differently. By 1926 King Oliver had tried substituting
a reed section (saxophones frequently doubling on clarinets), with written parts, for the single improvising clarinet
of his earlier New Orleans group. And Redman and Henderson had converted the American dance band, with its
reed, brass, and rhythm sections, into a jazz band by using
jazz effects and themes, and by employing improvised solos
by jazz musicians.

The Cotton Club shows were lurid affairs, full of "jungle"
nonsense, kidnapping "sheiks," and the rest of it, and the
music had to be occasionally bizarre and always immediate
in its effect. Small wonder that Ellington's stock orchestrations were later used at Minsky's burlesque houses. With his
own kind of urbane irony, Ellington could use preposterous
titles like *Jungle Nights In Harlem* for the "slumming"

white crowd at the club. At the same time he was expanding his knowledge of orchestration, orchestral color, and composition; he continued to learn from the theater orchestrators of the time, modifying, assimilating, and transforming what they offered him into an authentic expansion of the jazz language. All of the superficially sensational and quasi-primitive orchestral effects actually had a deeper role; they were kept quite musical and compositionally intrinsic, and they were a means of Ellington's musical growth.

The orchestra is, as has been said, Ellington's real instrument, and he has worked with his orchestra as the great playwrights have worked with their companies of actors, as the great choreographers have worked with their own troupes of dancers, as great European composers have worked for specific instrumentalists or singers, each learning from the other. In Ellington's band there developed a truly collaborative art among leader, soloist, and group, and it is a tribute to him that the careers of his sidemen were sometimes less illustrious after they left him. All the great Ellington works depend on a superb relationship between soloist and group, between what is written (or perhaps merely memorized) and what is improvised, between the individual part and the total effect, a relationship among beginning, middle, and end. A great Ellington performance is, therefore, not a series of sometimes brilliant episodes but, like the great works of all great jazz composers, a whole—greater than the sum of its parts. He learned how to discipline improvisation and how to extend orchestration—to the enhancement of both.

The extent of Ellington's talent showed itself not only in the fact that he began to cut across the compartmentalized sections of other jazz orchestras but in that he knew he was scoring (for example) not for a combination of muted trumpet, clarinet and trombone, but for Cootie Williams's cup-muted sound, with Bigard's clarinet sound, juxtaposing Lawrence Brown's trombone sound.

The size of Ellington's talent began to show also as he freed himself as orchestrator from his dependence on the fingers of himself as pianist and began to work more directly with the players and more abstractly with the music. He knew Harry Carney's baritone sound was crucial to the sound of his saxes, hence to the sound of his orchestra as well. But what genius was it that told him not to score Carney's sound always as the *bottom* of his harmonies, where it might seem to belong, but to move it from position to position for its best effect?

Ellington did take early lessons in scoring from his keyboard style. He later rid his writing of specifically pianistic aspects and wrote more directly for the resources of the horns themselves. And he also freed his work of a dependence on ragtime and its rather static and abrupt rhythm and phrasing. For example, *Rockin' in Rhythm*, an early success still in the Ellington books, has the accents of ragtime piano shaping its movement. New, more flexible and mobile ideas of rhythm and phrasing were Louis Armstrong's crucial and pervasive contribution to the music, of course, and one can hear an Armstrong-inspired propulsion bursting through the 1930 performance of *Old Man Blues*, specifically in Cootie Williams's marvelously agile trumpet solo.

There is a moment in *Shout 'Em Aunt Tillie* that I think is a beautiful revelation of Ellington's role. It is his striking and original piano accompaniment to Cootie Williams's solo. His left hand is not striding, and in rhythm, sound, melody, and harmonic relationship to the soloists, the piano becomes an excellent piece of contrasting orchestration. The maturing Ellington learned to think directly as an orchestrator—a jazz orchestrator—even when playing piano. Most of it he had to work out for himself, coax out of his men, or borrow from outside of jazz. There were some precedents in earlier jazz for the kind of thing he wanted to do, but Ellington doesn't seem to have been interested in them. And for a great deal of what he was to do, there were no models.

Ellington was coaxing a temperamental and brilliant group of soloists and players into discovering and developing their own best resources, into contributing constantly to the act of mutual composition involving the leader and his soloists, and also into subordinating their own talents to the total effect of a composition and a performance. As Gunther Schuller has pointed out, there was an imbalance in the earlier jazz works with Miley, as exciting and important as they are.

The first important Ellington-Miley collaboration, *East St. Louis Toodle-oo*, is still impressive, but Miley's anguished *wa-wa* horn dominates it as it does the second important joint work, *Black and Tan Fantasy*. Ellington's orchestral effects and secondary themes seem weak, out of place, and perhaps affected by comparison. *Creole Love Call*, another early collaboration, is better in that Ellington did not contribute thematic material.

In their later versions, both *East St. Louis* and *Black and Tan Fantasy* are greatly improved works: both are less dominated by the themes and the interpretations of a single musician; both are more balanced and appropriate in the contributions of the orchestrator and leader.

A more specific comparison might be instructive. Miley's contribution to *East St. Louis Toodle-oo* is a dramatic combination of themes in AABA song form. Ellington obviously added a third theme, a melody intended for contrast but rather inappropriate, employing almost archaic ragtime-like accents. In the 1937 "new" *East St. Louis Toodle-oo*, now featuring Cootie Williams, the theme is gone, the whole is much better orchestrated, the juxtaposition of the featured soloist against the orchestration and with the other soloists is excellently balanced and proportioned, and (to cite one detail) the plunger response executed by the full trumpet section on the first version of the bridge is startlingly effective.

Similarly with the "new" *Black and Tan Fantasy* of 1938. Ellington's rather schmaltzy secondary theme does not appear in the main section of the work but is now a part of a *Prologue to Black and Tan Fantasy*. The piece is played more slowly, giving a tone of conscious introspection to Miley's broader proclamations. And the *Fantasy* itself becomes a beautifully played and scored exploration of Miley's blues theme, climaxed by Cootie Williams's solo. En route, it is enhanced by a middle chorus which juxtaposes Nanton's plaintive solo, Ellington's accompaniment, and Barney Bigard's upper register b flat moving through D and into F, and from a whisper to forte.

Thus, it was again Ellington's very sophistication, sometimes so inappropriate in its early manifestations, that held the most promise for his development. And before he was through, Ellington proved that his own ideas could be assimilated and transmuted so as to become not only appropriate to the idiom of instrumental blues and jazz, but could authentically extend the music's range immeasurably.

However, I do not suppose that one could overestimate Cootie Williams's importance to Ellington, much as one could not overestimate Miley's. Not a great improviser, Williams is nevertheless a great player, and he brought both rhythmic sureness and an Armstrong concept of swing to the orchestra when it was needed. He also brought a sound brass technique and the ability not only to take over the plunger trumpet role that Miley had created but to expand it in technique, sound, and emotional range. It is fitting that one of the durable successes of early Ellington should be Williams's contribution, *Echoes of the Jungle* (1931). It is also fitting that his work on that piece is in a sense a pastiche of the work of his predecessors, "growl" trumpeters, Miley and Arthur Whetsol. And it is most fitting of all that one of Ellington's later masterpieces should have been his *Concerto for Cootie.*

As I have implied, late 1930, 1931, and early 1932 was a fruitful time for Ellington. He recorded *Old Man Blues, Mood Indigo, Rockin' In Rhythm, Echoes of the Jungle,* the first effort at a longer work—*Creole Rhapsody*—and the largely successful reworking of *Creole Love Call* as a vehicle for Cootie Williams in Miley's former role.

By 1932 a rhythmic turning point had been reached in *It Don't Mean a Thing,* with its prophetic subtitle, *If It Ain't Got That Swing.* The piece was obviously conceived as an instrumental although it was first recorded with a vocal by Ivie Anderson, taking over (it seems clear) passages first designed for Cootie Williams's plunger and Johnny Hodges's alto. *It Don't Mean A Thing* is an orchestral and not a pianistic piece, and it is written with the new swing phrasing throughout.

Sometimes raggy and overbusy phrasing continued to appear, particularly in the *Tiger Rag* and *Stompy Jones* variants like *Slippery Horn, Bragging in Brass,* or *The Flaming Sword.* These are usually brilliantly executed showpieces, but they are always in some sense melodic and rhythmic museum pieces as well. But by 1937 and *Harmony in Harlem,* it is clear that a collective and flexible swing was becoming almost second nature to the Ellington orchestra. One's only reservation, ironically, is the performance of drummer Sonny Greer, whose playing fits in excellently with the older or the "regressive" style. However, I should add that I don't think the Ellington orchestra has ever had a

really ideal drummer, except perhaps the Sonny Greer of
the late 'twenties and early 'thirties.

Excellent orchestration was also becoming almost second
nature, and there are swirling colors on *Merry-Go-Round*
and brooding sonority on *The Saddest Tale* that might in
themselves attest to Ellington's preeminence.

What is still imperfect is the just employment of the
leader's melodic sophistication, particularly in the blues
idiom. The B theme on even as exceptional an Ellington
piece as *Mood Indigo* (1930) has a rather trite, or tritely
employed, second phrase. *Bundle of Blues* in 1933, brilliantly juxtaposes Cootie Williams's resilient growls and
blues feeling against responses from the orchestra. But
Ellington then offers a second theme that is still a little too
chic, a little too sentimental. Similarly, *Echoes of Harlem*,
which begins so robustly, has a secondary Ellington theme
for the saxes that is jarringly out of place but takes on very
different life in Williams's earthy trumpet paraphrases later
in the performance.[2]

Azure from 1937, neglected perhaps because it is so simple, is one of Ellington's most affecting slow, introspective
mood pieces. It has a weak release, but its main strain is
superbly scored. And its melody is neither too "vocal" in
character as is *In a Sentimental Mood*, nor too sentimental
as is *Lost in Meditation*. A ritual sentimentality can be the
curse of sophistication, and an urbane sophistication is, as
I say, the cornerstone of Ellington's genius in its successes
and its failures alike.

A balanced and sustained assimilation of Ellington's musical urbanity is first announced, I think, on a piece called
Blue Light done in late 1938. Admittedly, he was working

2. This second theme to *Echoes of Harlem*, incidentally, was originally a
separate piece called *Blue Mood*, recorded three years earlier but unissued
at the time.

with a small group and only two other soloists besides himself. But the performance is compositionally conceived and not a simple succession of blues solos. The leader's piano introduces, organizes, comments, and at the end offers a contribution and summary of its own. Barney Bigard's lovely clarinet theme is so fragile it seems to be embellishments on a single low note. Then a simple theme for muted trumpet, clarinet, and trombone. Then Lawrence Brown's trombone solo, a firm and beautiful second melody. Then Ellington. *Blue Light* is a continuously developing whole: nothing extrinsic, all parts in balance. Following it, *Slap Happy* and *Old King Dooji*, by the full orchestra and from the same record date, or *Portrait of the Lion* from a month later are similarly cohesive and lack only first-rate melodic material and orchestration to rank with the very best Ellington.

Thus, Ellington was prepared for the great works that followed, beginning in 1940: *Blue Serge, Ko-Ko, Concerto for Cootie*; and for the shining satellites that gather around their brilliance: *Harlem Air Shaft, Rumpus in Richmond, Sepia Panorama, In a Mellow Tone, Across the Track Blues, Jack the Bear, Cotton Tail*, and the rest.

The *Concerto for Cootie* is in a sense the ultimate refinement of the influence of ragtime structures on later jazz composition. It opens, after its eight-bar introduction, with an AABA in song form, but the A theme is ten bars rather than eight, and each use of that A theme in the *Concerto* is a variation on its first appearance. The second section of the *Concerto* is its C theme, sixteen bars long. And the record ends with a brief variation of A, limited to six bars, followed by a beautifully sustained coda of ten bars.

Such comments may of course make the piece sound like a technical exercise in breaking down the four and eight-bar phrases—something which Ellington had been working on, perhaps not unsuccessfully, since 1929. In the *Concerto*, in any case, the extensions are successful and flow naturally; Williams and the orchestra share *ten*-bar segments, not eight-bar phrases with an extra two bars tacked on. The piece is *for* Cootie Williams, balanced against the orchestra but not dominating it, and once again he plays beautifully. He uses all his sonorous resources, from a tightly cup-muted sound, through the *wa-wa* of a plunger mute in motion, the plunger held closed, the hard "growl" with the plunger held partly open, open horn on the C theme, etc. The score is simple harmonically, but the balancing, setting, and transitions, dominated by the saxophones, are beautifully scored and beautifully played.

Portions of the *Concerto* had been previously tested. The forceful B melody is an adaptation of one of Cootie's blues phrases which introduces the 1938 *Mobile Blues*, and the coda is an adaptation of one Ellington used on *Moonglow*[3] in 1935. The new portions are the lyric themes, A and C, and they are the work of Ellington the composer, in 1940.

Ko-Ko is in a sense opposite to the *Concerto*. Its point of departure is simple, a succession of twelve-bar blues choruses; however, its handling is not so simple, particularly harmonically. In these two performances, Ellington and his orchestra pass two aesthetic tests: in the *Concerto* of undertaking a variety of material in a brief performance, and in *Ko-Ko* of undertaking a simplicity of material without letting the results seem monotonous. *Ko-Ko* begins with an introduction, followed by the orchestra's statement of its first, apparently simple theme. Then come solos by two of the orchestra's trombonists, Juan Tizol's valve instrument (one chorus) and Joe Nanton's plunger-muted horn (two choruses). The secondary theme of *Ko-Ko* is explored

3. What of the Hudson-Delange *Moonglow*, incidentally, since its structure obviously owes a great deal to the 1932 Ellington piece *Lazy Rhapsody* and its melody to *Lazy Rhapsody* and an interlude in *It Don't Mean a Thing*?

largely by the orchestra in four choruses, but using exchanges with Ellington's piano in the first and with Jimmy
Blanton's bass in the third.

An excellent touch is that the transition from the primary
to the secondary theme of *Ko-Ko* is made easier by a brass
figure which accompanies Nanton's solo and which is carried over, in modified form, to the first exposition of the
secondary theme. The performance ends with a balancing
restatement of the opening chorus.

In *Ko-Ko* Ellington's talent again reaches full expression.
The piece provides exceptional primary and secondary
themes, both of which are projections of basically simple,
traditional blues ideas. He handles them with appropriate
robustness and continuity. And his sophistication is used to
enhance the themes and to enhance the work of his soloists.
Finally, he develops the second theme orchestrally in a manner otherwise unknown in jazz.

The stature of the Ellington orchestra at this period
reveals itself in details as well as in full performances. There
is the original, contrasting saxophone melody behind the
simple trumpet riffing that opens *Harlem Air Shaft*. The
marvelous playing on *Never No Lament*, especially behind
Cootie Williams's solo. The beautiful saxophone ensembles
on *Rumpus in Richmond*, especially as they walk upward
behind Cootie Williams's second solo. Or the opening
choruses of *I Don't Know What Kind of Blues I Got*, a
minor marvel in the Ellington repertory. These begin with
a piano introduction in ad lib tempo, sketching color and
mood. In the first chorus, Barney Bigard states a brooding
theme in the clarinet's lower register while Lawrence Brown
counterpoints another theme behind him. In the second
chorus, the muted brass take up Bigard's theme for a variation while Ben Webster improvises another behind them.
Then Bigard returns to resing his opening theme in the

upper register while Brown provides a stronger and more elaborate version of *his* initial theme in counterpoint.

A third masterpiece after the *Concerto* and *Ko-Ko* is *Blue Serge*. For it, Ellington turned to the most challengingly simple and potentially monotonous of forms, the eight-bar blues. He and the orchestra meet the challenge with an ingenious variety of techniques including unobtrusive modulations, and with sustained and probing emotion.

The introduction to *Blue Serge* is six measures, but for good reason it is broken into four measures plus two. The opening four give the main theme, by clarinet and brass, but only for its basic melodic figure. This exposition is interrupted for a brooding, two-bar transition, a sort of vamp by the trombones, that sets the mood for the performance. It also sets up the idea of a "floating" two bars which ingeniously reappears in the performance several times, extending one chorus to ten measures, or breaking another into six plus two.

In the first chorus of *Blue Serge* Ray Nance's trumpet restates the theme in a full exposition, and for a fuller realization of its introspective character. The second chorus is a thematic variation scored for reeds and muted brass, a thing of marvelous color and one of the hundreds of examples in Ellington where only the closest listening will reveal what combinations of what instruments with what mutes are playing what, to produce this shifting sonority. This chorus also offers the first extension of the eight-bar chorus; it is unobtrusively and quite effectively eight plus two.

The next two choruses are tied. The first is a nonthematic plunger solo by Joe Nanton. As is usual with Ellington's settings for Nanton's dramatic simplicity, it is excellently accompanied. By a slight harmonic manipulation, this chorus is joined to the next, which is a written, but nonthematic, variation with plunger trumpets predominating.

This episode, however, ends after six bars, leaving two bars for the piano. This "premature" introduction of the piano ties the fourth chorus to the fifth, which is a thematic piano variation for a full eight bars. The next chorus is a secondary theme, a twelve-bar solo by Ben Webster played over the trombones. (But is it actually eight bars plus four bars?) The record concludes with a return to a beautifully orchestrated variation, just barely thematic but strong enough to leave the performance with a feeling of resolution and with no lingering need for a recapitulation.

The successes of 1938 to 1942 obviously have to do with a coming together of specific talents: the leader's in its maturity, and those of the sidemen with whom he had worked for years, like Williams, Stewart, Brown, Nanton, Tizol, Hodges, Bigard, Carney, and so on. Then there is the presence of the orchestra's second arranger, Billy Strayhorn, who joined in early 1939. Perhaps we shall never know exactly who has contributed what to the Ellington book from that day forward. Strayhorn was a talent compatible with Ellington's in several ways. It had its moments of chic and somewhat shallow sophistication, as his early songs *Lush Life* and *Something to Live For* will reveal. But he could alter the chords of *Exactly Like You* perceptively for *Take the 'A' Train*, and, with Ellington's guidance, he soon produced *Johnny Come Lately*. Undoubtedly tempering the more sophisticated talents in the orchestra were those of the musically robust midwesterners who joined at about the same time, Jimmy Blanton and Ben Webster.

Inevitably the less imaginative arrangers of the 'thirties and 'forties borrowed Ellington's melodies, effects, and backgrounds, two and four bars at a time, to turn them into simple, repeated riffs. Themes like *Slap Happy* and *The Jeep is Jumping*, for example, are ahead of their time in that they are continuous melodies and not simple repetitive

riff figures. The more perceptive students of Ellington did
not even undertake to grasp the subtler aspects of his orchestral language until the late 'thirties—and at first such efforts
were likely to go on in orchestras, like those of Charlie
Barnett and Erskine Hawkins, that were frankly engaged in
imitative tributes.

It has been Ellington's ambition to write a successful
musical comedy. Obviously he is a more than capable song
writer, but a higher destiny must have dictated the fate of
his ambition as a Broadway tunesmith. A truer and higher
expression of his talent can be found in his composition and
orchestration of a semi-improvised instrumental music for
his own orchestra. And one notes how many of Ellington's
themes, even those written more or less in the Viennese
operetta tradition, in fairly straightforward use of song form,
have to be revised, and revised downward, to become successful popular tunes.

Another of Ellington's ambitions is to write a significant
long work. Surely one dismisses none of his efforts in that
direction by saying that he remains the great miniaturist of
instrumental, orchestrated jazz. Beginning with *Creole
Rhapsody*, going through *Reminiscing in Tempo, Crescendo
and Diminuendo in Blue,* and the film score he did in 1939
called *Symphony in Black* (a suite that used earlier themes
like *Showboat Shuffle, Merry Go Round, Saddest Tale,
Ducky Wucky,* and others), each piece has something interesting in it. It is usually said that the greatest of the suites
is *Black, Brown and Beige* in its original 1943 orchestration.
Undoubtedly so, but the piece is a collection of Ellington
miniatures. It is ironic that *Suite Thursday,* of 1960, should
be the first long work in which Ellington directly undertook to integrate the various sections of one of his suites by
having his opening section state the various melodies and
motives which the later sections develop.

Some commentators have seen Ellington as an impression-ist. Surely we are invited to do so by his own descriptive and programmatic titles—*Daybreak Express, Misty Morning, Harlem Air Shaft*—and also by the manner in which he has coached his players, almost as though they were a group of actors, into evoking specific emotions appropriate to specific situations. Perhaps impressionism is his means on occasion, but his highest end includes *Concerto for Cootie, Ko-Ko,* and *Blue Serge,* which are pure instrumental music.

As I say, by 1940 he had dealt with the nature of his talent and brought it to fulfillment. During the 'thirties, he had learned to orchestrate less as a pianist and more as the leader of a group of instrumentalists: individually and collectively. He had also absorbed the challenging rhythmic idiom introduced in New Orleans and fully expressed in Armstrong's work. And by 1938 he was beginning to use the implicit possibilities of his own sophistication as a melodist, and to bring its distinct qualities into balance with the sturdier emotions of some of his sidemen. Ellington refined jazz beyond the achievements of anyone else. He orchestrated and enriched its message without taking away its spontaneity, its essential passion and life.

One problem in Ellington's subsequent career was that he sometimes ceased to work quite as closely with the specific talents of his players as he had once done. Choosing to maintain his style, as he had worked it out collaborating with his earlier sidemen, he was required to get new players to re-create what Cootie Williams had done earlier, what Joe Nanton had done, what Jimmy Banton had done. Fortunately, he lost Johnny Hodges only briefly, and the combination of communal earthiness, rhythmic drive, and sophisticated lyricism which Hodges possesses make him perhaps the perfect Ellington sideman.

Ellington remained, however, well into the 'sixties, the

major leader of a large jazz ensemble. And certainly there are excellencies from every period of his career. True, he may misjudge his audiences. He may offer a medley of Ellington "hits," or a facile and banal use of saxophonist Paul Gonzalves's fine but uneven talent, or of trumpeter Cat Anderson's phenomenal upper register before audiences who would rather hear the best portions of his *Such Sweet Thunder* suite or a full version of his exceptional score for the *Asphalt Jungle* television series.

Nevertheless, Ellington remains the supreme *popular* artist. His audience still has at its core couples who danced to his *Sophisticated Lady* on their honeymoons, and he knows it. If a program of popular dance band ballads interests him, he will provide one, and very possibly do so with brilliance. William Russo's suggestion that it was a later development of Ellington's talent to be able to rework the compositions of others and make them his own seems a just one.

He can still meet an audience on its own level and, on occasion, transport it up to his own. He has held audiences almost from the beginning of his career, whereas Thelonious Monk took fifteen years to find any audience at all, and whereas it was diluting popularizers who spread many of Charlie Parker's ideas. In that sense, Ellington may be the last popular artist jazz will ever see.

8

COUNT BASIE AND LESTER YOUNG

Style Beyond Swing

The Count Basie orchestra of the late 'thirties and early 'forties was highly praised for its wonderful spirit, and certainly the relaxed power of the ensemble was compelling enough to make one overlook—virtually forget—many things including a manifest lack of polish, of unity, even of good intonation. One theory holds that the orchestra's group spirit came about because it had perfected ensemble swing in the rhythmic style of the times. There is no question that the ensemble did swing. But it seems to me that the Basie orchestra had discovered that it could do more than swing, that there were more things to be done in jazz than had been done before, and that its collective joy came from such discoveries.

The year 1932 was probably the key year for big band swing. By then the Fletcher Henderson orchestra obviously knew how a large jazz ensemble could perform with something of the supple rhythmic momentum that a single jazz soloist, Louis Armstrong, had offered. Also by 1932 there were enough Ellington performances that manifest an Armstrong-inspired ensemble swing to underline the point. But in that same year, the midwestern orchestra of Benny Moten made some recordings which not only showed a developed ensemble swing but a basically simple style on which something else might be built.

The Moten orchestra was an unlikely one to make such a discovery. Some of its earlier scores owed an obvious debt to Jelly Roll Morton, but it took the Moten band until 1929 and a performance like *Jones Law Blues* for it to be able to play a Morton-derived style with sureness and accomplishment. Otherwise its arrangements were overstuffed affairs, full of effects that were at once simple and pretentious, and some of its soloists were apt to be embarrassingly indebted to the likes of Red Nichols or Frankie Trumbauer —when they were not simply faking.

Yet in December 1932 this orchestra, after the merest hints in its early records, had a marathon recording date on which it revealed a four-square swing so nearly perfect that some of its passages are classic—the final riffing on *Blue Room* for example.

The transformation came about less abruptly than the recordings make it seem, and it came about because the Moten band gradually borrowed the members of another band, the Blue Devils of bass player Walter Page. No matter how much credit one gives where it is due—to trumpeter "Hot Lips" Page, to trombonist Dan Miner, to trombonist-guitarist-arranger Eddie Durham, to clarinetist-saxophonist-arranger Eddie Barefield, to tenor saxophonist Ben Webster, to singer Jimmy Rushing, to pianist William (later Count) Basie—the crux of the matter on the 1932 Moten recordings is Walter Page and the firm, strong, and sometimes joyous four beats to a bar that his bass provided. Around its virtues all other things seem to have gathered.

Even the style had developed in Page's Blue Devils orchestra, and at its best it was simplicity itself. The most effective ensembles on the 1932 Moten records are simple riff figures, shouted out by the brass or saxes or tossed back and forth from one section to another in antiphonal call-and-response figures. Thus the finale of *Blue Room*. Thus the finale of *Moten's Swing*. Thus older-style pieces like *Milenburg Joys* and *Prince of Wails* could be reinterpreted in a new rhythmic manner. And thus the group could play a more elaborate piece like *Toby* and play it well. But the Moten band was to drop the style that *Toby* represents, leaving it to powerhouse orchestras like Jimmie Lunceford's.

Therefore the best Moten ensembles were simple and direct, and the more complex passages in the music were up to the soloists. And so it was not that the Basie band could swing in 1937; the Moten band had had such things in hand five years before.

The story is fairly well known that Basie's orchestra did not begin as a big band but as a smaller one of nine pieces which the pianist led after Moten's commercial potential had collapsed. But many of the stylistic virtues of that small ensemble were evidently borrowed from those of the Blue Devils and the later Moten band. So it is perhaps not quite miraculous that Basie was able to expand his small group to a large one, while retaining its informality, spontaneity, and verve.

The early Basie book was casual and frequently borrowed, either in bits and pieces or, sometimes, whole. The ultimate source was often Fletcher Henderson's orchestra. Basie's arrangement of *Honeysuckle Rose* is a slight simplification of Henderson's. Basie's *Swinging the Blues* comes from Henderson's *Hot and Anxious* and *Comin' and Goin'*.[1] *Jumpin'*

1. A more complete history of this piece is interesting and revealing. The 1929 Ellington-Miley *Doin' the Voom Voom*, in AABA song form (an obvious Cotton Club specialty), became the 1931 Horace Henderson-Fletcher Henderson pair of pieces called *Hot and Anxious* (a blues) and *Comin' and Goin'* (partly a blues). Those pieces also added the riff later called *In the Mood*. These, in turn, became Count Basie's *Swingin' the Blues*. Mean-

at the Woodside (as Dan Morgenstern points out) comes
from the Mills' Blue Rhythm Band's *Jammin' For the Jack-
pot*, with perhaps a glance at the arrangement of *Honeysuckle Rose* that Benny Carter did for Coleman Hawkins
and Django Reinhardt. *Jive at Five* from the same ensemble's *Barrelhouse*. The Mills' Blue Rhythm Band was a Hen-
derson-style orchestra.

On *One O'Clock Jump*, one hears a riff lifted from one
piece, and then another riff lifted from another piece. Or,
one hears a simple ensemble figure that reflects the style of
one Basie soloist, and then another figure that comes from
the vocabulary of another Basie soloist. The understructures
are also simple, often borrowed from *Tea for Two*, *Digga
Digga Do*, *I Got Rhythm*, *Lady Be Good*, *Shoe Shine Boy*,
and the like. And everywhere and always one hears the
blues, often in medium tempo and with a kind of joy unheard in the blues before.

A history of the jazz rhythm section is virtually a history
of the music. In the early 'twenties one might find a pianist's
left hand, a string bass or tuba, a guitar or banjo, a drummer's two hands, and perhaps his two feet, all clomping
away, keeping 4/4 time, or two beats out of the four. It was
partly a matter of necessity; keeping time was difficult for
some of the players individually, swinging more difficult,
and consequently both keeping steady time and making it
swing were difficult for many of the groups as well. When
such elementary time-keeping became less needed by the
hornmen, it began to drop away, to be sure, but not only
because the musicians didn't need it any more. It dropped

---

while, *Doin' the Voom Voom* had also obviously inspired the Lunceford-
Will Hudson specialties *White Heat* and *Jazznocracy*, and these in turn
prompted the Harry James-Benny Goodman *Life Goes to a Party*. In the
last piece, the background figure (a sort of up-and-down motif) to one of
the trumpet solos on *Voom Voom* had been slightly changed and elevated
into a main theme.

away also because the rhythm section men found something
to put in its place.

It is another of the Basie miracles that the pianist, Count
Basie, the bassist, Walter Page, and the drummer, Jo Jones,
came together. Jones not only played lightly and differently,
he gave jazz drumming a different role in the music. He
pedalled his bass drum more quietly and he moved his hands
away from his snare drum to keep his basic rhythm on his
double, high-hat cymbal. Unlike some of his imitators, he
achieved a momentum, a kind of discreet urgency in his
cymbal sound by barely opening the high-hat as he struck it.
All of which is to say that Jo Jones discovered he could play
the *flow* of the rhythm and not its demarcation. And he
perceived that the rhythmic lead was passing to the bass,
which he could complement with his cymbals.

From one point of view, the styles of the members of the
Basie rhythm section were built on simplifications of previous styles. Walter Page obviously owes much to Wellman
Braud, but Page counted off an even four beats, and only
occasionally used the syncopations that were sometimes so
charming in Braud's playing. Guitarist Freddie Green struck
chords on the beats evenly, quietly. Jones played his *ching-
de-ching* differently, in a sense much more simply, than, say,
Baby Dodds played his drums. And Basie, more often than
not, neither strides nor walks with his left hand. But the
simplifications, the cutting back to essentials, also involved
rebuildings.

Basie's melodic vocabulary came from Fats Waller, with
flashes of Earl Hines, and some soon-to-be-acquired bits from
Teddy Wilson. He could stride skillfully and joyously, as he
did on *Prince of Wails* with Moten. But when he dropped
the *oom-pa* of stride bass, Basie's right hand accents were no
longer heavy or light, but all equal, and, with Page taking
care of the basic beats, the pianist's rather limited melodic

vocabulary was suddenly released. Basie could form solo
after solo out of a handful of phrases that quickly became
familiar but were always somehow fresh because they were
always struck, shaded, enunciated and pronounced differently; he discovered the superbly individual piano touch
which defies imitation, and which can cause subtle percussive and accentual nuances in the most apparently repetitive ideas.

Similarly he shifted the very function of jazz ensemble
piano. He no longer accompanied in the old way: he commented, encouraged, propelled, and interplayed. And in
his own solos, his left hand commented, encouraged, propelled, and interplayed with his right. One need only listen
to those moments when Basie did revert to a heavy stride
bass (as when he did behind Lester Young on *You Can
Depend on Me*) to hear what a sluggish effect it could have
in the new context, or listen even to those moments when
Basie's left-hand stride was so light and discontinuous as to
be almost an abstraction of the style (as on *Time Out* or
Twelfth Street Rag) to realize how brilliant were his discoveries about jazz piano.

Basie's playing on *Lester Leaps In* seems perfect, perhaps
(one is tempted to believe) because he is in the company
of a select group from his own orchestra, men whom he
understood and who understood him. But when he sits in
with the Goodman sextet on *Till Tom Special* and *Gone
with 'What' Wind*, every piano animation and comment is
precisely right in timing, in touch, in second, in rhythm. If
there is anything left in Basie of the oldest tradition of jazz
piano, that of imitating an orchestra, it is an imitation of an
orchestra somehow made spontaneous and flexible and never
redundant. Probably the greatest moment for Basie the accompanist comes during the two vocal choruses on *Sent for
You Yesterday*, in a delicate balance involving Rushing's

voice, Harry Edison's trumpet obligato, the saxophone figures, and Basie's discreet feeds, interjections, punctuations,
and encouragements.

Perhaps the best introduction to Basie both as soloist and
accompanist is the alert exchange of two-bar phrases between
him and the horns on *Shoe Shine Boy* and of four-bar
phrases on its variant, *Roseland Shuffle*, on *You Can Depend
on Me*, and *Lester Leaps In*. In those moments, his piano
is discreet enough to dramatize the phrases of the hornmen,
yet too personal and firm to be self-effacing.

Basie's solo on *One O'Clock Jump* shows how rhythmically self-assured he had become, for it is clearly he who
leads the rest of the rhythm section. And *John's Idea*, the
second piano solo, shows what personal humor he had discovered within the broader genialities of Fats Waller's style.

Basie's opening solo on *Texas Shuffle* is a good example
of spontaneous logic of phrase and sound. His solo on
Doggin' Around is a classic of linking and occasionally contrasting melodic ideas, and is probably his masterpiece.

Basie does not wail the blues, to be sure, but he has an
obviously respectful concern for the blues tradition, and on
a slow piece like *'Way Back Blues* he shows what concen-
trated introspection he achieved in the style. Here is stride
piano (and touches of Hines piano) cut back to its essentials, and almost ready to "play the blues," as stride piano
can with later-day stride men like Monk and Bud Powell.

Many of the best early Basie arrangements were casually
worked out by the band's members in the act of playing, and
many others were revised by them in the act of replaying.
But when scores were written for the band, Basie himself
would frequently cut and simplify them, and one can well
imagine that this happened to Eddie Durham's *Time Out*.
Durham seems to have profited from, and improved on,
Edgar Sampson's *Blue Lou*, and his structure encouraged a

fine effect of suspense during Lester Young's solo. The re-
sultant *Time Out* is an exemplary Basie arrangement: its
ideas are sturdy and it is flexible; it might be expanded
almost indefinitely—by more solos, longer solos, and by
repeats of its written portions—without losing its casual,
high effectiveness. (And incidentally, the performance of
that piece shows how much technical polish the band
achieved by 1937.)

The great moments from drummer Jo Jones are the moments when he rises to the music most subtly. One is apt
to sense his splashing cymbal in its response to Lester
Young's arrival on *One O'Clock Jump* without really no-
ticing it. That response or the way he shifts and varies his
cymbal sound behind Young on *Shorty George* or on *Exactly
Like You.* His cymbal and bass drum accents propel Young
during his fine, rolling solo on *Broadway,* particularly at
the end of the bridge. (Was Jo Jones the first drummer to
use a bass drum for such accents?)

My examples all come from accompaniments to Lester
Young, and that is as it should be. On Basie's records we
listen to the group spirit and to the soloists. We hear what
a highly personal style Basie made of Waller. We may note
that Buck Clayton formed a personal approach within outlines suggested by Armstrong. That Harry Edison built a
more complex trumpet style with less obvious use of Armstrong. That Herschel Evans knew the Hawkins of the early
'thirties. But when we discuss Lester Young we enter his
own musical world.

An account of Lester Young's historical importance has
often been given, but it is an account always worth giving
again. He created a new aesthetic, not only for the tenor
saxophone but for all jazz. One compares him usually with
Coleman Hawkins, and the comparison is handy and instructive, but one might compare him with everyone who had
preceded him.

Like any original talent, Lester Young reinterpreted tradition, and we may hear in him touches of King Oliver, of
Armstrong (even of the most advanced Armstrong), of
Trumbauer, and Beiderbecke. But in pointing them out,
we only acknowledge a part of the foundation on which he
built his own airy structures.

There seems to me no question that Lester Young was
the most gifted and original improviser between Louis Armstrong and Charlie Parker. He simply defied the rules and
made new ones by example. His sound was light, almost
vibratoless. He showed that such a sound could carry the
most compelling ideas, that one could swing quietly and
with a minimum of notes, and that one could command a
whole orchestra by understatement. His style depended on
an original and flexible use of the even, four beats which
Armstrong's work made the norm. The beats were not in-
flexibly heavy or light in Young—indeed an occasional accent might even fall a shade ahead of the beat or behind it.
And he did not phrase four measures at a time. (If he had
any important precursor in the matter of flexible phrasing
besides Armstrong, by the way, it was trumpeter Henry
"Red" Allen, Jr.)

Lester Young's solo on Count Basie's *Doggin' Around* is
a handy example, and one of the best. He begins, actually,
by phrasing under the final two bars of Basie's piano chorus
(thus does "Lester leap in"). His own chorus starts with a
single note in a full bar of music—any reed player and
probably any horn player at the time would have used at
least four notes. His second musical phrase begins at the
second bar and dances gracefully through the seventh, unbroken. His eighth bar is silent—balancing the opening perhaps. In nine he begins his third phrase, which links logically with his second. But the basic impulse here is not
breaking through the four and eight-bar phrases, nor in the
daring symmetry of balancing one casual note at the begin-

ning against a silence eight bars later. It is in his accents,
in a sort of freely dancing rhythmic impulse, which seem
almost to dictate how his melodies shall move.

Harmonically, what Lester Young did was show how original one could be with the materials already at hand. By
means of a marvelous ear, and a refusal to allow a literal
reading of chords to detain him, he might freely, casually,
and tantalizingly phrase several beats ahead of a coming
chord change, and let its arrival show how right he was all
along. Similarly, he might phrase behind an already departed chord, and let the arrival of his melody notes tell us
that he knew it had been there after all. His opening chorus
on *Taxi War Dance* contains a bold enough use of such
horizontal, linear phrases to have captivated a whole generation of players, and to seem bold still.

Thus one might say that his originality was not harmonic,
but a-harmonic. He announced it on his very first recording
date in the dense and ultimately self-justifying dissonances
of *Shoe Shine Boy*, rather different from the simple harmonic ignorance of some of his predecessors. And he affirmed
it with a fine harmonic high-handedness in solos like *I Never
Knew*. In general what he did was hit the tonic chords, and
read through the others as his ear and sense of melody
dictated.

He was an exceptional sketch artist and a master of a
kind of melodic ellipsis. As Louis Gottlieb has said, he
could make one hear a scale by playing only a couple of
notes, as on his introduction to *Every Tub*.

Sometimes one even suspects a kind of perverseness, a perverseness perhaps born of a defensive introversion. He leaves
out beats other players would accent. He offers an ascending
phrase where one expects a descent. He turns a cliché inside
out. He uses melodic intervals no one else would use, in
places where one would not expect to hear them, even from
him.

But he was no mere phrase-monger. However original his phrases might be, his sense of order was sometimes exceptional. We are apt to think that the best of his solos delight us because they are so eventful that they maintain themselves only out of a kind of sustained unexpectedness and energetic surprise that somehow satisfies us. But on *One O'Clock Jump*, he begins with a light parody of the brass riff which accompanies him, and develops that parody into a melody. His first recording of *Lady Be Good* has a motific logic that is announced by his opening phrase. And a classic performance like *Lester Leaps In* is full of ideas that link melodically, one to the next. Perhaps the great example of this is his playing on *Jive at Five*. Every phrase of that beautiful solo has been imitated and fed back to us a hundred times in other contexts, by Lester's followers, but that knowledge only helps us to affirm the commendable decorum and the originality of the master's work, whenever we return to it.

Lester Young could directly reinterpret a simple, traditional idea, as he does in his clarinet solos on *Pagin' the Devil* and *Blues for Helen*. And he could play jazz counterpoint—as with Buck Clayton on *Way Down Yonder in New Orleans* and *Them There Eyes*, or with Billie Holiday on *Me, Myself and I* and *He's Funny That Way*—in such a way as to make one reassess all New Orleans and Dixieland jazz one has ever heard. He is—or he should be—the despair of his imitators as much as Basie the pianist should be.

We have few examples of Lester Young's slow blues playing from the years with Basie, and almost every one of them makes us wish we had more. Besides *Pagin' the Devil* and *Blues for Helen* there is a beautifully simple chorus on a never re-released Sammy Price pick-up date, *Things About Coming My Way*; and the accompaniments to Jimmy Rushing on both *Blues in the Dark* (before Ed Lewis takes over to reproduce Armstrong's *Gully Low Blues* solo) and on

I Left My Baby. The last is especially remarkable because
Lester Young imitates crying almost literally, yet aesthetically.

In 1939 Lester Young contributed a beautiful saxophone
theme on the slow blues *Nobody Knows,* and under his
guidance the sax section plays it, curving and bending its
notes with the plaintive depth of Lester himself. And in
1940 he provided the Basie orchestra with an original theme
called, with typical innocence, *Tickle Toe,* on which he had
the group play a melodic line in eighth-notes. On this basis,
one might have hoped for even further changes in style
within the large jazz ensemble itself, with Lester Young
showing the way.

His temperament was not universal. Indeed one sometimes feels he was gaily gentle to the point of deliberate
innocence and innocent to the point of self-delusion. Yet his
musical personality is so strong that, while one is in its presence, little else exists. He did create a world in which one
can believe fully, but when his personal world came in touch
with the real one, we know that the results might be tragic.
The Lester Young of 1943, after he left Basie briefly and
returned, was a somewhat different player, for some of the
leaping energy was gone. And the Lester Young who returned from Army service in late 1945 was a very different
player and man.

Young once indicated that he spent his early days with
Basie exploring the upper range of his horn, "alto tenor,"
as he put it. His middle days on "tenor tenor." And his last
years, on the low notes of "baritone tenor." Beyond question, his creative energy descended as he descended the
range of his horn, and his rhythmic sense gradually became
that of a tired and finally exhausted man. But there are
compensations, as perhaps there were bound to be from a
soloist of his brilliance. Slow balladry was seldom allowed

him in the years with the Basie orchestra, but his post-Basie years produced the superb musings of *These Foolish Things*. And, perhaps inevitably, they also produced a further extension of his blues language with the profoundly ironic, melancholy joy of *Jumpin' with Symphony Sid*, with its touches of be-bop phrasing, and the resignation of *No Eyes Blues*.

I suppose that any man who loves Lester's music will have favorite recordings from his later years in which something of his youthful energy was recaptured. Mine are from a 1949 session which produced *Ding Dong* and *Blues 'n' Bells*. Incidentally, the "cool" tenor players seem to have liked the later piece too, for it contains almost the only phrases from Young's later career which they borrowed.

Lester Young created a new aesthetic for jazz but, whatever one says about his rhythmic originality, about his expansion of the very sound of jazz music, about his elusive sense of solo structure, he was a great original melodist, like all great jazzmen. Great Lester Young solos—*When You're Smiling* with Teddy Wilson, or *You Can Depend on Me*, or *Way Down Yonder in New Orleans*—are self-contained. They seem to make their own rules of order and be their own excuse for being.

9

CHARLIE PARKER

The Burden of Innovation

It is still possible to discuss Bix Beiderbecke as a musician, although he has been dead for over thirty years. When Charlie Parker had been dead less than a year they still spoke of him often, but it became more and more unusual for anyone to discuss his music. They were beginning to speak of him as a god, perhaps because it saved them the trouble of reflecting either on his playing or on his life. Some prayed to him as a saint, but surely a saint must have a clear self-knowledge and acceptance of his destiny. Some say, in paranoid *non sequiturs* that pass for insight, that he was destroyed by big business and advertising. An uptown barkeep mutters, "I got no use for a man who abuses his talent." They proclaim, "Bird never practiced." (But he *did* practice, of course, and in his youth he practiced day and night.) They say of the more careless performances and the reed squeaks, "He was a man in a hurry." Perhaps he once said it better: "I was always in a panic." His friends say, "You had to pay your dues to know him." In a sense you have to pay them even to listen to him. Perhaps that is as it should be.

A Negro celebrity has said that Charlie Parker represented individuality and freedom. It is hard to know exactly what

he meant, for surely there was very little true individuality
in the life of the man, so constantly was he, it seems, the
victim of his own passions.

Parker was indeed a complex being, yet his personal life
seems to have been a chaos in which moments of perceptive
kindness vied with moments of panic and rage, moments
of gentleness contrasted with moments of suspicion. The
opposites in him were indeed far apart, tragically far apart.
But his music, for all its freshness, its expanded emotion
and its liberated feeling, its originality, its seemingly un-
ending invention, at its best presented an image of unexpectedly subtle and complex order and wholeness.

In his one chorus improvisation on *Embraceable You*,
Parker barely glances at Gershwin's melody. He begins with
an interesting six-note phrase which he then uses five times
in a row, pronouncing it variously and moving it around
to fit the harmonic contours of Gershwin's piece. On its
fifth appearance the six-note motive forms the beginning
of a delicate thrust of melody which dances along, pauses
momentarily, resumes, and finally comes to rest balanced
at the end with a variant of that same six-note phrase. From
this point on, Parker's solo interweaves that opening musical
motive in remarkable permutations and in unexpected
places. Sometimes he subtracts notes from it, changes notes
within it, adds notes to it. But it is the core of his improvisation, and, speaking personally, I have seldom listened to this
chorus without realizing how ingeniously that phrase is
echoed in Parker's remarkable melody.

I think we sense such subtle musical order even though we
may not hear it directly. Of course that order has nothing
to do with repetitiousness. It represents a kind of organization and development quite beyond popular song writing.
It fulfills the sort of compositional premise which a composer might take hours to work out on his own, but Parker

simply stood up and improvised the chorus. And a few moments later, at the same recording session, he stood up and played another chorus in the same piece, quite differently organized and, if not quite a masterpiece like the first, an exceptional improvisation nevertheless.

Improvisation has a meaning of its own; if we know that a piece of music is being at least partly made up for us on the spot, that we are attending the act of creation, we hear that music with special receptivity. But in the final analysis, an improvised music needs to be improvised well, and the final defense of improvisation in jazz is that the best jazzmen can improvise superbly; they can compete with less spontaneous melodists and even surpass them.

Of course, I am not contending that creating melodic order by a recurring motive, by "imitation," is new in jazz. And I am not contending that it is new with jazz, but I do believe jazzmen rediscovered it for themselves. Some of King Oliver's best solos (let us say *Dippermouth Blues*) use recurring motives and develop sequential phrases exceptionally well. Nor am I contending that the approach always works. There is a first take of *Hallelujah*, with Charlie Parker as a sideman in a Red Norvo group, on which he seems repetitiously and monotonously hung up on a single idea. But hear the second take of *Hallelujah*.

The six-note phrase is not the only principle of organization on Parker's first *Embraceable You*. The chorus begins simply and lyrically, gradually becomes more intricate, with longer chains of melody involving shorter notes, to balance itself at the end with a return to simple lyricism—a kind of curve upward and then downward. The second take of *Embraceable* has quite different contours, as Parker alternates the simple lyric phrases with more complex, virtuoso lines, and variations in light and shade, light and shade.

A great deal of misinformation has been put into print

about music in which Parker was a major figure. It was at
first called, onomatopoetically, be-bop, then modern jazz. It
has been said that the boppers often made their compositions
by adopting the chord sequences of standard popular songs
and writing new melody lines to them. So they did, and so
had at least two generations of jazzmen before them. It has
been said that they undertook the similar practice of improvising with only a chord sequence as their guide, with
no reference to a theme melody itself—in classicist terms
"harmonic variations," in the terms of jazz critic André
Hodeir "chorus phrase." But the practice had become a
norm and commonplace by the late 'thirties to men like
Teddy Wilson, Henry "Red" Allen, Roy Eldridge, Johnny
Hodges, Ben Webster, Lester Young, Coleman Hawkins,
Charlie Christian, and hundreds of others; indeed one might
say that in their work it had reached a kind of deadlock of
perfection. For that matter, one can find choruses of nonthematic improvising in the recordings of players who were
leaders in the 'twenties and earlier—Louis Armstrong, Earl
Hines, Bix Beiderbecke, Jack Teagarden, Sidney Bechet,
even Bunk Johnson.

The practices are, basically, as old as the blues. Certainly
King Oliver's three classic 1923 choruses on *Dippermouth
Blues* have no thematic reference to the melody of that
piece. One might say that jazz musicians spent the late
'twenties and the 'thirties discovering that they could "play
the blues" on chords of *Sweet Sue, I Ain't Got Nobody,
Sweet Georgia Brown, You're Driving Me Crazy, I Got
Rhythm, Tea for Two,* and the rest.

What Parker and be-bop provided was a renewed musical
language (or at least a renewed dialect) with which the old
practices could be replenished and continued. The renewed
language came, in part, as have all innovations in jazz, from
an assimilation of devices from European music. But a

deliberate effort to import "classical" harmony or melodic devices might have led jazzmen to all sorts of affectation and spuriousness.

Like Louis Armstrong before him, Charlie Parker was called on to change the language of jazz, to reinterpret its fundamentals and give it a way to continue. He did that with a musical brilliance that was irrevocable. But he did it simply by following his own artistic impulses, and Parker's innovations represent a truly organic growth for jazz and have little to do with the spurious impositions of a self-consciously "progressive" jazzman.

The music of Charlie Parker and Dizzy Gillespie represented a way for jazz to continue, but that way was not just a matter of new devices; it also had to do with a change in even the function of the music. Parker's work implied that jazz could no longer be thought of only as an energetic background for the barroom, as a kind of vaudeville, as a vehicle for dancers. From now on it was somehow a music to be listened to, as many of its partisans had said it should have been all along. We will make it that, Parker seemed to say, or it will perish. The knowledge that he was sending it along that road must have been at times a difficult burden to carry.

Today we are apt to see Parker as the most important of the pioneer modernists, chiefly because his influence has proved more general, widespread, and lasting; and because, for most of his brief and falling-star career, his talent grew and his invention seemed constant. Rightly or wrongly, we are apt to think of Dizzy Gillespie's influence as chiefly on brassman, Parker's on everyone. And we know that Thelonious Monk's ideas were rather different from either Parker's or Gillespie's, and that their real importance would emerge only later.

It is perhaps hard for some of us to realize now, so long after the fact, what a bitter controversy modern jazz brought about, but it is instructive to look briefly at that controversy.

Among other things, its opponents declared that the modernists had introduced harmonic values that were alien to jazz. Well, once jazz has embraced European harmony in any aspect, as it did far longer ago than 1900, it has by implication embraced it all, as long as the right players came along to show just how it could be unpretentiously included and assimilated into the jazz idiom. But the curiousness of this argument is clearly dramatized in the fact that bop's opponents are apt to approve of pianist Art Tatum and tenor saxophonist Don Byas, both of whom were harmonically as sophisticated and knowledgeable as Parker and Gillespie. But Byas does not really *sound* like a modernist, because rhythmically he is not a modernist. And rhythm is the crux of the matter.

The crucial thing about the be-bop style is that its basis came from the resources of jazz itself, and it came about in much the same way that innovation had come about in the past. That basis is rhythmic, and it involves rhythmic subdivision. Any other way would surely have been disastrous. We should not talk about harmonic exactness or passing chords and the rest before we have talked about rhythm.

Like Louis Armstrong, Charlie Parker expanded jazz rhythmically and, although his rhythmic changes are intricately and subtly bound up with his ideas of harmony and melody, the rhythmic change is fundamental. "Be-bop," however unfortunate a name for the music, does represent it rhythmically and hence rather accurately, much as "swing" accurately represents the rhythmic momentum that Armstrong introduced.

We may say that Armstrong's rhythms are based on a quarter-note. Parker's idea of rhythm is based on an eighth-note. Of course I am speaking of melodic rhythm, the rhythm that the players' accents make as they offer their melodies, not of the basic time or the basic percussion.

For that matter, to speak of rhythm, melodic line, and harmony as if they were entities is a critic's necessary delusion. But such separations can clarify much. To many ears attuned to the music of Coleman Hawkins or Buck Clayton and the rhythmic conceptions they use, Parker's music seemed at first pointlessly fussy and decorative—a flurry of technique. Players at first found Parker's sophisticated blues lines like *Relaxin' At Camarillo* and *Billie's Bounce* almost impossible to play, not because of their notes but because their strong melodic lines demanded such a fresh way of accenting and phrasing. But once one is in touch with Parker rhythmically, every note becomes direct, functional, unadorned musical expression. And of course I am giving only a rough rule of thumb; each style is more complex than such a description makes it seem. Parker, who showed that his notes and accents might land on heavy beats, weak beats, and the various places in between beats, was the most imaginative player rhythmically in jazz history, as his one dazzlingly intricate chorus on *Ornithology* might easily attest.

I do not think that one can hear the impeccable swing of a player like Lionel Hampton without sensing that some sort of future crisis was at hand in the music, that—to exaggerate only slightly—a kind of jazz as melodically dull as a set of tone drums might well be in the offing. In guitarist Charlie Christian, it seems to me, one hears both the problem and the basis for its solution, a basis which Lester Young had helped provide him with. Christian's swing was perfect. He was an outstanding melodist. And at times his rhythmic imagination carried him to the verge of some new discoveries.

To say that fresh rhythmic invention is basic to Parker's music is not to ignore the fact that he also possessed one of the most fertile harmonic imaginations that jazz has ever known. In this respect one can mention only Art Tatum in the same paragraph with him. Tatum must have been an enormous influence, one feels sure, harmonically and even in note values. But Tatum's imagination was almost exclusively harmonic, and Parker—although he had a melodic vocabulary in which (as with most musicians) certain phrases recur—was perhaps the greatest *inventor* of melodies jazz has seen.

Still, one is brought up short by the realization that a "typical" Parker phrase turns out to be much the same phrase one had heard years before from, say, Ben Webster. The secret is of course that Parker inflects, accents, and pronounces that phrase so differently that one simply may not recognize it.

What was Parker's heritage? Such questions are always vexing for so original a talent. Someone has suggested that he combined on alto the two tenor saxophone traditions: the sophisticated and precise harmonic sense of Coleman Hawkins and his follower, Don Byas; and the rhythmic originality, variety, and looseness of phrase and penchant for horizontal, linear melody of Lester Young and his follower, guitarist Charlie Christian. But the closest thing on previous jazz records to Parker's mature phrasing that I know of are a handful of Louis Armstrong's most brilliant trumpet solos—*West End Blues* from 1928, *Sweethearts On Parade* from 1930, *Between the Devil and the Deep Blue Sea* from 1931, *Basin St. Blues* from 1933. In them we clearly hear Parker's melodic rhythm in embryo. No one jazzman, not even Roy Eldridge, undertook to develop that aspect of Armstrong until Charlie Parker.

However, it is fitting that Parker's first recorded solo, on *Swingmatism* with Jay McShan, does owe so much to Lester Young. Whatever his debt to others (and to himself) for the genesis of his style, Parker had obviously absorbed Young's language soundly and thoroughly. Charlie Parker's second recorded solo is also indicative—brilliant but perhaps exasperating. On McShan's *Hootie Blues* he played what might have been a beautifully developed and rhythmically striking chorus, one which introduces almost everything Parker was to spend the rest of his life refining. But the solo is not finally satisfactory; he interrupts it in the seventh bar to interpolate a trite riff figure. Granted that he showed the sound intuition of knowing that a contrastingly simple idea was precisely right at that moment in his melody, a simply commonplace one was not.

The best introduction to Parker's music is probably his remarkable pair of choruses on *Lady Be Good*. Stylistically he begins rather conservatively, in a late swing period manner rather like Lester Young's, and he gradually transforms this into the style that Parker himself offered jazz.

These choruses are melodically fascinating in another aspect. Just as *Embraceable You* is organized around the interweaving and permutation of one melodic fragment, *Lady Be Good* uses several which emerge as the choruses unfold. Parker's first few notes are Gershwin's, but he uses these notes as the opening to quite a different melodic phrase. His second phrase is a simple riff. His third phrase echoes his opening Gershwin-esque line, but in a kind of reverse-echo reassortment of its notes, and it also has something of the character of his second riff phrase—in a sense it combines and continues both. And so on.

At the same time this brilliance was delivered in the most adverse circumstances, at a "Jazz at the Philharmonic" concert in the spring of 1946 in Los Angeles. The solo thereby refutes what is patently true, that Parker's playing really belonged only in the small improvising quintets he established as the norm. The circumstances were made even more trying by the fact that, as Parker begins to swing further away from the conventions of an earlier style, moving in his own direction, he is rewarded with a wholly unnecessary background riff from the other musicians on the stage at the time. It is apt to distract a listener, but it apparently did not distract Parker. Still, the solo is delivered with a kind of personal and technical strain and pressure in his alto sound that was foreign to Parker at his best. Almost opposite to the "classic" development of a *Lady Be Good* is another public recording made with a far more appropriate group, the Carnegie Hall concert of 1947 with Dizzy Gillespie. Here is Parker the daring romantic, using passing and altered harmonies, complex movements and countermovements of rhythm, unexpected turns of melody. Much of it is delivered with an emotional directness that makes the complexity functional and necessary. The celebrated stop-time break on *A Night in Tunisia* played on the same occasion shows Parker's intuitive sense of balance at its best: an alternation of tensions and releases so rapid, terse, and complete that it may seem to condense all of his best work into one melodic leap of four bars. One knows that on this occasion Parker was out to "get" his friend and rival Gillespie, and Gillespie was playing as if he were not to be gotten. This personal element influences the aesthetics of the music, sometimes for the worse. There was at times an edge to Parker's sound, an apparent strain.

No one who has listened with receptive ears to Charlie Parker play the blues could doubt that aspect of his authenticity as a jazzman. Nor should one fail to understand after hearing his music that the emotional basis of his work is the urban, Southwestern blues idiom that we also hear running through every performance by the Basie orchestra of the late 'thirties. *Parker's Mood* (especially take 1) is as indigenously the blues as a Bessie Smith record, more so than several James P. Johnson records. But one also senses immediately the increase in the emotional range of the idiom that Parker's technical innovations make possible.

Charlie Parker was a bluesman, a great *natural* bluesman

without calculated funkiness or rustic posturing. It has been
said that all the great jazzmen can play the blues, but that
is obviously not so. Earl Hines has played wonderful solos
in the blues form, but he doesn't have blues feeling. Neither
did James P. Johnson, Fats Waller, nor any of the classic
"stride" men. Johnny Hodges can play the blues; Benny
Carter not. But without counting, one would guess that perhaps 40 per cent of Parker's recordings were blues. The best
of them are reassessments and lyric expansions of traditional
blues phrases and ideas, ideas reevaluated by Parker's particular sensibility. The classic example is probably *Parker's
Mood*, but there are dozens of others. And his "written"
(more properly, memorized) blues melodies are also a valid
introduction to his work. On the first record date under his
own name he produced two blues. *Now's the Time* is an
obviously traditional piece (so traditional that its riff became a rhythm-and-blues hit as *The Hucklebuck*) which is
given an original twist or two by Parker, particularly in its
last couple of bars. But *Billie's Bounce* is a strikingly original, continuous twelve-bar melody, in which phrases and
fragments of phrases repeat and echo and organize the line,
and in which traditional riffs and ideas leap in and out
rephrased, reaccented, and formed into something striking,
fresh, and unequalled.

Writing was an aspect of playing to Parker. He contributed durable pieces and durable melody lines to the jazz
repertory. But likely as not, he contributed them simply by
standing up and playing them out of his head when it came
time to contribute them. A traditional or borrowed chord
structure would take care of the basic outline; his own sense
of order as an improviser would take care of melodic order;
his own melodic and rhythmic imagination would take care
of originality. *Scrapple from the Apple*, one of his best and
most influential melodies, began with the chords of *Honey-*

suckle Rose, but borrowed the bridge of *I've Got Rhythm.*
His basic repertory included the relatively complex challenges of sophisticated structures like *How High the Moon*
and *What Is This Thing Called Love.* But it also included
the simpler challenges of the blues and *I Got Rhythm.* He
met both kinds of challenges successfully, both as a player
and composer, and therein showed the range of an artist.

Parker's best piece of writing is *Confirmation,* an ingenious and delightful melody. For one thing, it is a continuous linear invention. Popular songs and jazz pieces
which use AABA song form have two parts, a main strain
and a bridge or release or middle. The main strain is repeated twice before the bridge and once after it, exactly or
almost exactly. *Confirmation* skips along beautifully with
no repeats, but with one highly effective echo phrase, until
the last eight bars and these are a kind of repeat-in-summary
to finish the line. And Parker uses the bridge of the piece
not as an interruption or interlude that breaks up or con-
trasts with its flow, but as part of its continuously developing
melody. Finally, *Confirmation* was in no way predetermined
by a chord sequence; its melody dictates one of its own. But
note that the song form dictates a cyclical harmonic under-
structure, whereas Parker's melody is relatively continuous.

One frustration with Parker's recorded work is that, although a lot of it is kept in print, the brilliant records he
made for the Dial label in 1946 and 1947 have been spo-
radically available and in a rather scattered manner. If that
were not so, and if the material were edited well, we could
hear *Bird of Paradise* evolving from three takes of *All the
Things You Are,* and we could hear the different variations
on alternate takes of *Embraceable You, Scrapple from the
Apple, Klactoveedsedsteen, Dexterity, Moose the Mooche,*
and the rest.

Also from the Dial catalogue there was a far better take

of *Quasimodo* than the one that has been made generally available on reissues. But the leaping solo on *Crazeology* tells as much as any single performance about the ease with which Parker handled harmony, rhythm, and line. *Klactoveedsedsteen* would be a wonder if only for Max Roach's drumming. It also has a breath-stopping Parker solo that at first seems built in brief spurts, placed ambiguously and vaguely around a bass line until he slides into the bridge. From that point he builds form simply by increasing complexity, and what previously seemed careless disparate fragments of melody now take their place in a firm, logically developed line.

One LP set has been issued which presents the final takes of four pieces from a highly productive recording date. There is *Moose the Mooche*, memorable not only for its writing but for Parker's bridge in the first chorus which seems to dangle us polytonally between two keys at once. There is the more tender Parker of *Yardbird Suite*, lyric in both the theme and the improvisation, understandably the favorite Parker of Lee Konitz. There is the famous fourth take of *Ornithology*, not only superb in its rhythmic ingenuity but in its alternation of long/short/long/short phrases, with some rests in between. There is *A Night in Tunisia*, with its famous unaccompanied break, and, again, the spontaneity with which Parker juggles tension and release, complexity and simplicity. There is a very different Parker on each of these pieces. He develops each in a manner he considered appropriate to the piece at hand, and those who will not allow that Parker had that kind of artistic discipline should listen carefully.

The personnel of the quintet that made Parker's 1947 records offered a fine collection of foils and counterfoils to Parker. The talent of a then still-developing and sometimes faltering Miles Davis was, in its detached lyricism, sonority, and lack of obvious virtuosity, an excellent contrast. What is perhaps more important is that, in a growing capacity for asymmetry and displacement, Davis was able to carry and refine a part of Parker's rhythmic message in a unique manner, quite opposite from Dizzy Gillespie's virtuoso approach to the idiom of "modern" jazz. Pianist Duke Jordan was a balanced melodic player. Bud Powell or John Lewis replace him on some of the Savoy records from the same period, and with the former at least, the whole group quality changes; Powell's ideas, his touch, and his strong emotion are perhaps too much like Parker's. Max Roach was at the peak of his early career in the mid 'forties. The simplest way to put it is to say that he could *play* the rhythms that Parker used and implied, and he knew exactly when and how to break up his basic pulse to complement what the soloists were doing with it. To call what he does interfering or decorative is perhaps to misunderstand not only the whole basis of this music but the function of all jazz drumming from Baby Dodds forward. Hear Roach on *Crazeology* behind the "guest" soloist on that date, trombonist J. J. Johnson, then behind Miles Davis and throughout the piece. *Klactoveedsedsteen* represents Roach's work at a peak development.

Surely one of the most interesting documents in jazz is the Savoy LP which preserves all the recorded material from the record date that produced *KoKo* and two blues we have already mentioned, *Now's the Time* and *Billie's Bounce*. It might be enough just to hear the various final performances gradually shape and reshape themselves (there are still dubious shifts of personnel—could Dizzy Gillespie really be playing all that piano on *Meandering?*) but the session was one of Parker's best, and its climax was *KoKo*. *KoKo* may seem only a fast-tempo showpiece at first, but it is not. It is a precise linear improvisation of exceptional melodic content. It is also an almost perfect example of virtuosity

and economy. Following a pause, notes fall over and between
this beat and that beat: breaking them asunder, robbing
them of any vestige of monotony; rests fall where heavy beats
once came, now "heavy" beats come between beats and on
weak beats. It has been a source book of ideas and no wonder; now that its basic innovations are more familiar, it
seems even more a great performance in itself. I know of
no other Parker solo which shows how basic and brilliant
were Parker's rhythmic innovations, not only how much
complexity they had, but how much economy they could
involve. *KoKo*, at the same time, shows how intrinsically
Parker's rhythms were bound to his sense of melody.

Parker's career on records after 1948 is a wondrous, a
frustrating, and finally a pathetic thing. It was perhaps in
some search for form beyond soloist's form, and for refuge
from the awful dependency on the inspiration and intuition
of the moment (as well as a half-willing search for popular
success) that he took on the mere *format* of strings, the *doo-
wah* vocal groups, the Latin percussive gimmicks. A major
artist can find inspiration in odd places, but Parker with
strings still includes the strings and banal writing for them.
What a perversion of "success" to place a major jazzman in
such a setting, whatever he thought about it or would admit
to feel about it! (Yet hasn't Louis Armstrong had worse,
and more often?)

There is an arrangement of *What is This Thing Called
Love?* whose triteness is gross indeed, yet Charlie Parker
plays brilliantly in it (as he usually did in that piece and
in its jazz variant, *Hot House*)—in effect he was a great,
creative musician battling pseudo-musical pleasantries. Then
there is *Just Friends*—Parker's part of it beautifully developed—which is the only one of his records he would admit
to like, and *In the Still of the Night* where he shimmers and
slithers around tritely conceived choral singing like a great

dancer in front of a chorus doing time-steps. The Latin gimmickry is not as bad, and on *Mongo Monque* Parker adjusts his own phrasing admirably. But to what end? One cannot hear Dizzy Gillespie improvise without realizing that his phrasing was influenced by his experience in rhumba bands, but Parker's is always a development of jazz and jazz rhythms. It was perfectly natural for Gillespie to use Chano Pozo, the brilliant Cuban bongo player, as a second drummer; for Parker such things remain extrinsic effects, however well he adapts himself.

What remains otherwise from those years is often an expansive soloist. One cannot hear the fluent sureness of *Chi Chi*, the easy conservatism of *Swedish Schnapps*, the developed virtuosity of *She Rote* without knowing that a major talent is enlarging and perfecting his language. And there is the celebrated excitement of *Bloomdido* and *Mohawk* on the "reunion" recordings with Gillespie. But on several of these personal successes, what a careless misunderstanding of Parker's music to involve him with a compulsive and rhythmically inappropriate drummer like Buddy Rich!

By this time, Parker created a finely developed and natural means of expression out of a high virtuosity of short notes and intricate rhythms. It is from this Parker that Cannonball Adderley learned, much as it was from the earlier Parker that Sonny Stitt learned.

Even in the midst of the orderliness of Parker's best solos we sometimes return to the proposition that a lot of Parker's work is oddly incomplete. Sometimes a solo will leave us with a feeling of suspense rather than one of order restored or even of passion spent. Parker fulfilled a mission, surely, to salvage a music and set it on its course. Perhaps he was also the victim of that mission. In any case, one wonders if he really fulfilled his talent even as one hears recordings on which he is so brilliant.

Perhaps to Charlie Parker invention sometimes came too easily, or perhaps he was tortured by its constancy. Perhaps, on the other hand, he did rely too completely on the intuitive impulse of the moment; it was his strong point, and he may therefore have come to believe it was his only point. Perhaps it was. When he could blow everyone else away just by standing up and playing, he admitted hearing no call to any other kind of challenge, and thereby he may have been persuaded to take on the spurious challenge of flirting with popularity by standing in front of those strings. In his utter dependency, night after night, on the inspiration he drew from the act of playing itself, in his frequent refusals to coast and determination always to invent, he may have given himself the kind of challenge that no man of sensitivity could answer without inviting disaster. Or perhaps Parker the man might have learned from the liberation *with* order and proportion that we can hear in Parker the musician.

I have said that Parker and his associates not only involved a replenishment of the jazz language, but that they proposed a change in the function of the music. Players undertook the former simply because they could, because they heard the music that way and therefore had to play it that way. There can be no question that they succeeded in permanently replenishing the jazzman's vocabulary and usage. But they undertook to bring about the change in the function of jazz a little more deliberately and a lot more self-consciously, and there remains a question of whether or not they succeeded. There was and is relatively little ballroom or social dancing done to modern jazz, but for a large segment of its audience it is not quite an art music or a concert music. It remains by and large still something of a barroom atmosphere music. And perhaps a failure to establish a new function and milieu for jazz was, more than anything else, the personal tragedy of the members of the be-bop generation.

New Orleans jazz began as a communal activity, played by men who were not professionals. The transition from such a communal music to a musical vaudeville was not too difficult. The early modernists wanted to take still another step, but as performers they had little or no tradition on which to draw in making that step: they had few traditions of presentation, of personal conduct before an audience, of stage manner, even of programming, to guide them. They did not favor the hoopla presentations of the vaudeville stage, and, I suspect, they did not want to borrow outright the stuffiness of the contemporary concert hall. On the one hand, they repudiated what they thought of as the grinning and eye-rolling of earlier generations of jazzmen; on the other, they sometimes refused to make even a polite bow to acknowledge the applause of their listeners. At the same time some of them, Parker included, apparently courted a public success and a wide following that were defined in much the same terms as the popular success of some of their predecessors.

But if they had little tradition on which to draw in presentation, they had a rich one on which to draw musically. I think they treated that musical tradition honorably, and obviously they left it richer still.

10

THELONIOUS MONK

Modern Jazz in Search of Maturity

The rediscovery of Thelonious Monk in the late 'fifties is surely a curious event in the admittedly short history of jazz. The fan and trade press, which once dismissed his recordings with a puzzled or scornful two or three "stars," began to wax enthusiastic at the slightest provocation and listed his name in popularity polls where it had seldom appeared before. Musicians who once dismissed him as having long since made his small contribution to jazz listened attentively for ways out of the post-bop dilemmas. They found that his music had continued to develop through the years of his neglect, that it provided a highly personal summary and synthesis of fifteen years of modern jazz, and that it suggested sound future paths as well. And a public which had once barely heard of this man with the intriguing name soon began to buy his records and attend his public appearances.

It is fitting that so unusual a thing in jazz as belated discovery should have come to so unusual a man as Monk. Monk's is one of the most original, self-made talents. Unlike almost every other jazzman, Monk was not only a productive musician after more than fifteen years of musical activity, but seemed still to be a growing artist exploring his talent and extending his range. Such a thing does not just happen in this music, one is apt to say; if a jazzman can simply maintain the level of his first maturity, he is exceptional. Monk's first recordings were not released until 1947 and are ours by accident. Jerry Newman was "on location" in the back room at Minton's Playhouse in 1941 to record guitarist Charlie Christian, and, above the din and through the low fidelity, he happened to take down some accompaniments and solos by Thelonious Monk. As it turned out, the two solos he subsequently issued indicate the basis for much of what was to come. On *Topsy* (called *Swing to Bop* on the LP recording) Monk plays a solo based on the melody itself; on *Stompin' at the Savoy* he improvises on the chords of the tune but with an original, harmonic, and rhythmic looseness. His "comping" (complementing) accompaniments and those of drummer Kenny Clarke sometimes involve unusual displacements of the regular four-beat pulse of the performance and of the period.

The style of the *Savoy* solo is curious: it stems more or less from Teddy Wilson's fluent, many-noted approach. That solo, the ones he recorded with Coleman Hawkins in 1944, and such later variations as those on *Straight No Chaser* and *Who Knows*, should answer the question of Monk's "technique." Obviously Monk has sacrificed techniques of manual dexterity for techniques of expressiveness—for the techniques of music, specifically of his own music.

Not that Monk's whole-tone runs are easy to play, with the unorthodox fingering that gives him the sound he wants. Not that his fast successions of ringing note clusters built on fourths are easy either. But Monk's virtuosity, and he has real virtuosity, has developed in the specific techniques of jazz. As when Monk offers a simultaneous, "inside" trill with the first fingers of his right hand, while playing melody notes with his outer fingers. Or when Monk actually *bends* a piano note: offers, by a special manipulation of fingers, piano keys, and foot pedal, a true blue note, a curving piano sound, not two tied notes or a momentary resort to minor. Or most important, in the virtuosity of Monk's jazz rhythm.

When the records with Hawkins were released in 1944, Monk's introductions and solos on *Flying Hawk* and *On the Bean* (based on *Whispering*) showed that an original talent was emerging. But the records were obscure, had limited distribution, and were pressed on fragile wartime material with extremely poor surfaces.

Thus Monk was known about long before he had really been heard by anyone but a handful of musicians and insiders. He was always named as one of those who had contributed to the evolution of the be-bop style of the mid-'forties during those jam sessions at Minton's, but it was fate that he happened to be there—Monk had been hired as the "house pianist."

Monk did not record again until 1947 when the series for Blue Note records began. Meanwhile, whatever the truth of the matter, it seemed that be-bop was a kind of virtuoso style full of fast tempos, cascading and jerky melodies, rapid runs of short notes, and was based on a certain few linear and chordal devices. In this setting, Monk's records were received with puzzlement and confusion; he did not seem to compose or play the way it had been decided he should. There is hardly a bop cliché in the whole early Monk series, and the ones that do appear are either deliberate parodies (like *Humph*) or they are in two pieces Monk himself did not write. Whatever his contributions to bop had been, Monk was not a bopper. He had been working on something else all along. Today, those Monk recordings, 1947–52, seem among the most significant and original in modern jazz.

In the first place, they establish for jazz a major composer —the first that jazz had had since Ellington—and one whose best work extends the concept of composition in the idiom. In speaking of his writing, the usual procedure is to point out that *'Round Midnight* is a beautiful piece and has long been a jazz standard, and to say that *Straight No Chaser, I Mean You, Ruby My Dear, Off Minor, Well You Needn't, Epistrophy,* etc. have been used by other jazzmen and groups. Popularity often determines value for the bookkeepers of jazz. But not all of these seem the most significant works in the series. It is in pieces like *Four In One, Eronel, Evidence, Misterioso,* and *Criss Cross* that the real import of Monk's composing emerges.

The ragtime pieces of Scott Joplin and James Scott are instrumentally conceived in comparatively simple ways. So are the best jazz works of Morton and Ellington instrumental *compositions,* not "tunes" and certainly not "songs." In modern jazz, most of Charlie Parker's best pieces are instrumental lines whose purpose is to set up a chord structure for improvising (most frequently a borrowed chord structure).

Joplin leaned heavily on the tradition of European and American folk dance melodies, polkas, and marches; Morton leaned on the same tradition. Ellington often works within the idiom of American (or more properly, Vinnese-derived) show tunes. Even when Monk writes within the framework of a thirty-two-bar, AABA song form, his conception is not only instrumental but compositional; he writes for instruments in the jazz idiom. Even when Monk borrows a popular song's chord structure, he transmutes it compositionally. Perhaps the best approach to this aspect of his music are his blues pieces. While they are as fundamental as Jimmy Yancey's, they have absorbed and transmuted the vocal background of the blues, and have gone beyond the facile excitement of the riff-style blues, restoring and extending the instrumental conception of such pieces as Morton's *Dead Man Blues* and Ellington's *Ko-Ko.*

Try to hum *Misterioso.* The instrumental quality of

Monk's writing is easy to grasp, the best rule of thumb being that we come away, not wanting to hum such pieces so much as wanting to hear them played again.

The compositional aspect is most succinctly revealed in the fact that the melody and the harmony of a good Monk piece do not, almost cannot, exist separately. In order to play Monk's pieces well, one must know the melody and Monk's harmony, know how they fit together and understand why. Most of Monk's melodies are so strong and important and his bass lines (even those bass lines that are fairly simple, straightforward or traditional) so integrated with their structures that it is almost impossible for a soloist to improvise effectively on their chord sequences alone: he will do better also to understand their themes well and, one way or another, make use of them. When Monk uses AABA song form in things like *In Walked Bud* or *I Mean You*, he is often careful to integrate the B, release, or "bridge" melody by basing it on an elaboration or development of bits of the final phrases of the A part.

It is even more striking that a close look at Monk's pieces shows that they are often unexpected elaborations, extensions, recastings of simple musical phrases, traditional jazz phrases, sometimes even clichés. This is obviously true of pieces like *Epistrophy, Shuffle Boil, Straight No Chaser*, but it is also less obviously true of pieces like *Misterioso* and *Criss Cross*.

Monk's sense of form is innate and natural, and therefore extends beyond composition to performance. Monk had perhaps no less a sense of group form than had Jelly Roll Morton or Duke Ellington, but in his smaller groups the form is looser and more spontaneous—the "orchestration," one might say, is extemporaneous. Two of Monk's best compositions are, in their early recorded versions, two of the best overall performances of Monk's music. They are *Misterioso* and *Evidence*, both, one should note, done in 1948.

Misterioso opens with Monk's blues theme, a succession of "walking" sixths, and a striking reassessment of a traditional blues bass figure. It is offered by Milt Jackson and Monk, the bass and drums phrasing with them. As the theme ends, Jackson begins to improvise on the blues, as the bass and drums begin to walk behind him, more or less conventionally now. But Monk is determined that this is not merely the blues, however beautifully Jackson can play the blues, but Monk's blues called *Misterioso*. Monk accompanies Jackson's vibraphone, not with the usual chordal comping, but in a stark, orderly, almost "melodic" pattern built on the next implied note, if you will, the "missing" note of his theme—the seventh. The sense of continuity continues in Monk's own improvisation which is built around a commanding ascending figure, echoing the upward movement of the main theme. When that theme returns at the end of the performance, Jackson carries it, with the rhythm once more phrasing with him, as Monk spreads out the sevenths of his previous accompaniment across the theme, in melodic and rhythmic counterpoint. Monk thus ties together all elements of the performance in a strikingly original, compositional, yet improvisational conclusion.

With *Evidence*, a little hindsight is an advantage; that is, the recording is even better if we know Monk's melody, at least in its later manifestations. Here it appears in Monk's introduction, darts in and out of Monk's fascinating accompaniment to Jackson's solo, is held in abeyance during Monk's relatively conventional solo. Then at the end of the performance, in the interplay between Monk and Jackson, this apparently jagged, disparate, intriguing tissue of related sounds has at last emerged, but not quite—a theme of great strength and almost classic beauty for all its asymmetry and surprise.

On *Criss Cross*, done in 1951, Monk allows the firmness of his harmonies and the percussive accents of Art Blakey to carry the performance once the opening theme is stated and the solos take over. But as the last soloist, Monk himself (entering at a quite unexpected point, by the way) realized it was time to reassert the claims of continuity and form, time to begin rebuilding his theme. He suggests it and then improvises on it more directly, preparing for its restatement. *Criss Cross* is perhaps Monk's classic piece, the one which above all others extends the idea of jazz as an instrumental music.

The early records also place Monk's piano style historically and establish his heritage in jazz. His earlier Wilsonesque solos don't fit that picture too well. Even if it were not for the stride bass line sections in *April in Paris* and the near-parody *Thelonious*, it should be clear that Monk's style (like Ellington's, a jazz influence whose later development has been strikingly parallel to Monk's) is a development of the style of Harlem stride men like James P. Johnson, Willie "the Lion" Smith, Fats Waller, and the rest.

The link between pianists like James P. and Monk is Count Basie. Basie's earliest work is either Earl Hines piano or Fats Waller stride piano, but in the 'thirties he modified or dropped the stated beat of his bass line and developed a rhythmic variety which modified the regular (not to say monotonous) accents of the Harlem school.

We are always brought up a bit short when a phrase or a quality in Monk's playing reminds us of these earlier stride players, because their work depends so much on the regular fulfillment of the expected. Monk's (like Lester Young's) depends on making the surprise twist, the sardonically witty phrase, and the unexpected rhythmic movement seem fitting and inevitable once one has heard them. Monk is authentically a blues man, as none of the older stride men were.

Monk, like the other great jazz composers, is a unique and largely unorthodox accompanist. He forms a frequently "simple," polyrhythmic and nearly polyphonic, horn-like line *between* the percussion (bass and drums) and the soloist or front line horns. Even when Monk does "comp" chordally, he is a subliminal melodist. The best introduction to his very personal approach is probably his accompaniments to Milt Jackson, with whom he works excellently. And as we have seen, such accompaniments involve something that was noticed in his work only later: Monk can hold both performances and inspiration together by the continuity he gives to his accompaniments. He is a kind of improvising orchestrator.

The only American critic who understood Monk in the 'forties was Paul Bacon, who wrote:

> His kind of playing isn't something that occurred to him whole . . . beyond its undoubted originality, it has the most expressive and personal feeling I can find in any musician playing now. It has cost Monk something to play as he does—not recognition so much . . . I believe his style has cost him 50 per cent of his technique. He relies so much on absolute musical reflex that Horowitz's style might be unequal to the job. . . . What he has done, in part, is quite simple. He hasn't invented a new scheme of things, but he has, for years too, looked with an unjaundiced eye at music and seen a little something else. . . . At any rate, Monk is making use of all the unused space around jazz and he makes you feel there are plenty of unopened doors.

As a matter of fact, to make his playing as personally expressive as he wished, Monk had even altered his way of striking the keys, his finger positions, and had largely converted his piano into a kind of horn which was also capable of stating harmonic understructures. And he did not fake, doodle, decorate, or play notes only to fill out bars or fill time.

The core of Monk's style is a rhythmic virtuosity. He is a master of displaced accents, shifting meters, shaded delays, and anticipations. Therefore he is a master of effective pause and of meaningfully employed space, rest, and silence. Fundamentally all of his innovations in harmony and line are organized around his innovations in rhythm. And as rhythm is fundamental to jazz, so one who develops its rhythms also develops jazz along just the lines that its own nature implies it should go. The work of Lennie Tristano and his pupils and of the "cool" post-Lester Young tenormen shows, I think, that if attempts to impose innovations in harmony and melodic line are not intrinsically bound to innovations in rhythm they risk distorting some secret but innate balance in the nature of jazz.

Actually, I am not sure that the term "harmony" is accurate when applied to Monk; he seems much more interested in sound and in original and arresting combinations of sounds percussively delivered, than in harmony per se. And this aspect has also saved him from the neo-Debussyan sentimentalities of many of his fellow modern jazz pianists. When he undertakes an unlikely popular ditty like *You Took the Words Right Out of My Heart*, he keeps the performance fairly straightforward melodically, except for Monkish nuances of accent and dynamics, but he pivots almost every sound around a single tonic note. Monkian alchemy somehow distills granite from sugar water.

In the early 'fifties, Monk's music and his recordings were even more misunderstood and ignored than before—after all, hadn't the question been settled that Monk had little to offer? But the records show that Monk was still productive and still growing.

He had not before recorded so obviously earthy a blues as *Blue Monk*. *Think of One* is, like the earlier *Thelonious*, ingeniously built on the metrical-accentual variations and harmonizations of one note. Pieces like *Nutty, Reflections, We See,* and *Gallop's Gallop* have melodies that maintain the good standards of *Introspection, Ask Me Now,* etc. *Trinkle Tinkle,* like *Four in One,* is built on the ingenious twisting of a virtuoso run of short notes. *Let's Call This,* one of his most satisfying lyric melodies, again achieves the truly Promethean task of being (in terms of jazz harmonies) continuous throughout, technically unresolved until its thirty-second bar, but emotionally full and complete.

Perhaps the greatest achievement of the time is Monk's exceptional 1954 recomposition of Jerome Kern's "tune" *Smoke Gets In Your Eyes* into a piece for instruments. One might call the performance a miniature concerto, with Monk's improvising piano leading the horns in their written parts, but with both sharing in the total effect. The additions that Monk makes to the original are not embellishments but integral parts of a recomposition, a new piece based on *Smoke Gets In Your Eyes.* Monk's splitting of the theme, his altered chords, his deeply forceful playing, his implicit humor, his commitment only to the best aspects of the original, rid it of its prettiness and its sentimentality and leave it with only its implicit beauty.

When Monk's solo on take 1 of *Bags' Groove* (1954) and his recital *"The Unique Monk"* appeared (1956), the re-evaluation of his work had begun. These recordings made more obvious what had been true all along: in Monk's work the changes in the melody, harmony, and rhythm of modern jazz were being ordered and organized. Monk was apparently the first modernist in whose work elements of the style were assimilated enough so that they could begin to be used in a musical continuity, beyond the requisite continuity and order of a good soloist. Far from being "difficult" and "obscure" or "eccentric," Monk's performances were logical and structured. And so was the music of his groups.

His work had obviously long had a sense of *emotional* completeness. Perhaps the highest tribute I have ever heard paid to Monk's music was offered by a novice who said, after first hearing recordings by Bud Powell, Parker, and Monk: "Monk seems to finish things, to get them all said. I feel satisfied and sort of full when one of his things is over."

Monk's long improvisation *Bags' Groove* is based on the sustained exploration of a single musical idea and on an ingenious use of rhythm and silence. It is a strikingly spare, suspended, hardly self-accompanied line, full of musical space and air, but it soon appears that Monk has brilliantly elaborated his opening phrase into a continuum of variations, turning it this way, that way, rephrasing it to fewer notes, elaborating it with more notes, hinting at contrasting phrases, but returning to the original, and all the while suggesting rhythmic patterns perhaps yet unheard.

A similar but less subtle *tour de force* is Monk's first version of *Functional*, a sustained nine minutes of original variations on a traditional six-note blues phrase.

The improvisations on the LP *"The Unique Monk"* are rhythmic and thematic variations in interrelated, developing sets, based directly on the melodies of standard popular tunes. *Just You, Just Me* is exemplary for its continuity. The version of *Tea for Two* also brings Monk's otherwise subtly penetrating but pervasive humor to the fore. Monk approaches the piece in parody, beginning as if he were doing a wildly witty version of an old-style jazz pianist. But soon one realizes that the joke is not so much on jazz as it is on the kind of listener who thinks that the jazz pianist is someone who plays a ditty like *Tea for Two* in a corny, ricky-tick style. However, everything Monk is playing is entirely and unfrivolously musical. And by the end, Monk has converted the respectful joke into a performance of Pirandello-like dramatic seriousness and penetrating melancholy, in a brilliant stroke.

Monk's penchant for making his variations directly on a theme itself in a sense echoes earlier practice: the embellishment styles of the 'twenties, as continued by Art Tatum, and the probing melodic paraphrases of Louis Armstrong. But Monk has his own perceptive ability in getting inside a melody to seek out its implications; he can elaborate, expand, reduce, or abstract a theme to an intriguing sketch and tissue of notes. At the same time he approaches a standard piece, as we have seen, not as a melody plus harmony, but as a point of departure for a two-handed, semi-improvised composition for piano, a logical, self-contained succession of unique pianistic, musical sounds.

We have spoken of Monk's sense of form as a composer, as leader of a group performing a semi-improvised music, and as an extended soloist. But orderliness is innate with him, and we ought to make at least a brief mention of Monk's more inventive, nonthematic variations. There is a two-chorus solo by Monk on *I Mean You,* as a "guest" with the Art Blakey Jazz Messengers, that has a striking inner logic. Monk bases his first chorus on a descending motif which he handles variously. The second chorus he bases on a brief, contrasting riff figure, which is turned several ways, is subjected to a counter-riff or two, and finally is complemented by a descending fragment which alludes to the first chorus and ties the two together. Once again Monk's music benefits from Blakey's presence and rapport, as it had on *Four in One, Criss Cross, Eronel, Blue Monk, Just You, Just Me, Tea for Two,* and the rest.

In the immediate foreground of Monk's rediscovery and subsequent popularity was an engagement with a quartet— Monk; John Coltrane, tenor saxophone; Wilbur Ware, bass; and Shadow Wilson, drums—at a New York club called the Five Spot during the summer of 1957. It was surely one of the most important and exhilarating events in jazz history. The group did record three selections, strong experiences and exceptional jazz, even if they are not as good as the performances one heard those summer nights at the Five Spot, when each man played with great enthusiasm, at the peak of his abilities, and through Monk's music each discovered and expanded his potential.

The leader and his saxophonist had exceptional emotional rapport. Technically they were something of a contrast. John Coltrane's techniques are obvious; Monk's piano techniques more subtle. And at the same time that Coltrane, with showers of notes and scalar "sheets of sound," seemed to want to break up jazz rhythms into an evenly spaced and fairly constant succession of short notes, Monk seemed to want more complexity, subtlety, and freedom. Monk is a melodist; his harmonies are intrinsic but his playing is ultimately linear and horizontal in its effect. Coltrane played vertically; he found harmonic stimulation in Monk's music, and he seemed to know where Monk was headed, as well as where he *was*, as very few players did then. But he also knew, as the recording of *Ruby, My Dear* shows, that Monk's melodies are strong and that it isn't enough merely to run their chords. Monk's pieces often disciplined Coltrane and ordered his explorations as weaker material did not. *Ruby* is a knowingly embellished performance, and Coltrane's opening solo finishes with a beautiful, Monkish effect of suspension. Monk's decision to begin his own solo with a lightly implied double-time was a beautiful stroke of musical contrast: Coltrane's many notes at a slow tempo, then Monk's fewer notes at a faster tempo.

Wilbur Ware was, like Monk, a melodist also able to find surprise twists in a use of traditional materials. Wilson, whose work once had the even smoothness of a Jo Jones, responded to Monk's music with some appropriate polyrhythmic comments.

Monk got a variety of textures from his four pieces, by

playing with the saxophonist, by playing contrapuntally against him, by "laying out" and leaving him to the bassist and drummer: sometimes to one of them predominantly, other times equally to both.

On their version of *Nutty*, Coltrane having strayed further and more elaborately into the harmonic implications of the piece, the composer typically enters for his own solo with an eloquent reestablishment of the theme in paraphrase.

He does the same on *Trinkle Tinkle*, with an even more intriguing recasting of that intricate melody. *Trinkle* is the best of the recorded performances by the group. Its melody, unlike most of Monk's melodies, is conceived perhaps a bit too pianistically to be fully effective on saxophone. But at the same time, its somewhat scalar quality suits Coltrane's style. The spontaneous interplay between Monk and Coltrane in the performance is exceptional, but Monk's intuitive logic in knowing just when to stop it and let the saxophonist stroll alone against bass and drums is intuitive perfection.

From this point on, Monk was heard and reheard carefully and widely. What could be so "difficult" about a man who often based his variations on melodies themselves? And what is so difficult about an improvisation based not on melody but on a chord sequence, if it worked out the single phrase or idea that it announced when it opened? In the face of this kind of basic continuity, what trouble could his unusual revoicings of chords and his rhythmic displacements cause? A listener who can follow a melody, and who is not put off by Monk's uncompromising emotion, need not know immediately how intrinsic are the harmonies and rhythms Monk uses. Form will guide him eventually to sense those things.

Brilliant Corners showed the innovative Monk still at work. Its basis is the alteration of the tempos; the piece is

constructed so that it is equally effective played slowly and
then exactly twice as fast, in a way that the abrupt shift in
pace does not interrupt the flow of the performance. It succeeds, partly because its melody notes dart about at unac-
customed intervals so that the changes of tempo are almost
anticipated by the nature of the melodic line. In turn each
player—Sonny Rollins, Monk, Ernie Henry, and Max Roach
—is required to improvise at the alternate speed but has to
keep the performance continuous.

Monk's *I Should Care* is perhaps his piano solo masterpiece and one of the most uniquely pianistic performances
in all recorded jazz. Monk once more transmutes a popular
song into a composition for piano. And in turn, he conceives
this composition as a striking, resourceful tissue of unique
piano sounds, in a kind of free tempo in which each phrase
seems to have its own momentum. Among its several virtues
I Should Care is evidence that Monk has carried the jazzman's concept of individuality of sound further than any
other player on his instrument; indeed, he has carried it
almost as far as the hornmen.

Thelonious Monk learned to explore and develop an
original and unorthodox musical talent. And he endured
years when his music suffered neglect and even disparage-
ment. Neither of those things is easy, and especially not for
an American. Then Monk was signed by a major record
company, and his appearances began to draw crowds. Today
his reputation is secure. He is faced, in short, with perhaps
the severest test of all—success. He is faced with personal
popularity, the problems of facing an audience night after
night, the problems of sidemen and of keeping the right
group together. Many a popular artist (and many a fine
one), faced with the recognition he has awaited, is tempted
to relax, admire his laurels, and pause now and then to count
the house. And during the past few years there have been
indications that Monk is all too willing to coast a bit, too.

His second version of *Bolivar Blues* does not have the anguish of the original, but Monk's solo is something of a minor wonder, moving from tripling dissonances (quasi-amateurish and quite humorous), through sustained splashes of sound which spread out in rings from a center (and echo his earlier accompaniment to tenor saxophonist Charlie Rouse on the piece), ending in quick spurts of sound that abruptly disappear beneath the surface, leaving no trace.

A new version of *Just a Gigolo*[1] condenses a range of sound into a quite brief solo performance by Monk, and again reveals, through Monk's left hand, that he belongs with the earlier Harlem stride players. Then, when his bass figures get a bit melodramatic, Monk kids them beautifully with a rattling tremolo in his right hand. *Sweet and Lovely*, another of the out-of-the-way standards in Monk's repertory, is perhaps better than his first version. He develops it to the point where his left hand boldly sings out an abstract of the melody line, while his right hand offers glittering pianistic embellishments above. On a solo version of *Body and Soul*, Monk has the daring to simplify a stride bass to the point of apparent amateurishness, yet its effect is of a powerful, incantive, yet humorous series of sound clusters, as accompaniment to a shimmeringly original paraphrase of the theme.

Then there is a new version of *Five Spot Blues*, on which an archaic triplet figure is elaborated within the traditional blues framework. It is perhaps a measure of Monk's talent that he is willing to undertake something so totally unpretentious. And yet in his solos, he stretches out that little triplet motif, then abruptly condenses it into half the space it is supposed to occupy, embellishes it until it is almost lost, then rediscovers it and restores its unapologetic simplicity.

1. A scholarly (and thoroughly unimportant) essay might be written on Monk's affinity for Bing Crosby's repertory. Or Sonny Rollins' for Al Jolson's.

Almost anyone with an ear for melody and rhythm could
almost follow him exactly, I think, yet in its small way *Five
Spot Blues* is almost a measure of his sense of order, of his
rhythmic virtuosity, his originality, and his greatness.

On a recent "in person" recording, containing the best
realization of Monk's music for a large ensemble, there is a
grand moment that shows the pianist's commitment to improvisation in his sudden, wildly witty interjections on Hall
Overton's scoring of his theme, *Epistrophy*, a piece which
Monk has obviously played many hundreds of times. And in
the same recital, there is once again his innate sense of form,
in his punctuations, his solo, and his accompaniment (particularly with Phil Woods) on *Evidence*.

It would not take too much psychological subtlety to see
what Monk's achievement means. It means that some of the
sensibilities that Parker, Gillespie, Powell, and Monk himself came upon and expressed with such masterful intuition
could be made more ordered and rational, and could be
handled with greater choice. Obviously a sense of form does
not mean conventionality or depreciation of the idiom.
Imagination, improvisation, spontaneity, and feeling—the
fact that form for the smaller groups of modern jazz is more
improvisational—these things alone might counter stylistic
rigidity. At the same time, Monk's unresting harmonic,
rhythmic, and melodic explorations have already led to
further reorganizations of jazz. And within his own idiom
Monk long continued to maintain the precarious, spiritually
dangerous status of an innovator.

But, most important, and the thing that shows that it is
all not a matter of mere "techniques," Monk at his best is a
deeply, uncompromisingly expressive player. He is not an
"entertainer"; he does not "show" us anything. Everything
he says, he says musically, directly, unadorned; he is all
music and his technique is jazz technique. His greatest im-

portance lies in the fact that Monk is an artist with an artist's deeply felt sense of life and an artist's drive to communicate the surprising and enlightening truth of it in his own way. And he has the artist's special capacity for involving us with him so that we seem to be working it all out together.

Jazz has had precious few of his kind.

11

JOHN LEWIS
AND THE MODERN JAZZ QUARTET

Modern Conservative

One could say that the Modern Jazz Quartet actually began in 1946 as the rhythm section of Dizzy Gillespie's orchestra: two years later, in fact, four titles were rather obscurely recorded by Milt Jackson, John Lewis, Kenny Clarke, Al Jackson on bass, plus Chano Pozo on Conga drum. However, in August 1951 the "Milt Jackson Quartet" assembled for a recording date, and its members decided they liked playing together. Percy Heath came in on bass for Ray Brown, Milt Jackson on vibraphone, John Lewis on piano, Kenny Clarke on drums. Lewis soon became musical director, and the group was called the Modern Jazz Quartet. Success was gradual, and the Quartet's career was interrupted several times as its members briefly took other jobs. Early in 1955, Clarke left and Connie Kay became the group's drummer.

On the early recordings the music was built primarily around Jackson's exceptional gifts as an improviser and his delight in medium and fast blues and medium-tempo ballads. The later recordings show the effects of John Lewis's leadership.

Lewis apparently felt that if the Quartet was to have an

identity and stability, it must offer something more than the quasi-jam session of four men improvising on fairly standard material, no matter how good those men might be as improvisers. Their music (like Jelly Roll Morton's music and Duke Ellington's music) might become more than the sum of the abilities of its players. He saw that the Quartet in some sense needed to create its own audience beyond the core of modern jazz "fans" that existed in the early 'fifties. He also saw, clearly, I am sure, that if the Quartet were to break out of the regular round of jazz clubs and all-star touring "packages," it must offer a music which could legitimately ask of an audience that it sit attentively in a concert hall, a music which must be more than a succession of half-hour night club "sets." One of the most singular facts in John Lewis's leadership is that he has a realistic sense of the facts of the milieu in which he functions, and that he usually knows what things can be changed and what things cannot be changed.

Lewis knew—his work shows he knew—that modern jazz itself needed more than the theme/string-of-solos/theme conception. That approach had served well as a vehicle for its best early players to work out its basic language. But the idiom needed some sort of synthesis of its elements, some sort of compositional order and form.

Inevitably, one cannot be entirely sympathetic with everything that Lewis does as a composer, nor with some of the ways he has searched for form outside the jazz tradition, nor with all of the results his leadership has produced. Long and frequently ponderous compositions like *The Comedy,* with neoclassic "effects," during which Milt Jackson is asked to employ his talent in executing some fairly mechanical ideas, are puzzling, to say the least. Indeed, I do not think one is wrong to hear in John Lewis's career at least an echo of the sort of misguided but understandable motives toward

prestige which led certain ragtime and Harlem stride pianists and composers to undertake "symphonic" works and
"operas," or which leads some contemporary jazzmen to
record "with strings."

But to turn to first principles, one cannot question the
marvelous group swing and drive which the Quartet is able
to achieve in an exceptional variety of moods and tempos
and at so many levels of dynamics. Nor can one question
the fact that the group is truly dedicated to improvisation:
its various recordings of the same repertory would be proof
enough of that without consulting its public appearances.

Lewis's failures, furthermore, are not typical of his talents
as either a composer or an improviser, nor of his leadership
of the group. Even in *The Comedy*, there are individual
sections with eloquently simple John Lewis melodies, and a
performance of the piece will feature improvisation that
shows the group's capacity to be at once both controlled and
marvelously spontaneous.

Lewis's achievements are real, and they have been important not only to the Quartet but to the course of modern
jazz. His credentials as a jazzman are authentic. Milt Jackson
is supposed to be the earthy, passionate, and spontaneous
member of the group, but anyone who has heard John
Lewis's solo on, say, *Bags' Groove* knows that John Lewis can
play the blues unashamedly—indeed with pride. Lewis's
own half-humorously protested ambitions to record with
people like blues singer Joe Turner make perfect sense. And
the expressiveness of his piano has deepened during his years
with the Quartet.

Lewis's virtues as a pianist do not include obvious finger
dexterity, and his virtues as an improviser find greater expression in relatively simple frameworks than in complex
ones. Early performances in which he undertook a Bud
Powell-like virtuosity of notes or a rapidly shifting pattern

of chords sometimes fail rather badly, and very fast tempos sometimes do still.

Lewis understands Count Basie. Contemporaneously, both Thelonious Monk and Miles Davis sensed that modern jazz rhythms needed a kind of relaxation and "opening up," that subtleties of space and rest in phrasing were called for. Lewis has achieved something of the same thing partly by recalling his knowledge of Basie, and of a time when Basie had done the same sort of opening up of jazz rhythms of the 'thirties. Lewis also knows the styles of swing period players like Earl Hines and Teddy Wilson; his *I Remember Clifford* is succinct evidence of that.

It is as if Lewis set about to reinterpret the modern idiom by directly using his knowledge of earlier jazz. Monk and Davis have used such knowledge, but less directly, I think. Lewis's approach to a use of the past is then comparable to Horace Silver's, but he has, both as a composer and as a musical director, a more developed sense of group form than Silver.

John Lewis's love and understanding of the music of the swing period, and his admittedly orchestral conception of the piano, allow him one spontaneous contribution to the music of the Modern Jazz Quartet. His accompaniments are seldom the percussively delivered chord patterns of the typical modern jazz pianist; he will automatically offer complementary countermelodies behind a soloist. These usually begin as riffs, the kind of repeated, rhythmic phrases that are as old as jazz and which big swing band reed and brass sections delivered all the time. Lewis often elaborates these brief phrases into a more complex but discreet jazz counterpoint. The results in the texture and the complexity of the Quartet's music are excellent, and it is as if Lewis had learned again, and independently, the lessons which King Oliver and Jelly Roll Morton had taught well—that con-

trapuntal effects can give the jazz ensemble a wonderfully
heightened excitement. Also, Lewis's spontaneous accompaniments often give cohesion and orderly pattern to a performance, as he elaborates a theme-proper behind a soloist's
variations or as he develops a single motif for several
choruses. A good example are the first few choruses of
Ralph's New Blues.

Mention of counterpoint brings up one of the most criti-
cally delicate aspects of the Modern Jazz Quartet's work:
John Lewis's obvious delight in European, baroque contrapuntal music. *Softly, as in the Morning's Sunrise* was one of
the earliest pieces in the group's repertory. As Milt Jackson
rephrased its melody and as the group spontaneously delivered it, this bit of operetta fluff became a real musical experience. But the Quartet now plays the piece with a brief,
Bach-derived introduction and conclusion that seems extrinsic and pointless, if not pretentious and arty.

The several fugal pieces in the group's repertory are more
indicative. British critic Max Harrison has said that although
the Quartet's first fugue, *Vendome,* sounds stilted and derivative, the later fugue, *Concorde,* decidedly moves in the
right direction, and that *Versailles* and *Three Windows* are
real jazz fugues, their materials assimilated and transmuted,
and reminding us more of Oliver and Morton than of a con-
servatory exercise. I think this more successful quality also
comes because the melodies of these later pieces sound less
derivative and more like jazz melodies. They are truly improvisational—the written portion of *Concorde,* for example, is a mere eight bars; the rest is made up in each performance.

The jazz-fugue has been around since the late 'thirties as
a kind of musical stunt, and pieces with the Bach-like steps
of, say, *All The Things You Are* have tempted many a borderline jazzman to trot out what he learned in student exer-
cises. The Quartet's accomplishments in *Concorde* and *Ver-*

sailles and *Three Windows* are a different and altogether more authentic matter. But, one should note, they are still only the Quartet's accomplishments—isolated phenomena which no other jazzmen have taken up except in a few pointless imitations.

On the other hand, one repeatedly finds this kind of paradox in Lewis's work: line in his quasi-baroque scoring of *God Rest Ye Merry, Gentlemen* sound quite straightforwardly musical when played by the Quartet, but the same effects sound almost ludicrous when a string orchestra executes them under Lewis's direction. One is tempted to blame this on the inexperience of string players with jazz phrasing, but surely the writing must take part of the blame.

Because of this aspect of his work, there is a strong temptation to think of Lewis as the kind of prodigy who would get straight A's in any music school, and never do anything really good thereafter. There were a number of musicians who functioned on both coasts during the 1950s' popularity of "cool jazz" about whom such things might be said with accuracy; their rather academic and transparent efforts to "do something artistic" were patently derivative and naïve. John Lewis is a different sort of musician. And with the Quartet's later fugues at hand, it is obvious that John Lewis can find something really creative—and not merely derivative—in the idiom of the eighteenth century.

John Lewis is the kind of man who can rename *Two Bass Hit* as *La Ronde*, *Moving Nicely* as *Baden Baden*, can name his pieces after French châteaux, can say "create" when it might be more discreet to say "write" or "compose." He is also a man with much knowledge of his own shortcomings, with a real sense of the facts of the milieu in which he functions, and a universal taste in music—and in jazz music. He is as much in touch with his own basic feelings as he is with anything he has learned. I say this, not in a personal defense of John Lewis, but because these things show quite directly in his work. They show in his own best playing and writing, and they are the best basis on which to hear him.

The directness of Lewis's phrasing as an improviser, and his capacity for understatement, make his playing an appropriate contrast to Milt Jackson's technical exuberance and emotional immediacy. Lewis's feelings seem naturally introverted, and I expect it has cost him something in technique and in musical histrionics to learn to project them so quietly yet so firmly. He is a player almost incapable of shouting (but neither incapable of raising his voice nor incapable of making the firmest of musical statements), and he is therefore the kind of player whose music some people almost automatically want to take as a pleasant "background" sound. This quality colors the Quartet's work as a whole, to be sure, and it undoubtedly accounts for some of the Quartet's borderline following. But the slightest sympathy in attending Lewis's improvising tells another story. Happily for him, Lewis can have it both ways, disappointing neither the casual nor the really attentive listener. Lewis's suggestion to the other members of the Quartet, that they attempt a more cohesive and singular emotional rise and fall in a given piece, may have begun as a piece of self-knowledge. But far from being a matter of audience pandering, it is the most legitimate sort of aesthetic refinement for jazzmen to undertake—and, incidentally, one that Ellington has used for many years.

Milt Jackson is obviously a man of great natural talent, and during his years with the Quartet that talent has been refined and made far more flexible in sound, in dynamics, in range, in expressiveness. I cannot agree that Lewis lacks insight into Jackson's playing, or that the Quartet "inhibits" him. Quite the contrary.

It might be legitimate to say that some of Jackson's best recorded work was done in 1948 and in 1951 when he made some classic pieces with Thelonious Monk (and the response between Jackson and Monk is always a very special one), and that since then, although he has remained a superb player, he has refined and improved what he could do already. One aspect of Jackson's work is what seems to me an occasional sentimentality in slow ballads. It shows in his early contribution to the Quartet's repertory called *Lillie*, and it is laid out at rather appalling length in the out-of-tempo opening of *How High the Moon*. In his accompaniments to Jackson, John Lewis is usually not as successful in compensating for this element as Monk has been—compare the two versions of *Willow, Weep for Me*. But Lewis's accompaniment often does provide Jackson's solos with decidedly helpful melodic and emotional shading. Jackson's exuberance is natural, but it can also be a rather general exuberance which sometimes overrides his attention to the piece at hand. It seems to me that very few of the LP recitals that Milt Jackson has made on his own in recent years have been as successful as his work with the Quartet—the outstanding exception being a date he did with Percy Heath, Connie Kay, and Horace Silver and which produced *My Funny Valentine* and *I Should Care*. One comparison which makes its point rather succinctly is Lewis vs. Jackson on *I Remember Clifford*—or for that matter, compare Lewis to any other jazzman on that piece, for it has tempted many players to sentimental excess. Paradoxically, when Jackson's slow balladry does win out over sentimentality, the victory is triumphant, as his performances of *Autumn in New York, Milano, I Should Care*, and *What's New* can bear witness.

Lewis's achievements as a composer include his blues line *Two Degrees East, Three Degrees West* and I fear that, beside it, Milt Jackson's endless composed permutations on his *Bags' Groove* melody, under various titles, become almost anonymous. Like some of Monk's best pieces, like Lewis's earlier *La Ronde*, and some of Lewis's best improvising, *Two Degrees* reinterprets tradition in a contemporary and personal manner. Its delightfully ingenious phrasing takes an indigenous blues fragment and uses it with striking insight into its nature and its possibilities.

Another successful Lewis piece is *The Golden Striker*, and, similarly, one might call it a kind of up-to-date version of the *Bugle Call Rag*, and in performance a somewhat fussy version. The piece presents a melody, a framework for improvising, and a brief effect of stop-time repeated in a way that gives the ad lib sections both variety and order. It encourages the improviser and helps to order his playing while not inhibiting him.

John Lewis's high achievement as a composer is *Django*. It is a funeral piece in memory of Django Reinhardt, the Belgian-French gypsy guitarist turned jazzman. The main theme seems to imply several things: an elegy as well as French, gypsy, and jazz music. The chord sequence for the improvised section is in effect new material, since it is not entirely derived from the theme. The last eight bars of the theme melody also serve as an interlude separating the soloists. There is still another motif, a simple and traditional blues bass-figure (my earliest acquaintance with it is in the introduction to King Oliver's 1926 piece *Snag It*) which appears and reappears in the improvised section—and in later performances Lewis sometimes counterpoints another traditional riff figure on top of it. Obviously, in *Django* Lewis also had in mind the tradition of consolation and rejoicing at death that was a part of culture in New Orleans and early jazz.

The subtle movement and range of feeling in a good performance of *Django* make it one of the truly successful and sustained extended works in the jazz repertory. Its melodies and motifs are excellent and excellently juxtaposed. And in performance the act of holding these opposites together cohesively becomes an achievement shared by both composer and players, by the compositional conception and the given performance—and that is the highest achievement of jazz composition.

Outside of his work for the Quartet, Lewis's best piece is a three-part suite called *Three Little Feelings*—I am speaking of the piece as it was originally written for a brass orchestra with Miles Davis as the main soloist. Its melodies are eloquently and deceptively simple, its scoring balances solo and group to the advantage of both, and there is hardly any waste motion or padding. There are sections of Lewis's score for the movie *Odds Against Tomorrow* that are also impressive, particularly the "prelude," in which Lewis scores and elucidates a great deal of musical material smoothly, tersely, and interestingly.

By the 1960s some of the Quartet's work had reached a kind of perfection from which there may very well be no place to go, for it is doubtful if these men could continue to find it challenging to play so well and to play so well together —at least in the same repertory and format. Their two-LP set called "European Concert," recorded during public performances in Scandinavia, might almost stand as a summary of some of the highest achievements of ten years of working together.

The set contains a third recording of *Django*, different from the previous ones, and in its way almost as good, with the structural strength of that piece still forceful and inspirational. Particularly on *Bluesology* (one of the earliest pieces in their repertory) and on *Festival Sketch*, the interplay between Lewis and Jackson is superb. Lewis's solo on *Bags' Groove* is again an unassuming exposition of blues feeling. There are three other twelve-bar blues pieces in the set, and of course Milt Jackson is very good on all of them. There is a nearly sublime performance of *It Don't Mean a Think (If It Ain't Got That Swing)* on which Lewis again begins his section unaccompanied, then has Jackson behind him, building marvelously suspenseful melodic patterns, until Heath and Kay reenter percussively to relieve the tension. They depart again, leaving Lewis alone. Etc. Brief suspensions of the rhythmic pulse were fairly commonplace by the 'twenties, and it is a delight to find the idea thus reintroduced and extended. There is another attempt at *Vendome*; it is better than the first, and it may even swing more (it at least sounds more jazzy), but it still seems a somewhat specious vehicle, even for such good playing as this. There is *I'll Remember April*, still a good workout and still, I think, too fast for that kind of quasi-impressionist popular song.

Lewis's career, since it risks larger success, also risks larger failure. The future will undoubtedly find him a composer and conductor of his own works for various kinds of ensembles and in various milieus. If his projects lead Lewis into more things like his strange, academic scoring of *God Rest Ye Merry, Gentlemen* for plodding strings, or like his curiously faltering ballet score for the San Francisco company, *Original Sin*, or his mish-mash of a film score, *A Milanese Story*, they may lead him to a stunted pretentiousness.

But I am again talking about shortcomings which are the shortcomings of something ventured. Lewis's failures are like Ellington's sentimental ballads, Armstrong's sometimes forced good spirits, Parker's sometimes overripe harmonies, Monk's overpercussiveness—they make successes possible. And John Lewis's success so far includes, besides musical leadership of perhaps the best small ensemble in jazz history, an important contribution to the synthesis that modern jazz achieved in its second decade, which includes *Django, The Golden Striker*, the *Odds Against Tomorrow* score, *Three Little Feelings, Two Degrees East*—not a small achievement.

12

SONNY ROLLINS

Spontaneous Orchestration

In the late summer of 1959 tenor saxophonist Sonny Rollins stopped taking night club, concert, and record dates. Inevitably there was much gossip. It was said that he had decided to escape a round of work where both public adulation and constant playing were forcing him to repeat himself; that he was preparing some long compositions; that he had been intimidated by critical praise and by the close technical analysis of his recorded work; that he intended to reappear solo, as an unaccompanied improvising saxophonist. The last rumor was perhaps the most provocative. Rollins had frequently appeared without a pianist and—most important—in a sense had taken over the functions of orchestrator and orchestra all to himself.

In mid-1956, Sonny Rollins, formerly the capable, or perhaps the promising, jazz tenor saxophone soloist, had had a musical coming of age. Soon he was winning all the popularity polls, and his records were being reviewed as examples of "uninhibited passion," "inner compulsion," etc. But descriptions of the impact and sureness of his playing tell only part of the story, and the rest of the story makes Rollins a unique hornman in the history of jazz.

By the mid-'fifties, modern jazz was no longer faced with

discovering or testing its basic musical language but, as we have said, with establishing some sort of synthesis within the idiom, with the task of ordering its materials which, for earlier styles, had been done by Jelly Roll Morton in the 'twenties and Duke Ellington in the late 'thirties. In the 'fifties, the problem was met, foremost, by Thelonious Monk; by pianist-composer John Lewis with the Modern Jazz Quartet; and by Sonny Rollins as an improvising saxophonist.

In one sense the history of the last thirty years in jazz might be written in terms of the length of the solos that its horn players have been able to sustain. Certainly one contribution of be-bop was that its best players (but only its best) could undertake longer improvisations which offered a flow of musical ideas without falling into honking or growling banalities. I do not mean that the younger players of the 'forties were either the first or the only jazz musicians to be able to do this, only that for some of them a sustained solo was a primary concern. However, a great deal of extended soloing in jazz has had the air of an endurance feat— a player tries to keep going with as little repetition as possible. But when the ideas are original and are imaginatively handled, such playing can have virtues of its own. However, a hornman's best solos are apt to be continuously developing linear inventions. Sonny Rollins has recorded long solos which, in quality and approach, go beyond good soloist's form and amount almost to sustained orchestrations.

Previously, jazz pianists have shown such concern with larger form in improvising. Some examples, a random sampling, are Jelly Roll Morton's solo on *Hyena Stomp*, Willie "the Lion" Smith's *Squeeze Me*, Fats Waller's *Numb Fumblin'*. But of course many pianists have thought formally and orchestrally, even some simple blues men—Jimmy Yancey in *How Long #2* and *State Street Special*—have exceptionally cohesive designs.

Sonny Rollins's early records indicate his later developments only in retrospect. At the time they seemed the work of a talented player, in more or less the style of the time, a style probably best exhibited in Dexter Gordon's work. This style variously combined the robust, extroverted manner of Coleman Hawkins (but without his vibrato) with many of the approaches to melody, rhythm, and asymmetry of phrasing of Lester Young, plus some of Charlie Parker's ideas as well.

One can hear the young Rollins of 1949 with a Bud Powell group on *Bouncin' with Bud, Wail*, etc., and the release of some alternate takes from this session shows that Rollins was really improvising, offering a rather different solo on each performance of each piece. Most of the other players involved had had experience in big bands. Rollins had not; indeed his first job with a regularly working group did not come until he joined Max Roach in late 1955. Big band work can teach lessons of discipline and terseness in short solos, and lessons of group precision and responsiveness. Rollins has learned some of those lessons, but, as I have indicated, he has surmounted not having learned others.

Rollins had his first record date on his own in 1951. *Slow Boat to China* (one of several unexpected pop vehicles to come) and *Shadrack* show a relaxed sureness of phrasing and rhythm, and *This Love of Mine* an increase in saxophone technique. *Mambo Bounce* is (significantly, I think) a twelve-bar blues. It includes four ad lib choruses by Rollins only the second of which uses ordinary ideas. More important, the solo has only one Parker-esque flurry of short notes. Parker himself often used such runs for contrast or variety in his solos; some of his followers might throw them in almost anywhere on impulse. Rollins usually uses such double-time phrases sparsely, and in *Mambo Bounce* the virtuoso run appears in his fourth improvised chorus, where it becomes the climax of his solo. A happy accident? Perhaps.

But I wonder, in view of his later work. Perhaps it was conscious and deliberate, but more likely it was the result of personal artistic intuition. It suggests one way that the technical resources of modern jazz improvising might be used structurally. Again, the hint might have come from Hawkins; he was one player of his generation who brought off long solos, and his usual manner was to build in technical complexity.

Sonny Rollins continued to acquire more techniques, learned to use them with more relaxation; as his sound and attack became increasingly personal, his ability to swing reached near-perfection. He also played with Thelonious Monk, and the experience was surely important to his development. And, in mid-1954, he participated in a very good Miles Davis recording session to which he contributed three interesting pieces: *Airegin, Oleo* (probably under the inspiration of such Parker lines as *Scrapple From the Apple*, finding something fresh in the *I Got Rhythm* chords), and *Doxy*, a modern return to the sixteen-bar blues patterns of the 'twenties.

A bit later there was *Tenor Madness* on which John Coltrane joined Rollins. Here is relatively early Coltrane, to be sure, but he shows the harmonic searching of the highly sophisticated, vertical player he later became. In the placing and accenting of his short notes, Coltrane is already identifiably Coltrane. Rollins is a confident master of his own materials and he climaxes his own section with a telling moment of technical complexity, just as he had on *Mambo Bounce*.

The two LPs which made Rollins's public reputation were *"Saxophone Colossus"* (done in June 1956) and *"Way Out West"* (March 1957). The latter is a collection, largely of pop "Western" songs in which Rollins plays with remarkable power and ease. Some reviewers heard "anger" or "aggression" in his saxophone sound. There is much humor to be sure; there is parody and even sardonic comedy. And surely Rollins's firm, confident phrasing, his masterful dynamics and excellent use of the range of his horn (from firm, cello-like low notes to bold cries in upper range), surely these things balance the "negative" emotion in his playing. Also on that record there is more than a hint that he was taking a cue from the airy, open phrasing of Lester Young's later work.

Another aspect of the *"Way Out West"* LP is the masterful way that Rollins shows he had absorbed ideas from Monk on how to get inside a theme, abstract it, distill its essence, perceive its implications, and use it as a basis for variations—without merely embellishing it decoratively or abandoning it for improvisation based only on its chords. Besides making public appearances with him, Rollins has several times recorded with Monk. And one might note that, for example, on their version of *Bemsha Swing* Rollins begins his solo with the last idea that Monk had played in his section, and that, as Rollins's line gets more complex, Monk reintroduces orderly reminders and hints of the theme beneath him.

By 1957 Rollins had moved so far along as a kind of one-man orchestra that on the title piece of *"Way Out West"* he returns for his second solo with a spontaneous imitation of Shelley Manne's drum patterns.

Blue 7 from *"Saxophone Colossus"* is a masterpiece, hence it is the kind of performance that one hears anew with each listening and that is difficult to discuss and describe. Its heritage, as Gunther Schuller pointed out in his detailed analysis, includes Monk's *Misterioso* and the Miles Davis-Sonny Rollins *Vierd Blues*. It begins with an almost nonchalant and tranquil bass line by Doug Watkins. Upon this, Rollins states the theme, a simple blues line that has a strong individual character. Yet it is also suspended in an ambiguous bitonality. The piano's entrance behind Rollins assigns it a specific key, and Rollins begins to explore its implied brilliance expertly.

The performance builds from one phrase to the next, yet that structure is so logical and so comprehensive, with its details so subtly in place, that it is as if Rollins had not made it up as he went along, but had conceived it whole from the beginning. Max Roach has said that he and Rollins both had in mind Monk's admonition: Why don't we *use* the melody? Why do we throw it away after the first chorus and just use the chords?

Almost everything that Rollins plays on *Blue 7* is based on his opening theme, but Rollins also structures and builds —he even builds on his elaborations and his brief interpolations, and he is not afraid of an almost direct recapitulation of his theme at one point during the performance. The order and logic of the performance extends also to Roach's solo, based almost entirely on a triplet figure and a roll, while Tommy Flanagan's nonthematic piano solo serves as a kind of effectively contrasting, lyric interlude.

Blue 7 is one of those rare performances which almost anyone can appreciate immediately, I think—anyone, from the novice who wants to know where the melody is, to the sympathetic classicist who can appreciate how highly developed the jazzman's art has become.

Blue 7 is one of the great pleasures of recorded jazz, but its elaborations and distillations of theme do not represent Rollins's only approach to extended improvised form. Another is the one he hinted at in *Mambo Bounce*, but he has never recorded it in the masterful way he has used it in public. In this approach Rollins would first state his theme, then gradually simplify until he was playing only a scant outline. Then he would gradually slip away from it and invent new melodies—at first very simple ones—out of the chord structure of the piece. He would proceed to develop these: his note values getting shorter, his melodic lines longer and their contours more complex. When he had built such a solo over several choruses to a peak of melodic and rhythmic virtuosity, he would gradually reverse himself, return to simpler melodies, to fewer and longer notes. Soon, one would realize, Rollins had begun to resketch his initial theme with certain suggestive notes and phrases, and finally he would restore it completely to a full recapitulation.

My account may make Rollins's performances seem mechanical. Of course his power and sureness alone might prevent such playing from being mechanical, but his spontaneous designs were never so pat as a general description is apt to imply. Long runs of notes are interspersed with short ones and even with short, staccato, humorously delivered single notes. Fragments of the theme are heard in otherwise harmonic variations. Brief virtuoso lines appear in otherwise simple choruses. But these form patterns of prediction and echo in an overall structure, and the way to hear a good Rollins performance is always to try to hear it whole.

There is another Rollins recording which is still differently structured, but which is again based on comparable material, *Blues for Philly Joe*. On it Rollins plays a kind of free, spontaneous blues rondo. Using A to indicate Rollins's main theme, A plus a numeral to indicate thematic variations, and other letters to indicate variations that are not thematic, one might outline the performance roughly this way:

A
A
A-1
A-2
A-3

B
C
A-4
D
D-1
E (A-5?)
Wynton Kelly's piano solo
Exchange of four-bar phrases with drummer Philly Joe
    Jones
A (A-6?)
A

There are several fascinating details which such an outline can't indicate. For example, the new material Rollins
introduces in A-1 appears again in variation in A-2, thus
tying these two choruses together. Subsequently this double-
chorus idea is echoed at D and D-1, at approximately the
middle of the piece, and again at the end of the piece. A-3
is almost, but not quite, a nonthematic chorus; it is as if
Rollins's strong departures from his theme were preparing
our ears for B, which is far enough away to be called nonthematic. Chorus E has strong reminders of the main theme
toward the end, and is therefore part E and part A-5.
Rollins's four-bar phrases in exchange with Joe Jones are
sometimes melodic and sometimes percussive, as might befit
exchanges with a drummer. The two final saxophone
choruses are thematic, but neither is an absolute restatement
of the A theme, although the final chorus is closer. Again,
let me warn that an outline like this one of a spontaneous
performance is apt to make Rollins's playing seem calculated and mechanical when it is anything but that. However,
his sense of order is there—as natural and spontaneous as
any other aspect of his playing—and it is a major part of his
aesthetic achievement.

    The Rollins who returned to public performance in the
fall of 1961 was the same Rollins, only more so. One's

memory of that Rollins is a memory of performances which nostalgia might exaggerate but which exact memory could obscure. Again there were the long performances, which Rollins seemed to conceive as entities, but which also develop with internal logic, phrase by phrase. There were also extended cadenzas in which Rollins would rapidly execute an entire thirty-two-bar theme on a series of two or three chords spontaneously offered him by his pianist, altering only those notes necessary to fit each chord in succession.

I wrote the following account in *Down Beat* of a Rollins concert held in mid-1962: "For Rollins, the promise was fulfilled brilliantly. From his opening choruses on *Three Little Words*, it was apparent that Rollins was going to play with commanding authority, invention, and a deep humor which even included a healthy self-parody. His masterwork of the evening was a cadenza on *Love Letters*, several out of tempo choruses of virtuosity in imagination, execution, and a kind of truly artistic bravura that jazz has not known since the Louis Armstrong of the early 'thirties. The performance included some wild interpolations, several of which Rollins managed to fit in by a last minute and wittily unexpected alteration of a note or two. To my ear, he did not once lose his way, although a couple of times he did lose [guitarist] Jim Hall—and that is nearly impossible to do for Jim Hall has one of the quickest harmonic ears there is. Rollins's final piece was a kind of extemporaneous orchestration on *If Ever I Would Leave You* in which he became brass, reed, and rhythm section, tenor soloist, and Latin percussionist, all at once and always with musical logic."

Again, one is left with the frustration that Rollins's recordings do not show the level of his achievements in clubs and concerts. There is a recording of *If Ever I Would Leave You*; it is very good indeed, but it is a shadow of the masterful performance described above.

Soon, however, Sonny Rollins had espoused "the new

thing." For me, it is as if, in undertaking this "free form" jazz, he denies his own basic aesthetic impulses as well as his already established place in jazz history. The musical liberation of a new generation may seem mere eccentricity when undertaken by its elders. True, there are precedents in his own work for a high-handed use of chord changes, as when (again echoing Lester Young) he phrases ahead of a chord change or behind one. He does this most effectively I think in parts of the excellent *Freedom Suite*. True, also, some of his free-form solos are far from uninteresting, and once again feature thematic fragmentations and echoes—but whether this serves to organize such solos, as it did his earlier ones, seems to me open to question.

To return to the earlier Rollins, one of the most instructive comparisons in recorded jazz, and one of the best indications of another aspect of Rollins's position in its history, comes about because several important players have made versions of *Cherokee* and variants thereof.[1] There are records by tenor saxophonist Don Byas, by Charlie Parker (as *KoKo*), and by Rollins (as *B. Quick*). At least by the mid-'forties Byas was perhaps as sophisticated harmonically as was Rollins at his peak—witness Byas's version of *I Got Rhythm*. Melodically and rhythmically Byas echoed Hawkins; he was an arpeggio player with a rather deliberate and regular way of phrasing. Accordingly, when Byas plays an up-tempo *Cherokee*, his solo is so filled with notes that it seems a virtuoso display, and in an apparent melodic despair he is soon merely reiterating the theme. Parker of course broke up his phrases and his rhythm with such brilliant

---

1. Among the recordings of the piece are those by Art Tatum, in a smoothly arpeggiated, harmonically imaginative version; by Lester Young with Count Basie; by Lee Konitz (*Marshmallow*); by Sonny Stitt (in several versions, both as *Serenade to a Square* and as *KoKo*); by Bud Powell at least twice; etc.

variety that he was able to establish a continuous, easy linear invention, avoiding Byas's effect of a cluttered desperation of notes. Rollins's *B. Quick* choruses, however, seem to be filling in again with notes. Of course this is partly because Rollins does not have Parker's rhythmic imagination (what jazzman has?) but, symbolically at least, it means that Rollins's maturity and his major contributions of improvised form came near the end of the great period of jazz which began with Charlie Parker.

13

HORACE SILVER

The Meaning of Craftsmanship

In April 1954 Miles Davis led an "all-star" recording date which produced *Walkin'* and *Blue 'n' Boogie*. I think that the music on those two classic blues performances could be said to represent the state of modern jazz as it entered its second decade. The pianist involved, however, was a relative newcomer named Horace Silver. Silver's recording activities were then prolific, but his role in jazz was really just beginning, and his work as a pianist, composer, and leader of quintets soon became pivotal in the jazz of the late 'fifties.

A few years later Silver had produced two LP recitals which seem to me to bring all the elements of his music to a perfection of conception and performance, and even to turn some of the shortcomings of his style into virtues. But at the very moment of such achievement the style he supposedly started was being almost ludicrously popularized. That style was at first called "funky" after an old Anglo-Saxon word for smelly; it was soon turned into a marketable commodity called "soul jazz." When it began, the funky style was supposed to save jazz from the tepid affectations of the "cool" players; it was also meant to restore its rightful heritage and rescue jazz from an affected softness, from what Silver once called a "fagotty" excess. But a borderline jazzman like

André Previn was soon playing glib, virtuosic Silver, and much "soul jazz" became a kind of self-satisfied pseudo-rustic posturing made up of a few pat devices derived from Negro gospel music, some conventional rhythm and blues effects, and about thirty saxophone clichés.

Nevertheless, Horace Silver's arrival in the 'fifties *was* important, and the funky style did what it set out to do. If its creativity as a movement was soon spent, Silver's own creativity was not—and his own style seems rather different from the style of his would-be followers.

The words associated with his music were "swing," "groove," "back-home," "low-down," "blow," "wail," "cook," and almost anything else people could think of to imply an uninhibited emotional expression.

Actually, Silver's is a very carefully designed and carefully rehearsed music, with a deliberate craftsmanship constantly in evidence. There are even built-in protections for the un-inspired soloist in several of his pieces. There is plenty of interest in his music also for the kind of casual listener who asks that his jazz be a fairly emotional background that occasionally encourages finger-snapping and head-shaking.

In the 'thirties it was just such listeners who formed the backbone of the jazz audience, of course. It is from the jazz argot of the 'thirties that those terms "swing," "groove," and "blow" were borrowed. If we say that funky jazz was an effort at a return to roots, we should remember these younger modern jazzmen did not return to the jazz of King Oliver or Blind Lemon Jefferson, but rather to the roots represented in gospel music, contemporary rhythm and blues, the music of Ray Charles, and to the roots as these players knew them in their own youth—to the swing period of the 'thirties.

It has occurred to some commentators to look for a formal synthesis of modern jazz in Horace Silver's work, but Silver has some of his roots set too directly and too firmly in the 'thirties. In his approach to the piano he owes an harmonic sophistication to modern jazz, and he pays an obvious debt to Bud Powell's style (in the sense that Powell played a pianist's version of Parker's alto saxophone, Silver played a pianist's version of tenor saxophone and he had been a tenor saxophonist) but often his manner of phrasing and some of his ideas of rhythm come very directly from an earlier time. If one says that Horace Silver sounds like a cross between Bud Powell and Pete Johnson, he had better acknowledge that there is an urbanity in several of Johnson's slow blues that Silver, in his determination to cook, may not manifest. Silver's groups sometimes give a similar impression—of a cross between a be-bop quintet and a little Southwestern jump-blues band of the 'thirties or early 'forties. But there is more to his music than ingenious hybrid.

Silver's earlier composing shows all this quite readily. *Room 608* has a be-bop line, but not an entirely comfortable one. And to balance it, there are pieces like *Stop Time*, which simplifies the bop line of *One Bass Hit*; or *Doodlin'*, which is a slightly sophisticated version of a riff figure that was commonplace in the 'thirties; or *Sister Sadie*, which is also based on a durable, traditional riff and which was used in a quasi-spiritual pop tune the Basie band once recorded called *Do You Wanna Jump, Children?*

Silver succeeds in using something of both worlds in *Hippy*, a piece which reveals several aspects of his music. The basic material of *Hippy* is a two-bar riff which I believe comes from Charlie Christian—at least a version of it shows up in the Benny Goodman sextet's *Air Mail Special*, and the old Basie band also used it in later playings of *One O'clock Jump*. Silver has taken that little phrase intact and, in the manner of bop composing, rather than repeating it over and over has extended it logically and delightfully into a bouncing melody that covers eight bars. This melody then becomes the main strain of a thirty-two-bar, AABA jazz theme. Thus *Hippy* is structurally bop. But rhythmically it remains rather close to swing.

Hippy also includes a secondary theme based in part on big band brass figures. Silver's pieces often include such secondary themes and written interludes, and I think the one on *Moon Rays* is particular attractive.

Most of Silver's music makes that kind of direct synthesis of some elements from the jazz of the 'thirties and some from the jazz of the 'forties.

Unlike some of his pieces, *Hippy* is harmonized in a fairly simple way. Several others have the harmonic sophistication of a rapid and dense texture of written chord changes. When a soloist begins his "uninhibited" cooking, he has a tight pattern of chords to run; he handles them according to his talent or his mood of the moment, either as a challenging inspiration, as a kind of musical game, or as a neat protection against a lack of ideas. If he runs all the chords correctly, he will sound as if he is playing something when he may be playing very little. Silver's accompaniment is simpler than Bud Powell's, and there are fewer interpolated passing chords. However, I do find myself in agreement with those who say that less solo space allotted to his sidemen would improve some of Silver's performances.

Horace Silver's style does owe a debt to Negro gospel music, to be sure, but far less a debt than has been said, and certainly a less direct debt than one can hear in several of his followers. I expect that the earlier piece called *The Preacher* may have been named with irony. It is a leaping, shouting theme on the outline of the inebriate's favorite *Show Me the Way to Go Home*—no wonder the Dixieland bands took it up. And, as I have indicated, *Sister Sadie* could have got her funkiness at a Count Basie dance as easily as at a sanctified church.

One striking effect of Silver's career is his special relation-

ship to trumpeters. Silver was in frequent attendance during the early stages of Miles Davis's reemergence in the mid-
'fifties. Kenny Dorham matured while he and Silver were
both members of the Art Blakey Jazz Messengers. Donald
Byrd produced a quite cohesive early recorded solo on *Señor
Blues* on a Horace Silver date. I don't think that it was
either inevitable or coincidental that Art Farmer settled
into being an exceptionally fluent and authoritatively lyric
soloist while he was with Silver. Similarly, Blue Mitchell
expanded his style while working with Silver. It should be
perfectly obvious how and why any player would gain
rhythmic sureness and dexterity from playing with Horace
Silver, but trumpeters seem to gain as melodists, even as
Silver bounces, barks, and chops his way around behind
them.

The problems inherent in Silver's piano style are obvious,
although not all of them of his own making. He does have
trouble with slow tempos and the lyricism of jazz ballads.
But few of Bud Powell's ballads are successful, and Powell
even indulged in a kind of pounded version of Art Tatum's
embellishment style on occasion. Thelonious Monk and
John Lewis can sustain a ballad meaningfully, but each has
a personal and somewhat isolated approach to such material.
Other modern pianists who have played ballads well—Al
Haig, Duke Jordan, and Joe Albany—have all shown an
interesting dependence on Teddy Wilson's brilliance in such
moods.

I have indicated that Horace Silver's accompaniments can
be rhythmically choppy and melodically static. In solo, the
same fault shows itself as a kind of fragmentation; a brief
and almost isolated melodic idea is propelled, by each bass
chord in succession—bass chord/treble figure/bass chord/
treble figure, in a sort of pianistic ping-pong—sometimes
with little effect of melodic or emotional continuity or pat-

tern. There is also Silver's almost malicious penchant for interpolation. In the midst of the fine momentum he gets going in *Blue 'n' Boogie*, for example, he drops an allusion to the *Hut Sut Song* (!), and in a slow mood piece we may suddenly be treated to a succession of bugle calls. Such jokes may be pretty good, but they seem uncalled for.

I began this by saying that I think two of his LPs show a kind of peak of development for Silver's music. There is certainly at least one peak performance on each of them. *Cookin' at the Continental* (on a set called *"Finger-Poppin'"*) and *Sister Sadie* (on a set called *"Blowin' the Blues Away"*) are both performed, by soloists and group, with an exceptionally sustained and surging energy and swinging inspiration of a kind seldom captured in a recording studio and almost as rarely in public performance. The two LPs are also performed with a rare collective skill and precision. *Cookin'*, by the way, also has the asset of saxophonist Junior Cook's occasional willingness to echo Lester Young's style, an approach which suits Silver's excellently. (I'm sure that Horace Silver sounded so good the way we first heard him playing with Stan Getz because Getz also owes much to the jazz of the 'thirties.)

Among the compositions, *Mellow D* has a very good line in which the swing and be-bop elements are so synthesized that one cannot really separate them. There is the usual flirting with "Latin" rhythms on several pieces, which are sometimes dropped after a chorus or so but which give a welcome variety to his programs. And there are the continuing efforts to break down thirty-two-bar structures and their eight-bar patterns in pieces of 16/6/16 etc.

But such things are not so much innovations, it seems to me, as they are acts of sound conservatism: in them Silver finds slightly different ways to present the fundamentals of his music.

More important, the writing is usually direct and economical. Some of the secondary themes are remarkably effective, and especially on *Sister Sadie* Silver makes two horns and his own piano sound *exactly* like the alternating brass and reed sections of a big band executing call-and-response riffs. One may question why a quintet should want to sound like a big band, but the astonishing results on *Sadie* can only produce a kind of awed admiration, and perhaps the conclusion that on several of his pieces Silver has in effect done some of the best big band writing of the period.

There is even more evidence of an approaching perfection in Silver's piano. The overall impression is one of cohesion and order—the blue notes usually seem to be there for cause rather than effect and the more adventurous intervals seem part of a larger plan (hear *Cookin' at the Continental* especially). In his accompaniments there is still some choppiness, and the rumbling and barking are there, perhaps a little too often. But particularly on *Blowin' the Blues Away* and *Sister Sadie,* Silver uses his piano excellently as a substitute sax or brass section, propelling his soloists along with background riff figures. John Lewis does much the same sort of thing in accompaniment, echoing the same sort of swing period sources, but the effect is quite different, and an aural comparison between Silver and Lewis as accompanists can be quite instructive.

A piece called *Saint Vitus Dance* is an exceptional five minutes by a piano trio, and its medium tempo may be just the right one for Silver. The romantic harmonies of *Saint Vitus* will convince you again that Silver can make anything sound naturally earthy, and his improvising has a melodic continuity and design that I don't believe he has shown elsewhere on records.

Perhaps the most remarkable of all is the slow piece called *Sweet Stuff*. There Silver's spurting right hand phrases and heavy chords may again seem isolated fragments at first; cumulatively, however, the performance soon takes on the hypnotic effect of a passionately chanted incantation. The right hand phrases on *Sweet Stuff* are rendered with a remarkably sustained emotional directness, and the performer avoids both the sentimentality and callousness which are inherent temptations to lesser players in such a piece. *Sweet Stuff* is a unique, almost unforgettable, performance. And Silver has achieved it not only in terms of his own style, but by taking ingenious advantage of the very things that otherwise seem flaws in his playing. After *Sweet Stuff* the interpolated bugle call that finds its way into *You Happened My Way* seems almost forgivable.

Horace Silver is that kind of inspired, creative craftsman that jazz, like any art, must have to sustain itself. Such a craftsman, whether Don Redman, Fletcher Henderson, Count Basie, Roy Eldridge, or Horace Silver, has been there at the right moment to play a crucial role in the development of the music. Certainly jazz would languish without its Armstrongs and its Parkers to renew its language, and without its Mortons, Ellingtons, and Monks to give it compositional synthesis. But without individual, creative craftsmen like Horace Silver among its soloists and its composers, there might be no common language to renew, and no affirmation of what things can be synthesized.

14

MILES DAVIS

A Man Walking

By the early 'fifties, it may have seemed that the productive career of trumpeter and fluegelhornist Miles Davis was just about over. Between 1950 and 1954 his work had become uneven. Obvious aspects of his style had already been siphoned off and popularized by several trumpeters, particularly on the West Coast. And in the East meanwhile there had arrived a young man named Clifford Brown, whose work brought together some of the best aspects of modern trumpet—a sort of synthesis of Davis, Dizzy Gillespie, and most particularly Fats Navarro.

Brown became something of a rallying point for Eastern musicians: in the face of a fad for "cool jazz," it was as if he rose up and shouted to his contemporaries—even to his elders—that jazz should not abandon the other side of its technical and emotional heritage, that it could find a renewed life in a reiteration of some of its first principles.

Most of the first-generation "modernists," at least those who received the earliest praise—Gillespie, Charlie Parker, Bud Powell, Max Roach—were virtuosos in obvious ways. But the musicians who became important in the second decade of the music, almost to a man, were not virtuosos; they became important by virtue of asserting principles aside from obvious technical dexterity. I am thinking of players like Thelonious Monk, John Lewis, and Miles Davis, or players like Horace Silver and Art Blakey. Even Milt Jackson, although he has developed the techniques implicit in his early, bop-influenced style, prefers simpler pieces and has contributed a classic blues in *Bags' Groove*. Also, each of these men has reflected the immediate past of jazz, specifically the music of the 'thirties and the swing period, some of them—Lewis, Davis, Silver—in a manner that is so direct that it implies a deliberate reaching back.

Miles Davis's earliest records were sometimes able and occasionally faltering, but they showed a very personal approach to the modern jazz idiom. From time to time he did espouse the virtuoso manner of Gillespie, and on occasion he showed a perceptive ability almost to abstract Gillespie's style, as on *A Night in Tunisia* with Charlie Parker. But more often he was involved in a simple, introspective but sophisticated lyricism which seemed to refute the ideas that many people had about modern jazz as a virtuoso music whose simplest passages had to alternate with a sustained barrage of sixteenth-notes. And he was sometimes so good a lyricist as to be able to follow, for example, Charlie Parker's superb solo on *Embraceable You* without sounding a hopeless anti-climax.

Davis was an effective foil for Parker's technical and emotional exuberance. But at the same time that Davis was occupied with a simple lyricism in improvisation, he was so preoccupied with particularly lush harmonies that it sometimes seemed his solos were about to become a succession of pretty but perhaps bland sound patterns.

Miles Davis's first recordings under his own name were made in 1947 when he was only twenty-one, and the fact that they have a decidedly individual character is even more notable when we remember that he was surrounded by such

accomplished players as Charlie Parker (on tenor for the
occasion), John Lewis, and Max Roach. The atmosphere of
these performances is more relaxed, the themes are more
fluent and more legato, and, although Davis has clearly
learned from Parker and Dizzy Gillespie, he seemed also to
be reaching back to the easy, introverted phrasing of Lester
Young. Davis's themes on those records have a built-in harmonic complexity. *Sippin' at Bells*, for example, is a twelve-
bar blues, but it is so written that the soloist has to find his
way through an obstacle course of some eighteen assigned
chord changes in a single chorus. And the shifting structure
of *Little Willie Leaps* (borrowed, by the way, but altered
from *All God's Chillun Got Rhythm*) almost throws so able
a man as John Lewis.

There is an effective tension on these recordings between
the surface lyricism of Miles Davis's solo melodic lines and
the complexity of their underlying harmonic outline. The
wonder is that a man who plays with such apparent simplicity as Miles Davis would have wanted such technical challenges. But he did, and he learned a great deal from the experience. And once he had learned it, he showed an artist's
wisdom in forgetting, but still knowing, what he had
learned.

Among the most celebrated of Davis's records are the
series he recorded with nine-piece groups for Capitol. They
have been celebrated for the work of the arrangers involved
—Gil Evans, Gerry Mulligan, John Lewis, Johnny Carisi,
and Davis—but if they proved nothing else, they would
prove that Miles Davis, already an interesting and personal
soloist, could produce two great improvisations, each one
great in a different way. His blues solo on *Israel* is a beautiful
example of classic simplicity of melody and of a personal
reassessment of the mood of the blues. His chorus on *Move*
is a striking episode of meaningful asymmetry, and it has
some phrasing that is so original that one can only say that,

rhythmically, it seems to turn back on itself while moving steadily forward.

Many a promising jazzman's career has come to a standstill after such achievements as these two solos, but Miles Davis had more, and still more to offer. Happily, he has found ways to offer it all, against both personal odds and a long-enduring public apathy (not to say hostility) toward his idiom.

Davis once confessed that he was not pleased with many of his own recordings, but he admitted to liking the series he did for Blue Note with trombonist J. J. Johnson. It happens that Davis recorded twice for Blue Note with Johnson. I don't know which is the session he likes, but on each of them he used pieces from Gillespie's early repertory (*Woody 'n' You, Ray's Idea, Chance It* or *Max is Makin' Wax*), others written along the same lines, and pieces from his own past (*Enigma* for one, is improvised around the framework of Davis's *Deception*). Like Louis Armstrong, Roy Eldridge and Dizzy Gillespie in their early repertories, Davis in effect reinterpreted in his own terms, the immediate past of jazz—and he did it for much the same reason as the others had, in order to move on.

In early 1954, a key year in the history of modern jazz in several respects, Miles Davis experienced a musical rebirth, a rebirth that brought him maturity as a jazz musician and ultimately led to a widespread popularity and acclaim. The essence of that maturity and, significantly, of that popularity as well, was the discovery of an intense, passionate, sometimes ravishing, highly personal trumpet sound. His style did not otherwise change much, except perhaps that it became simpler, or at least somewhat redistributed, more "open" and less compact. And it is surely important that the first full announcement of the rebirth came on two basic blues performances, *Walkin'* and *Blue 'n' Boogie*.

Dick Katz has written of these performances, *"Walkin'*

and its companion piece, *Blue 'n' Boogie* are acknowledged to be classics. To me they represent a sort of summing up of much of what had happened musically to the players involved during the preceding ten years. It is as if they all agreed to get together to discuss on their instruments what they had learned and unlearned, what elements of bop (horrible word) they had retained or discarded. An amazing seminar took place." The "they" also included tenor saxophonist Lucky Thompson, whose ideas of rhythm and phrasing belong to an earlier style; Kenny Clarke, who virtually invented modern jazz drumming; trombonist J. J. Johnson, the first and still most important modernist on his instrument; and pianist Horace Silver, a relative newcomer.

The overtly complex harmonic challenges, the shifting and substitute chords, were behind Davis. He was interested in a direct building up of melodic content, and he had learned to make pause, silence, and space a crucially expressive part of his musical language. Beginning now, one passionate note from Miles Davis seemed to imply a whole complex of expressive sound, and three notes a ravishing melody.

All of these things had perhaps been implicit from the beginning, but not the renewed emotional intensity of his sound. It frequently found expression in tightly harmon-muted horn, played close to the microphone. But far from being a phenomenon of electronics, it was a triumph of human feeling over its electronic vehicle. And Davis's control of his trumpet, and of the more difficult fluegelhorn, although it is far from obvious, includes a wide range of sounds along with a clear execution of unexpected rhythms.

On the whole, Miles Davis seems a lucky man, for apparently he can have it both ways: his records, like those of the Modern Jazz Quartet, seem to please people who want their music to be only a kind of fairly lively background sound issuing from their phonographs. But they also please those who expect the strongest kind of emotional statements from jazz and who expect the kind of musical and aesthetic interest that the best jazzmen provide. The lightness of his trumpet sound has something to do with his broad acceptance, to be sure, and because of that lightness he has been called "a man walking on eggshells." But Davis the musician walks firmly and sure of foot; if he ever encounters any eggshells, his intensity will probably grind them to powder.

The best introduction to Davis's particular distillation of jazz melody is a comparison in the blues theme he has called variously *Sid's Ahead* or *Weirdo*. In this piece, Davis has abstracted the theme of *Walkin'* and reduced it to an essence of three notes, and he has done it so brilliantly as to make the delightfully original *Walkin'* seem overdecorative. Davis's best improvising has the same evocative economy and hint of mystery.

The *Blue 'n' Boogie* date was no fluke; soon after, Davis produced a lovely solo on *The Man I Love* and an ingenious development of *Bags' Groove*—these also including first-rate Milt Jackson and (on *Bags' Groove*) brilliant Thelonious Monk. At the same time, a culturally lagging public was catching up to modern jazz and each of these soloists was destined for public popularity and success.

Popularity first came to Miles Davis with the quintet he formed in 1955 with tenor saxophonist John Coltrane (a dexterous foil to Davis's lyricism, as Davis had conversely been to Charlie Parker), and a rhythm section that played with apparent smoothness and continuity but that also provided subtly complementary polyrhythms and accents from Philly Joe Jones—a drummer who can roll back on himself while simultaneously moving forward in something of the way that Davis himself had done on *Move*.

The group also frequently played "in two," accenting the

second and fourth beats, once the weak beats, in a kind of upside-down Dixieland. In this, in several other aspects of his style, and in the Davis's repertory of the time (*Surrey with the Fringe on Top, Gal in Calico, I Don't Want to be Kissed, Just Squeeze Me, New Rhumba, Ahmad's Blues,* etc.) Miles Davis was clearly influenced by the trio of pianist Ahmad Jamal. One can readily understand why, since Jamal is a sophisticated harmonicist and, like Davis, uses space and openness in his music. Despite the impeccable swing of Jamal's group, however, his music seems chic and shallow— all of which is another way of saying that good art, and particularly good popular art, can be strongly influenced by bad. Miles Davis, after all, can undertake such unspeakably mawkish material as *Some Day My Prince Will Come, Put Your Little Foot Right In* (which he calls *Fran Dance*), or *Spring Is Here* and make them palatable by his intense involvement as he recomposes their melodies. In repertory, as in other obvious respects, Miles Davis's music often represents the triumph of an innate artistic sensibility over middle-brow taste.

Possibly the most miraculous transformation of all is *Bye Bye Blackbird*: an admittedly light, militant, but shallow ditty, which Davis transmuted into a beautifully pensive theme, playing one chorus of melodic paraphrase (accompanied "in two") and two choruses of invention (accompanied in an even, four beats with discreet countermovements from Jones's sticks).

With public success, came a new alliance of Davis and Gil Evans on a series of LPs the most celebrated of which is the first, called "*Miles Ahead.*" Evans has frequently provided a fascinating and effective setting for Davis's improvisations. On the other hand, it seems to me that Evans does not utilize the rhythmic idiom of modern jazz. And in his approach there is the implicit danger that one may end up

providing only a succession of beefed-up, quasi-impressionist color-harmonies and background for Davis's horn, a danger which is fully encountered in some selections on the
languid Davis-Evans LP called *"Quiet Nights."*
The Evans-Davis collaboration called *"Sketches of Spain"*
is a truly arresting performance, however. It begins with a
reorchestration of the first movement of Joaquin Rodrigo's
Concierto de Aranjuez for Guitar and Orchestra to feature
Davis as the soloist; the recording is something of a curiosity
and a failure, as I think a comparison with any good performance of the movement by a classical guitarist would confirm. But Evans provided fanfares for a *Saeta,* a traditional
Holy Week vocal lament for the dead Christ, and Miles
Davis plays with a stark, deeply felt communal anguish that
jazz has not heard since King Oliver.

There was a public Miles Davis during the 1950s therefore, a Davis who performed familiar pieces from his repertory at fast tempos—fast enough to get away from him at
times. One found himself asking why. If he is bored with
that one then why does he play it? Is he impatient with
this one? Why is his opening statement on that one so seemingly lackadaisical? But his playing answers such questions
almost as soon as they are asked. When he is successful in
such returns to his popular repertory Davis is once again the
brilliant sketch artist whose abstractions of standards like
Autumn Leaves and *All of You* can be as knowingly precise
as they are evocative.

Popularity invites artistic complacency, and in our world
it particularly invites the complacency of reducing one's
successes to a safe formula and repeating it. I cannot say that
I believe Miles Davis has always avoided repeating himself.
But in 1959 he recorded *"Kind of Blue,"* a remarkable LP
recital which took its place as one of the most provocative
events in jazz since the mid-'forties.

I have spoken of the surface simplicity of the jazz of the late 'fifties, of a cutting back, opening up, and airing out of the density of modern jazz—which involved less emphasis on complex harmonic background and a greater emphasis on melody. When such retrenchments of style take place (an earlier example would be the Count Basie of the late 'thirties), major changes are probably at hand. It is a credit to Davis that at a moment of public success, his work should move in the direction of those changes.

Most of the material on *"Kind of Blue"* was new to the musicians; it was presented to them when they arrived for the recording session. Most of the pieces were done in a single take, and most of the improvisation was done using points of departure that jazzmen had only rarely undertaken before. *So What*, for example, in a sense restricted as well as free in its outline, asks the improviser to make his melody from one assigned Dorian mode for sixteen measures, then a half-step up for eight measures, then back to the first mode for a final eight measures. The result was a superb Davis performance. *Flamenco Sketches* (which was mislabeled *All Blues*, and vice versa) sets up five different scales and asks the player to improvise on each of them in turn, moving from one to the next as he wishes.

"Kind of Blue" was an influential record both in and of itself and because it paralleled other, independently conceived, events in jazz. But for a while it seemed a rather isolated event for Davis himself—one might say that it was more immediately important to John Coltrane's development than to Davis—and for the next few years the repertory of ballads and standards was resumed to a great extent.

Then, beginning in 1965, Miles Davis returned to the principles he had asserted six years earlier. In association with his tenor saxophonist, Wayne Shorter, and his remarkable young drummer, Tony Williams, Davis began to build up a repertory of original, instrumentally conceived jazz compositions of unusual and generally unhackneyed structures. These placed Davis in the advanced guard of the period.

The pieces, and the LP performances in which they were introduced, inevitably vary in quality, but they form a remarkable series of recordings nevertheless. Perhaps most important, they indicate that Miles Davis has continued to explore and develop his talent for over thirty years thus far. That is unusual, virtually unique, in a music where many instrumentalists have been able to sustain and refine the achievements of their twenties and early thirties, but few have been able to go beyond them.

However, when one reminds himself that the lyric *Circle*, the "extended" piece *Country Son*, and *Petit Machins*, which are among the high achievements of Miles Davis in the 'sixties, were all written by Davis himself, things appear in a different light. Perhaps, as he entered his forties, the composer in Miles Davis was reborn, and is both sustaining and challenging the instrumentalist in him.

One must acknowledge, if only in passing, the great contribution of drummer Tony Williams to these recordings. The dense, complex, polyrhythmic textures of his best performances are wonders in themselves, yet they are always in motion, always swing, are always responsive to the soloist and the ensemble, and are never interfering or distracting. And for his splashing, complex cymbal work alone, Williams belongs among the great drummers in jazz history.

Because of its unique, evocative character, Miles Davis's music has challenged many a reviewer to deal with its emotional content and deal with it in fairly specific terms. One man says he hears in Davis the defeat and despair of an effete nihilist. Another hears forceful lyricism. Another ecstacy. Still another, the whine of a complaining, disgruntled child.

I began by saying that Davis's music, like that of other important contemporaries, echoed the past and particularly echoed the 'thirties. We hear Gillespie and Parker in him, but often their ideas are so transmuted that they become unrecognizable. There is also a deep respect for Lester Young in him. And sometimes the edge and curve of his trumpet sound hints that he is reinterpreting the whole range of the Ellington trumpets of 1939—the textures of the section, the purer leading voice of Wallace Jones, the growl of Cootie Williams, and the wail of Rex Stewart's squeezed half-valves—all on Davis's nearly vibratoless, open, or tightly-muted horn.

But there is one echo of the past that seems to me to be central, and for it Miles Davis has reached back two generations and brought a seminal style up to date. More than any other player, Miles Davis echoes Louis Armstrong; one can hear it, I think, in his reading of almost any standard theme. And behind the jaded stance, beneath the complaints, and beneath the sometimes blasé sophistication, Miles Davis's horn also echoes something of Armstrong's exuberantly humorous, forcefully committed, and self-determined joy.

15

JOHN COLTRANE

A Man in the Middle

John Coltrane had his followers, imitators, and popularizers from the time that he was first a member of Miles Davis's quintet in 1955. There are musicians who show the influence of his playing at almost every period of his career, and that fact reminds us that he was an important jazzman. It also reminds us of how much his playing changed during his lifetime. Or perhaps one should say, how often it changed, because on the surface at least, some of the changes seemed to come abruptly, almost as though some phases of Coltrane's career were not evolutionary exactly, but deliberate.

When he first attracted attention with Miles Davis, Coltrane was sometimes spoken of as another "hard" tenor player—hard as opposed to cool—but even then Coltrane's sound was personal, and it was hard almost to the point of brittleness.

Otherwise, Coltrane was a vertical player, a kind of latter-day Coleman Hawkins. And that means that he moved somewhat counter to the direction that jazz saxophone had been following since the mid-'forties. Dexter Gordon was the leading player of a generation of tenor men who, receiving guidance from Charlie Parker, had made a synthesis of the styles of Coleman Hawkins and Lester Young. They liked

Hawkins's big sound, but Young's limited vibrato; they liked Hawkins's harmonic sophistication and exactness, but they preferred Young's linear melodies to Hawkins's arpeggios; and they favored Young's variety of rhythm and phrase-length over Hawkins's four-bar, heavy/light/heavy/light regularity.

However, Coltrane owes more to the Hawkins heritage and to a brilliant Hawkins follower like Don Byas, than to Lester Young or any of Young's followers, or to Dexter Gordon or any of *his* followers first or second-hand.[1] And I think that in Coltrane's early work his rhythmic conception was a personal adaptation of Byas's, with its heavy accents on the first and third beats and frequent flurry of notes on the weak second and fourth beats. If one doubts this, I think he will find it confirmed in the playing of Coltrane's one-time associate, Benny Golson, for Golson will sometimes slip from a very much Byas-inspired style into a Coltrane idiom, and the transition seems logical.

Coltrane's 1955–56 solos with Miles Davis are largely exploratory. He seemed more interested in discovery than in making finished statements, as though for the time being he were occupied with turning up a vocabulary with which future sentences, paragraphs, and essays might be built.

There is another aspect of his recorded style, particularly at this period, which might confirm the view that his approach was tentative. It is a tendency for Coltrane's terminal phrases to end with an apparent fumble of notes, or to diminish into a kind of mutter or hesitantly delivered cliché. Perhaps the exploratory Coltrane swallowed his endings because he found himself suddenly up against a banality which he saw no way of avoiding, but which he did not really want to pronounce.

1. Noncommercial tape recordings from Coltrane's younger days exist that indicate he did go through a brief Gordon period himself.

Even Coltrane's most provocative solo from this period, on the Davis version of Thelonious Monk's *'Round Midnight* (Columbia version), has a hesitant note or two here and there, but it was prophetic of the next step in his career. In mid-1957 Coltrane became a member of Monk's quartet. I don't suppose the importance of that event to Coltrane's development could be underestimated, although the importance of the group itself has been assessed here in the chapter on Monk. Coltrane's work remained exploratory, expanding his techniques along the lines his past work had indicated. But with Monk's music (as the truism has it) one has to know the melodies and their harmonies, and understand how they fit together in order to improvise well, and Coltrane understood this. Thus, a solo like Coltrane's on *Trinkle Tinkle,* for all its bursting virtuosity, which runs into elusive corners of Monk's piece and proceeds to build its own structures, is constantly orderly and keeps us constantly oriented because of the nature of Monk's piece and Coltrane's understanding of it.

Leaving Monk, Coltrane rejoined Miles Davis, and his solo with the trumpeter on the Monk blues in F, *Straight No Chaser,* is a powerful and arrestingly full statement of where Coltrane *was* at the time. But several of the harmonically architectonic solos on the Coltrane LP *"Blue Train"* also give indication of where he might be headed and of some of the problems he would encounter.

The title blues, *Blue Train,* has a prophetically eerie and mysterious statement from the leader. The faster *Locomotion* (a 12/12/8/12 blues) gives an exposition of Coltrane's unique melodic-rhythm at perhaps its fullest development. *Moment's Notice* has a rather undistinguished theme which it uses to set up a series of challengingly difficult chord changes for the soloist.

The post-Monk Coltrane, then, was a prodigious saxo-

phonist and a prodigious harmonicist. He had also extended
the range of his instrument, the textures of sound he was
able to evoke from it, and the human quality of his saxophone voice.

Coltrane could superimpose a complex of passing chords,
substitute chords, and harmonic extensions upon a harmonic
structure that was perhaps already complex. And at times he
seemed prepared to gush out every possible note, find his
way step-by-step through every complex chord, careen
through every scale, and go even beyond that prolixity by
groping for impossible notes and sounds on a tenor saxophone that seemed ready to shatter under the strain.

There were times, also, in the performances with Monk
and those with Davis that immediately followed them, when
it seemed that, in an effort to get it all in, Coltrane was
reaching for a kind of subdivided bop rhythm, into a six-
teenth-note accent pattern. Such a thing had to be tried, and
was even predictable, but to say so is not to belittle Coltrane
for having undertaken the task—particularly not if I am
correct that Coltrane's basic rhythmic concept came from
Hawkins and Byas, who, in contrast to Armstrong, were
almost "European" in their use of heavy and light accents
within a 4/4 time context. Such a subdivided rhythm would
obviously create problems in both melody and swing—it is
difficult to improvise melodically and to swing (at least to
swing in the traditional sense) when one is thinking rhythmically in such a rapidity of notes. But Coltrane avoided a
direct confrontation with such problems to concentrate on
his saxophone sound and technique, and on harmonies.

From one point of view, the post-Monk Coltrane had
pushed jazz harmonies as far as they could go. From another,
such complex, sophisticated knowledge set its own trap, and
Coltrane, still a vertical thinker, careened around like a
laboratory hamster trapped in a three-dimensional harmonic

maze of his own making. ("You don't have to play *every-thing!*" Miles Davis is reported to have said to him.)

To this Coltrane, a Miles Davis piece like *Milestones,* or pieces like *So What, All Blues,* and some of the others on the Davis recital *"Kind of Blue"* must have come as revelations. Here were "modal" pieces, with harmonic challenges cut to a minimum, and with the soloist allowed to invent on a single chord or scale for sixteen measures, or even for as long as he liked. Coltrane sounded a bit hesitant on *Milestones,* but he met the challenges of *So What* and *All Blues* like a man who saw—or thought he saw—an exit from the maze.

"Kind of Blue" is key evidence of one of the most remarkable events to take place in Western music in this century. Why should a comparable modality suddenly appear—coincidentally and almost simultaneously—in the music of Ornette Coleman, of Miles Davis and John Coltrane, of the Detroit rock and roll groups, of the British rock groups, of the American "folk" ensembles, and even crop up in the music of the more traditional Chicago-based blues bands? In any case, Ornette Coleman is a horizontal melodist of exceptional rhythmic freedom, and his use of modality *cum* atonality is rather different from Coltrane's use of scalar or pedal-point modality. That was true in the beginning (as I think is demonstrated by Coltrane's 1960 versions of some of Coleman's pieces on the LP *"The Avant Garde"*), and it remained true.

Coltrane's first LP as a leader that followed on *"Kind of Blue"* did not immediately build on it. *Giant Steps,* the title piece, echoes *Moment's Notice* in setting up a difficult and ingenious series of chords for the soloist to run through. *Naima* attempts a kind of compromise by suspending a series of sophisticated changes over an *e* flat pedal tone, with a *b* flat in the bridge, and allowing the soloist to take either

course. Coltrane's solo on *Countdown,* in which he several
times employs a complex double-motive, has been praised
for its form. But I think the solo raises fundamental questions about when the reiteration of a motive is a means to
order, and when it is a matter of repetitiousness.

At this point in his career Coltrane encountered *My
Favorite Things,* and that piece could serve his purposes in
almost the same way that *How High the Moon* had served
Parker's and Gillespie's. Here was a popular song that had,
built-in so to speak, the same sort of things that he had been
working on: very little chordal motion, folk-like simplicity,
a quasi-Eastern mystery, and incantation. Simple but at the
same time sophisticated, the piece could contain Coltrane's
prodigiousness as an improviser. In no sense was *My Favorite Things* an artistic compromise for Coltrane—and in no
sense should it be a surprise that his first recording of it
was a best seller.

As he pursued modality, however, evenings with Coltrane,
a vertical player working with minimal harmonic understructures, began to sound to some listeners like long vamps-
til-ready, or furious, unattached cadenzas, or lengthy *mon-
tunas* introducing rhumbas or *sons* that never got played.
As one wag put it at the time, "I went to hear Coltrane last
night. He played forty-five minutes of C-minor ninths."
And forty-five minutes on a C-minor pedal-tone, it became
increasingly clear, do not lead to musical freedom.

I know that Coltrane's audiences were usually enthralled.
I know the sincerity, the powerful and authentic emotion,
and the frequent skill involved; I am aware of the truly
astonishing contribution of Coltrane's drummer Elvin Jones
to his music, and of the innovative importance of his work;
and yet—to be entirely subjective about Coltrane's music
at this period—I was, and am, repeatedly disengaged. After
three or four minutes my attention wanders, and giving the
records try after try does not seem to help.

Two extended performances from 1961 represent the
turning point, *Impressions* and *Chasin' The Trane*. On each,
his improvising had become more horizontal, more linear
than previously. *Impressions* borrows an opening melody
from Debussy, to revisit, two years later, the same modes and
the song form structure that Miles Davis used on *So What*.
Before the performance is over, Coltrane is reiterating a
little half-scale figure.

Virtually the same figure dominates a portion of *Chasin'
the Trane*. *Chasin' the Trane* is the key Coltrane performance from this period and has become a highly influential
one among younger musicians. Coltrane's use of reiterated
phrases on these pieces is neither sequential nor significantly
organizational nor truly developmental. (And in this, he
is in direct contrast to Ornette Coleman.) Coltrane's use of
such motives seems deliberately repetitive and incantive.
And one man's incantation is another man's monotony.
With Elvin Jones laying down a rich and complex pattern
beneath him, Coltrane's sing-song lines sound thin, and his
occasional saxophone cries and shrieks seem protestations
against that very thinness.

I may hear this Coltrane wrongly, but if I do perhaps I
can at least put questions to those who hear him better,
questions that they may find worth answering. And perhaps
the key question is whether so able and knowledgeable a
vertical player could still walk upright when setting himself so decidedly horizontal a task.

The Coltrane that I better admire from this period is the
deliberately conservative Coltrane. The Coltrane who stated
Duke Ellington's *In a Sentimental Mood* so perceptively yet
personally and without overembellishment. (Yet with *Take
the Coltrane*, on the same LP, we are back with *Chasin' the
Trane*.) And there is a similarly conservative Coltrane on
the LP called *"Crescent."* There for the moment at least he
seemed to have profited by the years of complex harmony

and by the years of modality, to return like a hero from a
perilous but necessary journey, ready to share the fruits of
his experience. Harsh dangers and exotic beauties are related on the title piece, *Crescent,* and the once "impossible"
saxophone sounds seem natural and firmly established techniques. Reflections and evaluations of the journey take
place on *The Wise One.* And *Bessie's Blues* might be called
a joyful celebration of the new insight the hero had provided. Perhaps it was also an element of comparative calm
and of reflection that made Coltrane's *"A Love Supreme"*
a best seller.

On the other hand, *Ascension* is probably Coltrane's most
daring recording. It is a thirty-eight minute performance
on which the leader's regular quartet was augmented by two
trumpeters, two tenor saxophonists, two altos, and an extra
bassist. There is a single, slight thematic idea; there are several turbulent, loose, improvised ensembles; and there are
solos by most of the participants. The performance soars
and it sings. And it rages, blares, shouts, screams, and shrieks.
It is at the same time a contemporary jazz performance and
a communal rite.

Ascension is directly indebted to Ornette Coleman's *Free
Jazz,* and that fact inevitably invites comparison between the
two. For me Coleman's work invokes the contemporary
demons as unflinchingly as Coltrane's, but is a thing of
beauty and affirmation and hope. *Free Jazz,* to use James
Joyce's superb phrase, better sees the darkness shining in
the light.

The later *Meditations* was offered as an "extension" of
A Love Supreme. I would say that it undertakes to lead us
through the torments of *Ascension* and into the world of
A Love Supreme, and that the effort is honorable and commendable. The piece seems to state the dichotomy and the
dilemma; it parallels the two moods. But it does not truly

bring them together in resolution. And the final section, "Serenity," seems both unconvincing and arbitrarily arrived at—and, perhaps not incidentally, the piano solo that introduces it is both a bit pretentious and dubious as jazz.

Thus, some of Coltrane's work from the 'sixties seems brilliant, and some of it repetitious and banal. And there are times when Coltrane's authentically wild passion seems not so much a part of the music as a part of the musician, the reaction of a player who is improvising with a minimum of built-in protections but who sometimes cries out in frustration against the very limitations that he has set for himself, limitations that once seemed so necessary. Sometimes my impression is of having heard musical statements that have brilliant moments but that become static and remain unresolved, statements that are contained only by a fantastic and original saxophone technique on one hand, or by a state of emotional exhaustion on the other. And it is perhaps indicative that several of his later records were faded out by the engineers rather than ended by the musicians.

I began by saying something about the ways that Coltrane's music changed. And there have been several musics—Oriental and African, as well as American—that interested him and directly influenced him during his last twelve years. The changes in his work may, of course, have been signs of growth, and if they were, few important jazz improvisers have grown and developed as much as Coltrane did in so short a time. But, on the other hand, the changes may have been naïve. Or they may have been signs of personal indecision or frustration.

Does one, then, with Coltrane take his choice between the alternatives of a true artistic growth or of mere change? Perhaps not, or not necessarily. Perhaps a deeper frustration and tormented indecision are part of the unacknowledged truth of the temper of the times which it was Coltrane's destiny simply to articulate rather than interpret. If so, he was an artist of primary rank.

In any case, Coltrane was bold enough to state his message so that the present knows of him, and so that the future must acknowledge that he was with us.

16

ORNETTE COLEMAN

Innovation from the Source

A popular artist is apt to find his own ways of expression, and no one would claim that for him an increase in conventional techniques necessarily has anything to do with an increase in expressiveness. As our comic strip artists become better draftsmen, they may produce more soap opera; as our sound films become more technically resourceful, they seem to talk more, say less, and show hardly anything.

Jazz, on the other hand, seems to thrive on acquiring new techniques and on periodic change, and, with each legitimate change, to expand its scope and retain its creative life. Change in jazz has involved losses, but so far they have been the inevitable losses of an organic growth—they have been sure signs of life. In describing such changes, one must use the terms he has to describe what he hears—or go to the trouble of inventing and explaining new ones.

It is not enough to say that Ornette Coleman's music will affect jazz profoundly, for it already has so affected it, and not only the jazz of younger men but that of some of his elders as well. His music represents the first fundamental reevaluation of basic materials and basic procedures for jazz since the innovations of Charlie Parker. "Let's play the music and not the background," Coleman has said. And when

someone does something with the passion and deep conviction of an Ornette Coleman, I doubt if there could be any
turning back; it seems mandatory somehow for others to
follow and explore in the direction he indicates.

In any case, it is surely no longer required, when Coleman
writes a fourteen-bar blues, that one suggest that he did it
deliberately. Or, when, in improvising, he fails to treat a
theme as though it automatically set up a series of predetermined chord changes or a rigid outline of four and
eight-bar phrases that must be followed, it is surely no longer
required to explain that he does so purposefully and not out
of ignorance. "If I'm going to follow a preset chord sequence,
I may as well write out my solo."

Ornette Coleman's first recordings do not so much outline
his own music as they juxtapose some of his own ideas with
those of his predecessors. The tunes are his own. Like all his
pieces they are functional vehicles to introduce his improvising—and good, appropriate, sometimes excellent, composed
melody seems to flow out of him. But these early vehicles
still have the rhythms and forms of be-bop clinging to them,
and some of them use popular song sequences recognizably:
Jayne echoes *Out of Nowhere,* and *Angel Voice* is Ornette's
I Got Rhythm. (It is interesting that the latter seemed to
appeal to him as a rhythmic pattern rather than as an harmonic one.) *The Sphinx* and *Chippie,* however, indicate
a desire to change the four, eight, and thirty-two-bar phrase
boxes of song form.

The quest to achieve his own music is clearly stated in his
first entrance on the opening bridge to *Invisible,* where
Parker-esque accents vie with a loose and highly vocalized
phrasing of his own.[1] Throughout the LP, it is clear that
Coleman does not want to run chord changes to make his

---

1. I have heard Coleman play an uncannily exact reproduction of Parker's
style, by the way, and others attest to having heard him do the same for
previous alto styles.

melodies, although he does regularly run the phrases of the pieces. His effort to get his horn to "speak" is also everywhere evident. And it's interesting that his playing is at its most "free" and most personal on a blues (a somewhat tonally ambiguous blues) *The Disguise.*

Coleman's second LP, *"Tomorrow is the Question"* [2] is a step forward. First, and perhaps most obvious, the chordally anchoring piano has been eliminated, never to return. Coleman's themes and improvisations are freerer of be-bop accents, and more original rhythmically.

On *Lorraine,* particularly, Coleman's phrasing and melodic rhythm are his own. The piece is the first of a series of exceptional dirges that includes *Lonely Woman* and *Sadness,* and *Lorraine* effectively uses a contrasting fast section both in the writing and the improvising. On the blues with the inspired title *Tears Inside,* Coleman's personally intoned solo is initially unsettling and ultimately self-justifying.

Thus he was becoming an original, interesting, intense, and orderly improviser, if not quite yet a brilliant one.

"The Shape of Jazz To Come," recorded in 1959, is a pivotal record in Coleman's development and in the evolution of the new jazz, and it clarified much about the music.

In the first place, it reassesses the theme-and-variations form for jazz—indeed it ultimately rejects the form, and with good reason. For in a theme-and-variations approach the theme is primary and the variations secondary. But in jazz, the improvised variations are often the substance of the music, and variation and interpretation, at least in the form of embellishment and paraphrase, may extend even to an opening theme-statement itself.

In Coleman's music, a theme may be interpreted by even

2. I do not like the deliberately futuristic titles of several of his LPs and pieces, and whether they proved to be accurate or not, I expect that at the time they were a tactical error.

two horns in an opening and closing "unison" passage. It is
obviously difficult to do such a thing without sounding amateurish, but Coleman and Don Cherry do it extremely well.

Further, an opening theme may set a mood, fragments of
melody, an area of pitch, or rhythmic patterns, as points of
departure for the player to explore. It need not set up patterns of chords or patterns of phrasing. Or if it does, these
may be expanded, condensed, used freely—it does not necessarily take eight measures to explore an idea that it took
eight measures to state, and an improvisation initially built
on a melody itself need not also follow a harmonic outline
that melody might suggest. (One remembers Charlie Parker's remark that "You can do *anything* with chords.") Nor
would tempo in improvising have to be constant, but
whereas Coleman (like Monk before him) had at this time
used dual-tempos in his pieces, the question of tempo had
to wait for further development, as we shall see.

But the question of accents and phrasing did not have to
wait, and Coleman's melodic rhythm is freer, more varied,
and more original—without on the surface being necessarily
more "complex." "Rhythmic patterns should be as natural
as breathing patterns," he has commented. And if the past is
a standard, an original development in rhythm is the surest
key to valid innovation in jazz.

Many of Coleman's individual melodic rhythms, and the
responses they inspire in his bass players and drummers, are
quite old-style and simple. But he uses them as parts of a
free, varied, and developing pattern. He does not offer a
further subdivision of the beat, as Armstrong, Lester Young,
and Parker had done, but a greater variety and freedom in
rhythm and phrase. It should go without saying that a free
and original use of meters and accents is quite a different
matter from setting up a tricky or difficult time-signature
and then (as happens more often than not in such "experi-

ments") skating over it with bop phrasing, after making a slight initial adjustment. Melodic rhythm and polyrhythmic juxtapositions are essentials in jazz. And time-signatures, on paper or in performance, are sometimes a fiction or a mere convenience. Intonation is a matter of context and expression to Coleman. "You can play sharp in tune and you can play flat in tune," he has said, and a D in a context representing sadness should not sound like a D in a passage of joy. (A modern classicist would say that Coleman uses "microtones.") This of course has nothing to do with "good" intonation, and if there be any doubt about that, there are enough key notes and phrases in Coleman's solos on exact pitch to dispel that doubt. Further, split-tones, harmonics, tense upper register cries, and gutteral low register sounds may be used expressively—not an entirely new idea but one which Coleman has developed with taste.

Coleman's improvising is predominantly modal, even diatonic, but under the inspiration of the moment he may move out of key, hence into a momentary atonality. Furthermore, since a chord pattern is not preset to a soloist, or at least may be freely departed from, there is a texture of atonality set up by the juxtaposition of the alto's lines and those of the bass which moves in a kind of interplaying, melodic and dissonant counterpoint rather than accompaniment. There are of course momentary, *passing*, intervalic "clashes" of tones between players in traditional contexts too, between a pianist and his bass player, and among the horns in a New Orleans ensemble. Further, Ornette tends to suspend his lines to leave them airborne, without making customary cadences and tonic resolutions. And he has also functioned with ease in a context of complete "classical" atonality, as his remarkably perceptive improvising in Gunther Schuller's twelve-tone *Abstraction* demonstrates.

Analogies between Coleman's music and procedures in other musics, particularly East Indian music, are obvious. But I think a better understanding comes when we reflect on how much of what he does is implicit in Coleman's own sources. One thinks of the many "primitive" bluesmen (Clarence Lofton, or vocally, Sonny Terry) to whom the blues is a flexible, not a rigidly twelve-measure form—whether out of ignorance or inspiration may not matter. In the free-handed use of chord changes, one thinks of Lester Young. In the matter of expressive intonation, Coleman has raised the idea of the blue notes and other vocally inflected tones to the level of first principles that may encompass whole melodies. One thinks also of Charlie Parker's tendency to play slightly sharp. Indeed, one hears all the reed players in jazz history differently, from Sidney Bechet and Johnny Dodds onward, for having heard Ornette Coleman.

Certainly, Coleman did not contrive any of his procedures, nor force them on the music academically out of a conscious effort to "improve" it. His artistic daemon tells him to do these things. And the procedures show a penetrating, intuitive understanding of the nature of the music and its implications. "It was when I found out I could make mistakes that I knew I was onto something."

Several players preceded Coleman more immediately in undertaking something of the same kind of spontaneity one hears in his music, and to mention some of them is undoubtedly to neglect others. But one thinks of Lennie Tristano's efforts at an unpremeditated group music. One thinks of Charlie Mingus's similar efforts and of his "extended form" in which a soloist may spontaneously extend a piece by turning any of its chords into a pedal-tone for as long as he wishes to explore it—a procedure in which the rhythm section is to follow the soloist. And one thinks of Cecil Taylor's music, particularly in the way that Taylor's piano and his bassists' accompaniments may move in a-harmonic directions. But to mention such efforts is not to raise the question of their "influence" on Coleman, and indeed several of those efforts were largely isolated. It is only to give further evidence that the procedures in his music are not so radical as they may seem, and were probably inevitable.

One does not enjoy such "theoretical" discussion before going to the music, of course, but one can hope that it serves its purpose. In any case, *"The Shape of Jazz to Come"* is a remarkable record in many respects.

Peace is a beautifully conceived piece, and Coleman's improvisation is remarkable for its natural swing. Compositionally it has an opening section of twenty-five measures, a bridge of ten, a return to the opening twenty-five measures, and a closing coda of five. Of course, jazz musicians have been working on the idea of a modification of song form and its measured phrasing at least since Ellington in 1929. But I think Coleman's efforts have a rather different and somewhat more natural quality than some of the others. He does not "break through" or "extend" existing forms so much as he lets each piece take its own form as its own inspiration dictates, with earlier forms as a general source in the background.

Focus on Sanity is an interesting "extended" work. Its two sections, with their separate tempos, do not really make it a "suite," and each ensemble portion truly sets up the impetus for the soloist.

Lonely Woman is a remarkable piece in plan and in execution, and a strong experience. It opens with bass and drums, each playing a separate but related rhythm, which they continue throughout. The horns enter, unexpectedly, in a third, dirge tempo, and, freely intoned, they interpret the stark theme, with momentary break-aways by the alto. Coleman's solo is in perfect time and tempo, of course, but the freely accented individual phrases and an adroit use of implied double-time give an immeasurable complexity and richness to the performance. "He is the first jazz musician since King Oliver," a friend has said, "whose playing does not seem egocentric to me."

I think that the responsive textural richness of the drums in this piece make one long for more complex, improvised polyrhythmic textures on other performances here, although Billy Higgins is an exceptional drummer of exceptional swing. (It is interesting that from Higgins to Ed Blackwell, to Charles Moffett, and the single "guest" appearance by Elvin Jones, Coleman's drummers have played with an increasing variety of textures. But Coleman has not, as I write, yet found his Tony Williams.)

Congeniality has a much-admired Coleman solo, including the marvelous "mistake" between bars 127 and 142 in which Coleman enters "early" and turns the beat around, but produces a momentary confusion in the rhythm section. He therefore stretches out a bar to accommodate them. They, meanwhile, have turned around to him, and Coleman, hearing this, turns his beat around again.

Similarly, there is the moment at the end of *Chronology* when Coleman is ready for the closing "head" but Don Cherry does not respond, so the saxophonist uses a few bars to give him a gutteral saxophone yell and call him in.

Such things are perhaps not "errors" so much as they are natural parts of a freely improvised music, and they can be heard on quite another level than a technical one. They are also complements to the otherwise almost telepathic understanding between Cherry and Coleman on matters of tempo and length of solo statement, and the responsive inspiration that Coleman and bassist Charlie Haden provide for each other.

One central impression that emerged from this recital was that Ornette Coleman, an obviously impassioned and inven-

tive player, working in a fresh and "free" and even fragmented idiom of his own, is also a logical melodist. His
music does not invite an a-harmonic chaos, but is decidedly
orderly, and orderly along quite traditional lines.

An idea appears, inspired perhaps by the meaning of the
tune or even by a single note or accent. It is phrased, and
rephrased, offered from every conceivable angle, developed
sequentially until it yields another idea. Or it appears and
reappears periodically in various guises within an otherwise
contrasting context as a kind of point of reference. Patterns
of tension and release are thus set up by the introduction
and ultimate development of brief motives, or by their appearance and reappearance. Ornette Coleman has extended
fundamental principles of orderly jazz improvisation that
have been around at least since King Oliver. And it seems
to me, that he took these matters up just where Thelonious
Monk left them with his *Bags' Groove* solo.

If such continuity does not immediately occur to a listener from a performance like *Congeniality*, he might try
one of Coleman's few solos on a piece by another man,
Gunther Schuller's *Variants on a Theme by Thelonious
Monk*, from Monk's *Criss Cross*. Coleman's entrance virtually dictates to the rhythm section the quality of the beat
he wants. Melodically, he is clearly interested in Monk's
theme and the ideas it suggests to him as his point of
departure.

I have said above that a modality comparable to Coleman's had appeared almost simultaneously and apparently
independently in the work of other jazzmen. This, plus the
fact that Coleman unquestionably influenced him later, invites a comparison between Coleman and John Coltrane.
Coleman's use of key motives is developmental and sequential. But Coltrane's was repetitious and incantatory. Further,
it seems to me that his modality *cum* atonality released Coleman melodically and rhythmically. But Coltrane undertook

"drone" modality out of a desire to cut back and limit a sizeable harmonically-oriented technique.

Coleman's best statements seem to me complete. He may avoid conventional resolutions, but his solos are entities because of their rhythmic and motivic continuity and development. And one is much less aware of the drone in his playing, I think, than in that of other modal improvisers.

Coleman's *"Change of the Century"* was recorded at about the same time as *"The Shape of Jazz To Come,"* and, if it does not expand on any of that album's ideas, it still has some good music. *Ramblin'*, for example, is a sort of light, blues impression of a Southwestern hoe-down. And *Free* has Ornette using some striking accents in his opening solo and an interesting moment when the fast tempo stops and then resumes with the exchange of soloists.

On *Beauty is a Rare Thing*, from mid-1960, we hear a collective improvisation by all four members of the quartet. That idea led to the remarkably conceived and remarkably influential *Free-Jazz* (1960), a flawed and brilliant work. A double quartet—two trumpets, two reeds, two basses, and two drummers—in a collective improvisation that lasted thirty-six minutes plus. There are solos, or rather there are exchanges of a lead voice with comments, encouragements, and countermelodies from the other players as they feel inspired. And there are written themes that introduce each section—these, plus the order of solos being the only premeditated aspects of the performance in the turbulent, purposeful, harrowing, and joyous textures. Here is a realization of the polyphonic possibilities that were implicit in Coleman's music since its beginnings.

There is effective contrast between the more traditional phrasing of Freddy Hubbard's trumpet and Eric Dolphy's bass clarinet, and the accents of Cherry and Coleman. On bass, Scott La Faro's virtuosity and Charlie Haden's almost lyric directness work beautifully together—indeed, the sections by the bassists and drummers (Billy Higgins and Ed Blackwell) are extraordinary. Coleman's section, which is roughly twice as long as the others, is both inspired and inspiring to the ensemble, although one wishes that the shuffle beat that gets set up behind him might have been tempered. Jazz is a music full of the stuff of life, and *Free Jazz* has the stuff of life in it as no other recorded performance I know of.

C. & D., from 1961, returns Coleman to a quartet, here with La Faro and Blackwell. Its theme has been praised for its melodic logic; its originality is equally evident. Similarly, Ornette's solo is almost traditional in its materials but not in his use of them.

R.P.D.D., from the same session, has a much praised solo. It benefits, I think, from the richly textured virtuosity of La Faro's bass, which is less sympathetically complementary than Haden's, but in its way no less inspiring to Coleman.

One thing that was eminently clear at this point was Coleman's mastery of the alto saxophone. But when he chose to make a subsequent recording on tenor sax (the instrument he had played for several years in rhythm and blues bands), he sounded entirely comfortable on that instrument. *Cross Breeding* has an admired tenor solo, and on *Mapa* he returned to the proposition of simultaneous improvising by the members of the quartet in a performance that moves back and forth from almost antiphonal textures to polyphony.

The trio recordings Coleman made in 1965 in Denmark show a striking renewal in his music. I do not admire his violin or trumpet playing as such, but on *Snowflakes and Sunshine* they are functionally effective parts of a singular, and even sophisticated, musical performance, to which David Izenzon's bass also makes an important contribution.

Dawn, truly an ensemble creation, is a beautiful piece, full of fear, expectation, and splendid, shining beauty.

The Riddle is a wonder: an extension of the traditional

idea of double-timing perhaps, a radical attack on the idea
of fixed tempo, and a real contribution to the jazz language.
Under the inspiration of the moment, the soloist and group
collectively and almost telepathically move in and out of
several tempos with such ease, naturalness, and musical logic
that one may barely notice what is happening, or recognize
its significance.

Also on *Antiques* from the Danish performances, a deliberately meandering, fragmented piece, there are casual
changes of tempo. But the idea gets a further development
on Coleman's later *Garden of Souls*, where tempo changes
are, again, clearly an integral part of a musical development.
But on *Broadway Blues* (built on the reevaluation of an old
riff), the tempo changes seem to be extensions of the retards
built into the theme itself.

Round Trip takes up the idea of polyphony again, but I
think the most significant work in that idiom since *Free
Jazz* is a piece called *Trouble in the East* from a 1969 concert.

Trouble in the East, played by Cherry, Coleman, Dewey
Redman on tenor saxophone, Charlie Haden on bass, and
Coleman's son, Denardo, on drums, is unlike any other collective improvisation ever undertaken in this idiom or any
other idiom. It seems spontaneously ordered in all its aspects,
due it would seem (I am guessing at this) to the assignment
of certain recurring motives to be freely used, particularly
by Redman. I wrote of its first performance that it "had the
timeless joy and melancholy of the blues running through
it. It had its feet planted on the earth and it spoke to the
gods. It was one of the most exciting, beautiful, and satisfying musical performances I have ever heard."

I have said little in the foregoing about the development
of Don Cherry, who began as an adroit "modernist" on
Coleman's first LP in whom one hears a synthesis of the work

of so many trumpeters of the 'forties and 'fifties. But I will here mention his piece *Complete Communion*, for it seems to me one of the most interesting efforts at an extended work in jazz history. Cherry has used counterpoint, both written and improvised; he has used both his bass and drums as melodic voices; Cherry's themes and improvised sections change tempo and flow one to the next; little ideas and riffs from each section echo through the rest of it. The solos are frequent, usually brief, and although I think a couple of them do rush to their climaxes a bit too soon, both the written passages and improvisation are related parts of a commendable overall compositional plan.

A music like Coleman's, which depends so much on reflex, and has so few built-in protections, risks much and demands inspired players. Coleman is inspired. And there is not in his music the sizable element of throw-away expendability one hears in the music of some younger players, wherein one waits through twenty minutes of effort for three minutes of excellence.

Coleman is an orderly player, but I do feel that, particularly since about 1962, his solos and his use of recurring motives may sometimes extend past the point of inspiration to the point of ingenuity and, beyond it, to the point of repetition—and I think that is true of some initially brilliant solos.

Coleman's example means that jazzmen may improvise with less premeditation and with fewer harmonic and phrasal protections—and this is the element of his music that has received wide acceptance among older and younger players alike. Like all the great innovators, Coleman has brought fresh and varied ideas of phrasing and melodic rhythm to the music, and he has also extended the idea of tempo. Finally, there are his ideas of emotional pitch and of individual and group tonality.

Such things represent major insights into the nature of jazz and into its source of growth. How future musicians will use those elements and insights is of course a matter for musicians—and perhaps the genius of the music itself—to decide. Meanwhile, for Coleman they have been a means by which he has brought us an authentic and impressive body of jazz.

DISCOGRAPHICAL NOTES

The availability of a phonograph record, once it has been issued, can be a matter of frustration for a buyer, and sometimes seems a matter of sheer caprice on the part of the record company, its distributor, or dealer. Records go in and out of print, in and out of stock, and even in and out of dealers' bargain bins frequently and rapidly. I have tried to list the most recently available issues of the titles I have discussed in the text. For some titles that have no recent American issue I have made note of British and European LPs, if their issue seemed recent enough to indicate current availability.

2. JELLY ROLL MORTON

"*Jelly Roll Morton, King of New Orleans Jazz*" (RCA Victor LPM 1649) contains fourteen of the great 1926 to 1928 orchestral recordings. However, three of the titles included are composite tapes which put together several different takes. *Dead Man Blues* particularly suffers in that George Mitchell's trumpet solo is spliced in from a rejected version.

Meanwhile, the otherwise uneven set "*Stomps and Joys*" (RCA Victor LPV-508) has *Mournful Serenade*, *Boogaboo*, and *Blue Blood Blues*. On the similarly uneven LPV-524, there are *Wild Man Blues* and *Tank Town Bump*; and on LPV-546, there are *New Orleans Bump*, *Deep Creek*, and the two takes of the trio version of *Wolverine Blues*.

"*Classic Jazz Piano*" (Riverside RLP 12-111) was a collection of the early Morton piano solos. It contains *King Porter Stomp*, *New Orleans Joys*, *Wolverine Blues*, *Jelly Roll Blues*, *Grandpa's Spells*, *Kansas City Stomps*, but unfortunately omitted *The Pearls*. *Muddy Water Blues* and *Big Fat Ham* are on Milestone 2003, as are (with their titles reversed on the album cover and label) *Froggy Moore* and the best version of *Mamanita*.

The delicate beauty of *Mamie's Blues* and the tango, *The Crave*, are probably enough in themselves to recommend Mainstream 56020 on which Morton plays, sings, and reminisces.

The Library of Congress series last appeared on Riverside 9001-9012. Riverside also released a couple of LPs drawn from the Library of Congress recordings: RLP 12-132 and RLP 12-140 being the best of them. The low fidelity is no problem, of course, although the occasional slowish speed of the recording turntable is a problem from time to time.

3. LOUIS ARMSTRONG

Basic Armstrong includes the Columbia series, CL 851 through 854. Volume 1 has *Hotter Than That*; volume 2 *Potato Head Blues, Gully Low* and *S.O.L. Blues*, and *Twelfth Street Rag*; volume 3 *Muggles, Tight Like This*, and *West End Blues*; volume 4 the 1929 *I Can't Give You Anything But Love* and two versions of *Stardust*, both from the same recording session.

The two *Stardusts* are duplicated on Epic EE 22019, which also has the two versions of *Between the Devil and the Deep Blue Sea*.

1933–34 recordings are collected on RCA Victor LPM 2322: *I Got a Right to Sing the Blues, Basin Street Blues, St. James Infirmary, That's My Home, Sleepy Time Down South*. RCA Victor LPM 2971 includes *I've Got the World on a String*. The exceptional Armstrong performance on *Sweethearts On Parade* is available on European LP, Odeon XOC176 or O 83 262.

Supplementary Armstrong: his presence with King Oliver's Creole Jazz Band can be heard on Riverside RLP 12-122, on Milestone 2006, on Epic 16003, and on Orpheum 105. There are nine Armstrong pieces in Columbia's *"Fletcher Henderson Story"* (C4L 19), and Milestone 2010 features some small group Armstrong from the same period, sometimes in the company of Sidney Bechet.

Decca DL 9233 has solos with Henderson and includes Armstrong's best version of *Wild Man Blues*. The rhythmic contrast between Armstrong and the other musicians on *Lucy Long* and *I Ain't Gonna Play No Second Fiddle* on this set is particularly enlightening.

The 'thirties are represented on Decca LPs. DL 8327 is uneven in its choice of selections but has *Jeepers Creepers, I Can't Give You*

Anything But Love, and others. Decca DL 9233 has *Jubilee, The Skeleton in the Closet, Ev'n Tide,* and *Lyin' to Myself.* An impressive 1947 concert at which he announced his return to leadership of a small group is available on RCA Victor LPM 1433.

My more recent examples *(Struttin' With Some Barbecue, Basin Street, Lazy River, Georgia on My Mind, King of the Zulus)* are drawn from the singularly uneven Decca set called *"Satchmo, a Musical Autobiography"* (DL 8604-7). The collection also includes a new *I Can't Give You Anything But Love* with an arrangement based on the 1929 version. The separate LPs of the *"Autobiography"* album are beginning to appear singly, and the two LPs in Decca's *"The Best of Louis Armstrong"* (DXB 183) also use some of the *"Autobiography"* material.

The 1948–52 Armstrong-Hines alliance is also represented on *"A Monday Date"* on Decca 8284 and on other Decca sets.

4. BIX BEIDERBECKE

Riverside RLP 12-123 (reissued as Orpheum 104) collected all of the Wolverines' recordings (except for one unimportant second take of one piece), including *Jazz Me Blues, Riverboat Shuffle, Royal Garden Blues, Tiger Rag,* and *Big Boy.*

There is a series of three Beiderbecke volumes on Columbia, the first (CL 844) by a small group under Bix's name, the second (CL 845) with Trumbauer's usually larger groups and including *Singin' the Blues, Way Down Yonder in New Orleans, For No Reason at All in C, I'm Comin' Virginia,* and *Riverboat Shuffle.* The final volume (CL 846) is largely devoted to solos with the Whiteman Orchestra, including *Sweet Sue.*

An RCA Victor set (LPM 2323) includes the rediscovered *I Didn't Know,* two takes of *Lonely Melody,* and *Dardanella.*

5. COLEMAN HAWKINS

All of the Henderson titles with Hawkins that I have cited except *Hocus Pocus* and *It's the Talk of the Town* come from Columbia's *"The Fletcher Henderson Story"* (C4L 19).

Hocus Pocus is in RCA Victor's Coleman Hawkins set, *"Body and Soul: A Jazz Autobiography"* (LPV-501), which also has the first *Body and Soul, Wherever There's a Will, Baby, One Hour, Dinah,* and *The*

Sheik of Araby. (Incidentally, the tenor soloist on the Lionel Hampton *Early Session Hop* included in this album is not Hawkins but Ben Webster.) An alternate take of *Hocus Pocus* was used in Victor's Red Allen album (LPV-556). *Hello Lola* is on Camden CAL 339. The European *Honeysuckle Rose* and *Crazy Rhythm* are on Prestige 7633. *It's the Talk of the Town* is on Prestige 7645.

Hawkins's second version of *Body and Soul* was last available on Grand Award 33-316. The Hawkins-Eldridge-Wilson *I'm In The Mood for Love* is on Emarcy 26011. The Hawkins-Eldridge *I Surrender Dear* (1940), on Mainstream 56037, is another exceptional performance from the great period.

The session which produced *The Man I Love, Sweet Lorraine*, and *Crazy Rhythm* was last available on Contact CM-3.

My choice for relatively recent Hawkins, on the Shelly Manne LP, is Impulse A-20.

6. BILLIE HOLIDAY

Verve V-8410 contains the 1956 Carnegie Hall concert, with *Yesterdays, I Cried for You, What a Little Moonlight Can Do*, and *Fine and Mellow*. The earlier *Yesterdays* is a part of Commodore 30,008 or Mainstream 6000, either of them an excellent set which also contain *I Got a Right to Sing the Blues*, the first *Fine and Mellow*, and *I Cover the Waterfront*.

Many of the early Billie Holiday and Teddy Wilson selections which I have mentioned are included in Columbia's three LP set, C3L21: *Your Mother's Son-in-Law, Riffin' the Scotch, These Foolish Things, A Fine Romance, Easy to Love, The Way You Look Tonight, Pennies from Heaven, I Can't Give You Anything But Love, Why Was I Born?, The Mood That I'm In, I'll Never Be the Same, Without Your Love, Swing! Brother, Swing!, They Can't Take That Away from Me, Getting Some Fun Out of Life, Trav'lin' All Alone, When You're Smiling, If Dreams Come True, I Can't Get Started, Back in Your Own Backyard, On the Sentimental Side, The Very Thought of You, All of Me, I Cover the Waterfront, The Man I Love, Body and Soul, Love Me or Leave Me, Gloomy Sunday*.

Columbia's second omnibus Holiday volume, C3L40 offers *Painting the Town Red, You Let Me Down, Let's Call the Whole Thing Off, Moanin' Low, Mean to Me, I'll Get By, He's Funny That Way, I Can't Believe That You're In Love with Me*, and *More Than You*

Know. (I prefer an earlier released take of the later piece over the one in current release.)

A supplement is Columbia CL 637 which has the Billie Holiday-Lester Young *Me, Myself and I,* and *The Sailboat in the Moonlight,* along with a spirited and celebrated *I Cried For You.* *Lover Man* is on Decca 8702. The April 1946 concert is on Verve V-8338-2, which also offers a good cross section of her post-1952 work, including the later *These Foolish Things.*

7. DUKE ELLINGTON

Essential Ellington is included in two RCA Victor LPs. *"At His Very Best"* (LPM 1715) includes the *Concerto for Cootie, Ko Ko, Jack the Bear, Harlem Air Shaft, Across the Track Blues,* and others. *"In a Mellotone"* (LPM 1364) offers, besides its title piece, *Mainstem, Blue Serge, Cottontail, Rumpus in Richmond, Sepia Panorama,* etc.

Columbia's *"Ellington Era"* (C3L 27), the first of a pair of LP albums, includes *East St. Louis Toodle-oo, Black and Tan Fantasy* (with Jabbo Smith taking Miley's part), *Hot and Bothered, Rockin' in Rhythm, Old Man Blues, Mood Indigo, It Don't Mean a Thing, Bundle of Blues, The Saddest Tale, Slippery Horn, Merry-Go-Round, Echoes of Harlem, Harmony in Harlem, I Let a Song Go Out of My Heart, Slap Happy, A Portrait of the Lion, Diminuendo and Crescendo in Blue.* I should add the warning that I detect a "wow," a wavering in pitch, in slow pieces like *Sophisticated Lady* on the third of the set.

The second *"Ellington Era"* volume (C3L 39) includes the 1932 *Creole Love Call, Showboat Shuffle, Reminiscing in Tempo, Azure,* and *Old King Dooji.*

Earlier Columbia LPs offered *The New East St. Louis Toodle-oo* and *The New Black and Tan Fantasy* (CL 558). *Blue Light* was last available on Columbia CL 2126; it was also included in Columbia CL 663. Victor LPV-568 has invaluable early Ellington.

More recent Ellington on Columbia includes *Such Sweet Thunder* on CL 1033, *Suite Thursday* on CL 1597, and splendid Ellington orchestrations of dance band standards on CL 1282.

The Victor version of *Black and Tan Fantasy* last appeared on LPM 1393. Victor LPV-506 includes *Echoes of the Jungle,* and Camden CAL 459, *"Duke Ellington at the Cotton Club"* has *Shout 'em Aunt Tillie* and a version of *Creole Rhapsody.*

Two relatively recent informal albums give some insight into how

Ellington works with his sidemen; they are by Ellington and Johnny Hodges, *"Back to Back"* (Verve MG V-8317) and *"Side by Side"* (Verve MG V-8345). There are several sets on Victor and Epic that have Ellington working earlier, and more formally, with small ensembles.

The earliest Ellington, including *Choo-Choo* and *Rainy Nights,* was last issued on Riverside 12-129.

8. COUNT BASIE AND LESTER YOUNG

The Benny Moten band can be heard on RCA Victor LPV-514. Decca DBX 170, *"The Best of Count Basie,"* includes *One O'Clock Jump, Time Out, You Can Depend on Me, Sent for You Yesterday, Swinging the Blues, Blues in the Dark, Doggin' Around, Jive at Five, Every Tub, John's Idea, Shorty George, Texas Shuffle,* etc. Epic's *"Lester Young Memorial"* (album SN 6031, available singly as LN 3107 and LN 3168) has the October 1936 quintet versions of *Lady Be Good* and *Shoe Shine Boy,* and picks things up again at March 1939, including *Taxi War Dance, Lester Leaps In, Dickie's Dream, Tickle Toe, Twelfth Street Rag, Broadway,* and *I Left My Baby.*

'Way Back Blues, Nobody Knows are included in Columbia CL 901, *"Blues by Basie."* Basie with the Goodman sextet is on Columbia CL 652, which includes *Till Tom Special* and *Gone with 'What' Wind.*

Me, Myself and I is in the Columbia Billie Holiday album CL 637. *When You're Smiling* is in the Holiday anthology C3L 21 (incidentally some earlier issues of that piece have used a different and equally good take), and *I Must Have That Man* in the Holiday anthology C3L 40.

The *Way Down Yonder in New Orleans—Pagin' the Devil—I Want a Little Girl—Them There Eyes* date with Lester Young and Buck Clayton was collected on Commodore 30014, and is spread across two Mainstream reissues 6002 and 6012. This 1938 session was originally released as by the Kansas City Six; the nominal leader was Eddie Durham, whose guitar solos show a very different and older sense of rhythm than the other players. The instrumentation is horns plus rhythm with no piano—the idea has been tried since and less casually, but not so successfully.

Blues for Helen is a part of Vanguard's album *"Spirituals to Swing, the Legendary Carnegie Hall Concerts of 1938–39"* (VRS 8523-4); also included in that set, incidentally, is *Mortgage Stomp*, a sketch for the masterpiece, *Lester Leaps In*.

9. CHARLIE PARKER

Charlie Parker's *Lady Be Good* solo is included in the album *"The Charlie Parker Story"* (Verve V16 8100-8002.) That set is a cross-section of Parker's work belonging to Verve and has the *Just Friends* with the strings, and the *What Is This Thing Called Love* with strings. The Norvo *Hallelujah* is on Parker Record PLP 408.

From the Parker recordings for Dial, Parker Record's PLP 407 had *Moose the Mooch, Yardbird Suite, Ornithology, A Night in Tunisia, Bird of Paradise, Embraceable You, Scrapple from the Apple.* Roost 2210 has *Embraceable You, Dewey Square, Scrapple from the Apple, Crazeology, Klacktoveedsedsteen.* (Two albums on a label called Baronet also had Dial recordings by Parker, Baronet 105 and Baronet 107.)

The historic Gillespie-Parker quintets and sextets are on Savoy MG-12020 (except for *Shaw 'Nuff*, which was somehow not included), and the Dizzy and Bird Carnegie Hall concert, including *A Night in Tunisia* and *Confirmation* is on Roost 2234.

There are five volumes in the Parker series on Savoy. The entire *Billie's Bounce—Now's the Time—KoKo* date is on MG-12079. Volume 1 (MG 12000) has a take of *Parker's Mood.* Savoy 12001 has some 1944 solos, plus some of the Parker recordings on tenor. The remaining two takes of *Parker's Mood* are on 12009. The final set is Savoy 12014. In general the Savoy series has Miles Davis, Tommy Potter, and Max Roach, but the pianist will be Duke Jordan, John Lewis, or Bud Powell, depending on the date.

From the *"Genius of Charlie Parker"* series on Verve, Volume 2 (8004) is the with strings set with *Just Friends.* Volume 3 is a collection of quartets, and includes a version of *Confirmation* (Verve 8005). Volume 4 (8006) is the "reunion" with Gillespie, with Monk on piano, including *Bloomdido, Mohawk, Melancholy Baby.* Volume 7 (8009) has *Cardboard, Visa, Passport.* Volume 8 (8010) has *Swedish Schnapps, Lover Man, She Rote.*

10. THELONIOUS MONK

Basic Monk includes the version of *Misterioso* on Blue Note 1510 and the versions of *Evidence, Criss Cross, Eronel,* and *Four In One* on Blue Note 1509. *Smoke Gets In Your Eyes* (along with *Let's Call This*) is on Prestige 7363 and Monk's solo on *Bags' Groove* (take 1) on Prestige 7650. Riverside 12-209 includes *Tea for Two* and Monk's "classic" set of variations on *Just You, Just Me. I Should Care* and Monk's best recording of *'Round Midnight*, plus the blues *Functional*, are on Riverside 12-235. *Trinkle Tinkle* by the Monk quartet with John Coltrane is on Riverside 490. And the best version of *Blue Monk* is on Prestige 7508.

Monk as a member of Coleman Hawkins's quartet can be heard on Prestige 7805. Monk can be heard as a participant in the Minton's jam sessions on Everest 5233. *Gallop's Gallop*, in a far from ideal performance of a superior piece, is included in Savoy 12137. *You Took the Words Right Out of My Heart* is on Riverside 312; *Brilliant Corners* is on Riverside 3004. Monk's presence with the Art Blakey Jazz Messengers, including the solo on *I Mean You*, can be heard on Atlantic 1278.

My examples from Monk's more publicly successful days are drawn from *"Monk's Dream"* (the second version of *Bolivar's Blues, Just a Gigolo, Sweet and Lovely, Body and Soul, Five Spot Blues*), Columbia CL 1965. And the big band in concert (*Evidence, Epistrophy*) is Columbia CL 2164.

11. JOHN LEWIS AND THE MODERN JAZZ QUARTET

The suite called *Fontessa* on Atlantic 1231 now forms the concluding sections of *The Comedy*. The themes called "Harlequin," "Pierrot," and "Colombine" were originally a part of Lewis's Atlantic 1272.

Most of the several recorded versions of *Bags' Groove* by the Quartet would bear out my point about John Lewis and the blues, beginning with his solo on the version on Atlantic 1265. The John Lewis version of *I Remember Clifford* is on Atlantic 1375, as is the best version of *Two Degrees East, Three Degrees West*.

The four titles from 1948 by Jackson, Lewis, Clarke, Al Jackson, and Pozo, have been issued on Galaxy 204. Savoy 12046 collects the Quartet's 1951 work, including the first *Softly, as in a Morning Sunrise*, but mechanical distortion crept into some of the tracks in transfer to a twelve-inch LP. The later *Morning Sunrise* is on Prestige 7005, as are *Concorde* and *Ralph's New Blues*. The 1954 version of *Django* is on Prestige 7425, as is *Milano*. The first version of *Vendome* is on Prestige 7059. *Autumn in New York* is on Prestige 7421.

The Quartet's version of *God Rest Ye Merry, Gentlemen* is on Atlantic 1247.

Lillie is on Blue Note 1509, as is *What's New* and Jackson's version of *Willow, Weep for Me* with Thelonious Monk. The session with Horace Silver that included *I Should Care* and *My Funny Valentine* is on Prestige 7655. The later *Willow, Weep* by the Quartet is on Atlantic 1231. *How High the Moon* is included in Atlantic 1325, along with a version of *Django* and *It Don't Mean a Think (If It Ain't Got That Swing)*. The *Golden Striker* and the triple-fugue *Three Windows* are on Atlantic 1284.

Three Little Feelings was reissued on Columbia C28 831. The sound track music for *Odds Against Tomorrow* appeared on United Artists 4061.

The *"European Concert"* set by the Modern Jazz Quartet, with versions of *Django, I Remember Clifford, It Don't Mean A Thing, Festival Sketch, Bluesology, Bags' Groove*, etc., is Atlantic 2-603.

Among the many exceptional Milt Jackson blues solos, there is *Opus Pokus* on Savoy 12036, which reinterprets some traditional blues ideas with new insight.

12. SONNY ROLLINS

Of the several piano solos I mention, Morton's *Hyena Stomp* (Riverside 12-132) and Willie "the Lion" Smith's *Squeeze Me* (on Dot 3094, or on Commodore 30,003 as *The Boy in the Boat*) have most recently been in print.

The Bud Powell date with Rollins now appears variously on Blue Note 1504, 1531, and 1532.

Rollins's *Mambo Bounce* date is on Prestige 7029. *Airegin, Oleo,* and *Doxy*, with Miles Davis are included in Prestige 7109. The Rollins-Coltrane *"Tenor Madness"* is Prestige 7657. *"Saxophone Colossus"* with *Blue 7* is on Prestige 7326.

Rollins's *Freedom Suite* was last issued on Riverside RS-3010.

Gunther Schuller's detailed analysis of *Blue 7* appeared in *The Jazz Review* and was republished in the anthology *Jazz Panorama* (Collier Books). *Vierd Blues* by Miles Davis is on Prestige 7044. Monk and Collins do *Misterioso* together on Blue Note 1558. Schuller also suggests that in organization and form *Sumphin'* by Rollins and Dizzy Gillespie (Verve 8260) was almost on the level of *Blue 7* if a bit less original. *"Way Out West"* is Contemporary 3530. *Blues for Philly Joe* is in Rollins's Blue Note 4001. B. *Quick* is now included in *"Sonny Boy,"* Prestige 7207. RCA Victor LPM/LSP 2572 has *If Ever I Would Leave You.* Probably the most representative of the "free-form" Rollins LPs is RCA Victor LPM/LSP 2612.

On Atlantic 1299 there is an interesting musical disagreement between Rollins and John Lewis, on a version of *Bags' Groove* recorded at a public concert, as Lewis accompanies him, not with the modern jazz pianist's pattern of complementary chords but polyphonically, with complementary melodies.

13. HORACE SILVER

The Miles Davis "all-star" *Walkin'* and *Blue 'n' Boogie* are on Prestige 7076. On Blue Note 1518 are pieces by Silver, Kenny Dorham, and the Art Blakey Jazz Messengers, including *The Preacher, Room 608, Hippy, Stop Time,* and *Doodlin'.* *Señor Blues* is on Blue Note 1539. Both Blue Note 1562 and 1589 were made with Art Farmer as a member of the Silver quintet, and the latter includes *Moon Rays.* *Sweet Stuff, Cookin' at the Continental, You Happened My Way,* and *Mellow D* are on Blue Note 4008; *The Saint Vitus Dance, Sister Sadie,* and *Blowin' the Blues Away* are on Blue Note 4017.

14. MILES DAVIS

Charlie Parker's *A Night in Tunisia* and *Embraceable You* are on Parker Record LP 407; the former is also on Baronet B105, the latter also on Roost 2210.

The early Miles Davis session which included *Skippin' at Bells* and *Little Willie Leaps* is spread across Savoy 12001 and 12009.

Capitol T 1974, *"The Birth of the Cool"* offers *Israel, Jeru, Godchild, Move,* and the rest of the Davis Nontet performances. The sessions for Blue Note with J. J. Johnson which included *Ray's Idea, Chance It, Woodyn' You, I Waited for You, Enigma,* and *Weirdo* are on 1501 and 1502.

Prestige 7608 has *Walkin'* and *Blue 'n' Boogie;* Prestige 7650 collects the all-star session on *Bags' Groove, The Man I Love,* etc.

Sid's Ahead is on Columbia CL 1193. Of the several LPs by the Davis quintet that featured John Coltrane, *" 'Round About Midnight"* (Columbia CL 949) is perhaps the best; it includes *Bye Bye Blackbird.* The later *Bye Bye Blackbird,* along with *Neo, Well You*

Needn't, and *No Blues,* are on *"In Person,"* Columbia C2L 20. The concert performances of *Autumn Leaves* and *All of You* are on Columbia CL 2183.

"Miles Ahead" is Columbia CL 1041, and *"Porgy and Bess"* is CL 1274. *"Sketches of Spain,"* with *Saeta* is Columbia 1480.

"Kind of Blue," with *Flamenco Sketches* and *So What,* is on Columbia CS 8163.

Petits Machins is on *"Filles de Kilimanjaro"* (Columbia CS 9750); the same LP has a good "drone" piece by Davis called *Frelon Brun.* *Country Son* is a part of *"Miles in the Sky"* (Columbia CS 9628). And *Circle* can be heard on *"Miles Smiles"* (Columbia CS 9401). Indeed, the general level of composition and performance on *"Miles Smiles"* is very high. *"Sorcerer"* (Columbia CS 9532) is also representative of Miles Davis's better work in the 'sixties (one brief vocal track by Bob Dorough excepted), and has outstanding work by drummer Tony Williams in several selections.

15. JOHN COLTRANE

Miles Davis's *'Round Midnight* is on Columbia CL 949. Coltrane and Monk can be heard on Riverside 490, which includes *Trinkle Tinkle.*

Miles Davis's version of *Straight No Chaser* is on Columbia CL 1193, as is *Milestones. Blue Train, Locomotion,* and *Moment's Notice* are on Blue Note 1577. The Davis *"Kind of Blue"* set is Columbia CL 1355.

Giant Steps, Naima, and *Countdown,* are on Atlantic 1311; *My Favorite Things* on Atlantic 1361.

Chasin' the Trane is Impulse A-10; *Impressions* on Impulse A-42. *In a Sentimental Mood* and *Take the Coltrane* are on Impulse A-30; the *"Crescent"* LP is Impulse A-66. *A Love Supreme* is Impulse A-77. Coltrane's *Ascension* is Impulse A-95. And *Meditations* is Impulse A-9110.

One personal addition, *Three Little Words* on the LP *"Bags and Trane"* (Atlantic 1368), for the pacing of Coltrane's adventurous solo.

16. ORNETTE COLEMAN

Basic Ornette Coleman:

Peace, Focus on Sanity, Lonely Woman, Congeniality, and *Chronology* are on *"The Shape of Jazz to Come"* on Atlantic 1317. *Free Jazz* is Atlantic 1367.

The Stockholm recordings are Blue Note 84224, with *Dawn*; and Blue Note 84225, with *Snowflakes and Sunshine, The Riddle,* and *Antiques.*

Trouble in the East is on Impulse AAS-9187 a two-record set not available singly.

Supplementary Coleman:

Jayne, Angel Voice, Chippie, The Sphinx, and *Invisible* are on *"Something Else!"* (Contemporary C 3551).

"Tomorrow is the Question," with *Lorraine* and *Tears Inside* is Contemporary M 3569.

Ramblin' and *Free* are on *"Change of the Century"* (Atlantic 1327). *Beauty is a Rare Thing* is on Atlantic 1353.

C. & D. and *R.P.D.D.* are on Atlantic 1378. And Coleman on tenor, with *Cross Breeding* and *Mapa,* can be heard on Atlantic 1394.

Coleman's performance on *Abstraction,* and his interpretation of Thelonious Monk's *Criss Cross* are on Atlantic 1365.

Ornette Coleman, Town Hall, 1962 on ESP Disc 1006 has a version of *Sadness,* and a piece called *Doughnut* in which (as far as I know) the idea of spontaneous, collective changes of tempo first appears. I am told that Coleman likes his playing on *The Ark* from the same LP. Another version of *Sadness* and also of *Doughnut* can be heard on *"An Evening with Ornette Coleman"* released in England on a two-record set on International Polydor 623 246/247. (These two albums also include works by Coleman for string quartet and woodwind quartet—both of which are outside the limits of this discussion.)

"New York is Now!" (Blue Note 84287) has *Round Trip, Broadway Blues,* and *The Garden of Souls* (plus a rather boyish joke that doesn't come off called *We Now Interrupt for a Commercial*).

Don Cherry's *Complete Communion* is Blue Note 84226.